International Communism
after Khrushchev

Edited by

Leopold Labedz

THE M.I.T. PRESS

Massachusetts Institute of Technology

Cambridge, Massachusetts

Printed in Great Britain by The Eastern Press, Ltd., London and Reading

15379

CONTENTS

The End of an Epoch .... *Leopold Labedz* 3

Schism and Secession .... *Kevin Devlin* 29

The State of the Parties

Western Europe .... *Eric Willenz and Pio Uliassi* 51

Eastern Europe .... *J. F. Brown* 65

Asia .... *Donald S. Zagoria* 89

The Strategic Triangle: 1. India .... *Sathi* 105

                       2. Indonesia .... *Ruth McVey* 113

                       3. Japan .... *Kyosuke Hirotsu* 123

Australasia .... *T. H. Rigby* 131

North America .... *Joseph R. Starobin* 144

Latin America .... *Ernst Halperin* 154

Africa .... *William E. Griffith* 168

Sino-Soviet Rivalry and the National Liberation Movement
Elizabeth Kridl Valkenier 190

International Consequences of the Sino-Soviet Dispute
Helmut Sonnenfeldt 205

Appendix: The State of the Parties 217

Contributors 224

THE END OF AN EPOCH

Leopold Labedz

THE fall of Khrushchev, like the death of Stalin, terminated a political era, though in a very different, yet possibly more fundamental historical sense. In contrast to his predecessor, Khrushchev has not imposed the stamp of his personality on it; he just released some forces which remained latent under Stalin, and then he could not contain them. Nor are his successors likely to do so, much less to put the clock back. The end of Khrushchev's reign coincides with the end of communism as a unitary movement. The years after Stalin witnessed the loss of Soviet control over the movement and the erosion of its unity. The dismissal of Khrushchev will not stop the process of polycentrism; in the long term it may even be seen as having accelerated it. One need only compare the reactions of different communist parties to this event with their behaviour after Stalin's death to realise how far are the days when differing opinions and interests were unable to manifest themselves through the facade of communist uniformity, now as slender as the proverbial seventh veil. At present such differences are increasingly visible, and no amount of tactical manoeuvres and compromises by the Soviet and the Chinese rulers can change this fact.

The new leaders in Moscow are of course capable of switching their policies overnight (a glance at Soviet history shows that this has always been the case), but basically they are facing the same problems as Khrushchev did, and these cannot be solved by ideological incantations or the merging of contrary formulas. 'Tutti-frutti' declarations, such as the Statement of the 81 parties, and bans on polemics, were all tried under Khrushchev and found wanting. It takes a Soviet ideological functionary, relegating for the second time the personality cult to the dustbin of history, to pretend that the removal of Khrushchev can make all that difference in Sino-Soviet relations. For how long can he serve as a scapegoat for a détente? After all that has happened, neither side can have many illusions about its permanence. The interests of the two states have clashed and the two parties are engaged in a struggle for hegemony. At best, a compromise can only be temporary and its present significance quite different for world communism from that of 1960, which, as they know, was fragile enough and less difficult to achieve. Moreover, now that the Sino-Soviet conflict has run its course for so long and has reactivated communist divisions, a Sino-Soviet rapprochement, whose durability is doubtful, may be almost as embarrassing to many communist parties, facing their factionalist rivals or local electorate, as previously the dispute itself was. The point has been reached when Soviet and Chinese actions, whether they clash or get closer, provoke a polycentric 'feed-back'. An exclusive concentration on what the Russian or the Chinese communists may or may not do is clearly insufficient to realise what its effect may be on the international communist movement. More than ever, the parties must be studied in detail; the communist scene is not confined to the Kremlin or the Heavenly Palace. The accumulated effects of the post-Stalin decade on international communism, with its inter- and intra-party struggles, the outcome of which is no longer decided only in Moscow or Peking, must be taken into account as a necessary starting point for any realistic appraisal of its future.

UNDER Khrushchev, communism was still claiming to be ' mono-lithic ' and based on ' proletarian internationalism ', but all that remained of such claims were letters to ' Dear Comrades ', in which mutual charges of betrayal and slander were accompanied by ' fraternal greetings '. Whatever patchwork arrangements may be made by Khrushchev's successors, there can be little doubt that any real unity of the communist movement cannot be restored. The historical significance of this fact can hardly be exaggerated. What are the lessons of the past?

It is ironical that the fragmentation of communism should coincide with the centenary of the foundation of the First International. This can only emphasise the fact that ' proletarian internationalism ' as well as ' monolithic unity ' have come to the end of the road. It puts a seal on the failure of all the post-war attempts to re-create the discipline of the Third International, in one form or another, within one institutional framework. It makes it clear that communists have to abandon the original hope that ' the International shall be the human race '. The idea of the International in its Marxist or Leninist form is for all practical purposes dead. The future of communism will depend on the differentiated evolution of the national communist parties or of regional communist groupings.

This will not make communism disappear any more than the 1914 collapse of the internationalist professions formulated at the Basel Congress of the Second International made the socialist parties disappear. Nor will the harm to the communist ideology caused by the present schisms be such as to lead to the withering away of communism. It will no more mean its end than the Reformation signified the end of the Church. But it does mean the end of an epoch.

Marx considered that the consolidation of the international was the result of the ' movement of history ':

> The evolution of socialist sectarianism and that of the genuine working class movement go in opposite directions. So long as the sects are (historically) justified, the working class is not yet ready for an independent historical movement. When it achieves such maturity, the sects become reactionary. Yet what history shows everywhere is also reproduced inside the international. The old always tries to reconstitute itself inside the new forms. The history

of the International has been a continuous struggle of the General Council against the sects and against the attempts of the amateurs to resist inside the International the real movement of the working class.[1]

The amateurs in question were Mazzini, Owen, Proudhon, Bakunin, and their followers, against whom Marx waged an implacable battle, inside as well as outside the General Council. But whatever his successes in these struggles, they were certainly not due to the movement of history towards internationalism, but rather to the fact that in the liberal 19th century nationalism was not yet as strong as it became later, and to his own tactical skill. And when the battles with the Italian nationalism of the Mazzinians, with the English empiricism of the Owenites, and with the French individualism of the Proudhonists were over, Marx took up the struggle against Bakunin and his followers, who resented his authoritarianism and objected to the hierarchical organisation of the International. 'How can a free and egalitarian society develop from an authoritarian organisation?' they asked. In this they were right. But up to a point Marx too was right. No organisation can exist without some structure of authority, and the Bakuninists themselves, for all their libertarian language, were not exactly democratic, being the heirs of the French and Italian secret societies and of Russian conspiratorial methods. As anarchists they were impractical, as conspirators they were themselves authoritarian.

Where Marx was wrong was in not seeing that national divisions were bound to release centrifugal forces and to undermine the unitary authority in the International and that an international organisation, centrally controlled, would not stand the strains of the struggles for power which sooner or later would coalesce on the lines of such divisions.

In these conflicts he resorted to the methods with which we became so familiar later on: excommunication, expulsion of the (arithmetic) majority, and so on. On 27 July 1869 he wrote to Engels: 'This Russian [Bakunin] wants to become the dictator of the European working class movement. Let him take care, otherwise he will be officially excommunicated.' To Marx and Engels, with their Western European background, the idea that the centre of gravity of the International could move to 'barbaric Russia' seemed preposterous. They expected that it would move from France to Germany (after the defeat of the Paris Commune), and in this they were right. But they were indignant at the thought of a further shift to the east. Engels exclaimed [2]: 'A fine presumption that the European proletariat should achieve its unity under Russian command!'

---

[1] Letter to F. Belte of 28 November 1871, quoted in *La Première Internationale*, ed. Jacques Freymond (Genève, 1962), p. xx.
[2] Marx/Engels Gesamtausgabe, Dritte Abteilung, Band 4, *Der Briefwechsel zwischen Marx und Engels 1868–1883* (Berlin, 1931), pp. 213, 313.

The active membership of the International was rather small. The proletariat it represented was actually concerned with such measures as the prevention of the importation of foreign labour, which could be employed at lower wages, the first manifestation of how 'proletarian internationalism' might be threatened by the economic divergences between the more and the less developed countries.

Faced with the challenge of Bakunin, Marx succeeded in expelling him from the International on charges of financial swindles.[3] He decided to wind up the International by transferring its General Council to New York, where it expired. But it was not to the West, but to the East, that revolutionary 'Marxism' was eventually to move.

THE Second International consolidated the working class movement in Europe, but its official revolutionary and internationalist ideology only concealed the deep cleavage between its theory and its practice, a cleavage revealed in the conflict between its Western right-wing and its Eastern left-wing. When war came in 1914, the socialist parties did not (and could not, if they wanted to retain their following) conform to their ideological obligations and became what Lenin called 'social patriots'. After the First World War, the Second International gave up its revolutionary ideology, and after the Second World War its Marxist theory as well.

From the East came the call for the foundation of a new revolutionary international. When it was founded, Lenin produced what may be called a relay theory of the International[4]:

> For a time—it goes without saying that it is only for a short time—hegemony in the revolutionary, proletarian International has passed to the Russians in the same way as at various periods in the nineteenth century it was enjoyed by the English, then by the French, and then by the Germans.

This emphasis on the temporary character of the shift to Russia was based on his expectation of the coming proletarian revolution in the West. Little did he know that one day his argument would be invoked by the Chinese against the Soviet 'revisionists'.[5]

Lenin, who in November 1918 asserted in *The Proletarian Revolution and the Renegade Kautsky* that 'Bolshevism has created the theoretical and tactical foundations of a Third International', now went

[3] Bakunin wrote on 12 June 1872: 'The sword of Damocles, with which we have been threatened for so long, has finally fallen on our heads. Strictly speaking, it is not a sword, but the customary weapon of Mr Marx, a bucket of filth' (Freymond, op. cit. vol. II, p. 301).
[4] *Communist International*, No. I, May 1919.
[5] 'When Kautsky was still a revolutionary, he said that the centre of revolution would shift from Germany to Russia. While Kautsky later became a renegade from the revolution, Lenin still quoted with approval this earlier revolutionary prediction of Kautsky's. Then the storm of revolution reached the East'. Chou Yang, 'The Fighting Task Confronting Workers in Philosophy and the Social Sciences', *Peking Review*, No. 1, 1964, p. 15.

on to impose Bolshevik ideas and discipline on that body through the instrumentality of the 21 conditions of admission to the Communist International adopted in 1920 by its second congress. The Leninist model of a tightly-knit, disciplined revolutionary party was projected onto the International. Its sections, with all the variety of their backgrounds, were now supposed to conform strictly to the Bolshevik pattern.

The process was not without its setbacks, but any manifestation of deviationism, any tendency towards autonomy in the communist parties, was stamped out in the campaign for their 'bolshevisation'. Under Stalin the process was brought to its conclusion: Comintern became an instrument of his dictatorship, a simple appendage to the Soviet Foreign Affairs Commissariat, and the pretence that it was 'the general staff of the international revolution' was dropped after the proclamation of the 'theory of socialism in one country'. Communists all over the world had to accept the complete identification of Soviet *raison d'état* with the interest of their own parties, and it was, of course, Stalin who decided what the interest of the Soviet 'bastion of the revolution' required. Those who hesitated or refused to give their unquestioning submission were either liquidated or expelled, and the 'monolithic' facade was constructed.

The system created a habit of automatic obedience on the part of communists the world over. When trouble was expected, the International, i.e. Stalin, went to the length of dissolving a whole national section, as happened in the case of the Polish Communist Party in 1938. When the period of the Soviet-Nazi Pact was over, and the Soviet Union found itself in alliance with the 'capitalist democracies', Stalin decided that it was tactically advantageous to dissolve not one party, but the Communist International itself, which he did in May 1943. He was evidently convinced that the old conditioning would continue to ensure automatic conformity even without the formal existence of the International. The resolution of the Executive Committee of the Comintern hinted as much in its announcement that the decision to dissolve the International had been made 'taking into account the growth and political maturity of the communist parties'.

SORCERERS usually reckon without their apprentices (Khrushchev's case has shown this in a particularly striking way). But some loyal foreign Stalinists were even then trying to push their parties along the roads not approved by Stalin, and because of the exigencies of war they were getting away with it. Thus in November 1943 Tito created his National Committee to act as the provisional government of Yugoslavia, disregarding the expected negative reaction to this step from Moscow (which duly came) [6]; in the United States Earl Browder was in 1944 transforming the American Communist Party into an 'association'

---

[6] Milovan Djilas, *Conversations with Stalin* (New York, 1962), pp. 10–11.

(for which he was to be scolded by Duclos), and there were other examples, from India to Brazil.

But it was only after the war that the institutional problem really emerged (although still in a latent form). So long as communists were only struggling for power, they felt the need, psychological, political, financial, to rely on the Soviet Union. When some of them attained power and acquired control of the state, their identification with the Soviet Union was bound to be affected. It was now no longer psychologically necessary to regard the interest of the first communist state as a universal communist interest to the exclusion of everything else. There were now other states.

Because they were satellites, however, the possible divergences of interest were, for the time being, concealed beneath the surface. But in 1948 Yugoslavia, the second country where communists came to power independently, had to be expelled from the new, limited version of the international, the Cominform, established only the year before. In 1949 came the victory of the Chinese communists, who created another autonomous centre of communist power. Polycentrism became a fact seven years before Togliatti used the word.

But of course the real trouble came only after Stalin's death. The clashes of interest, first between communist states and then also between parties, in and out of power, could now come to the surface. The excommunication of Tito only postponed their appearance, it could not dispose of the underlying problem. There was no institutional mechanism to settle fraternal disagreements and there was little hope of establishing one. Inside the Soviet Union, the disappearance of the apex of authority posed the problem of succession, but outside, unitary authority could no longer be re-established within the bloc, and this was bound to lead, sooner or later, to the end of the unity of the entire movement.

Efforts were made to bring it together: the 1957 and 1960 Moscow meetings were such attempts. In the present perspective it seems that they contributed to further deterioration, rather than to a solution of the problem.

The first of these meetings to reconsolidate communism came after the 1956 upheaval in Eastern Europe and it tried to paper over the cracks caused in the once monolithic facade by destalinisation. But following it internal communist polemics became more, not less, acute. The second meeting, convened after the Bucharest clash between the 'revisionist' Russians and the Sino-Albanian 'dogmatists', was already on the verge of a split, which was averted only by what Lenin would have undoubtedly described as a 'rotten compromise'. It was immediately clear that the Statement of the 81 parties was a confusion of incompatible political formulas. It could only lead to a continuation of polemics, with both sides stressing their own parts of the document. Eventually the inevitable happened: Sino-Soviet polemics came into the open. Equally inevitably, this had a snowballing effect on all the communist parties of the world.

There was no question of establishing an international organisation to cope with the communist conflicts. The idea of the international was no longer practical; the most communists could hope for was an occasional conference of the parties. But there was a snag here too. The conference itself became a tactical element in the Sino-Soviet conflict and therefore the prospect of its taking place became remote. The parties would not agree on its timing, much less on its composition and rules of procedure. In the circumstances, any such agreement would, from the point of view of the contestants, prejudge the outcome of the struggle. There was, therefore, no room for compromise even on the subject of holding the conference. The Chinese, being in a minority, steadfastly refused to be drawn into a game which they were bound to lose if the overwhelming number of the small pro-Soviet parties were to have the decisive voice. The manoeuvres about the conference became, therefore, only tactical moves to put the blame for the split on the opposite side, to establish a sort of alibi before the Marxist tribunal of history.

THE Soviet decision to cross the Rubicon and issue invitations to Moscow for a meeting to prepare a general communist conference was made after much procrastination. The Chinese announced in advance that they would not participate in any meeting which the Russians might call ' for the purpose of splitting the international communist movement '. The Russians reversed the charge, asserting that not the conference but the Chinese refusal to attend would precipitate a split. As expected, the Chinese declined the invitation and declared that by issuing it unilaterally the Russians ' must be held responsible for all the possible consequences of openly splitting the international communist movement '.

The Russians wanted the conference to maintain discipline in ' their ' part of the movement. They could not preserve their position in it without some common act of ideological solidarity to be adopted by the parties not supporting the Chinese position. Such an act would isolate the Chinese and their followers and prevent further undermining of the Soviet position. Inside the bloc Khrushchev wanted to reconsolidate ' socialist internationalism ' more substantially. In his speech on 3 April 1964 he referred to the desirability of establishing ' organisational forms to improve the continuing exchange of opinions and the coordination of foreign policy between the member countries of Comecon '.

But there were many snags, and steps to convene the conference were repeatedly postponed. Soviet procrastination was due to the fact that not only pro-Chinese communist parties, but many critical of the Chinese were also critical of the idea of the conference. Dragging their feet were the Italian, Yugoslav, British, Dutch, Norwegian, Austrian, Belgian, South African, and other parties, not to mention the communist

' neutrals ', like Rumania or Cuba. The Poles and the Hungarians were also clearly unhappy about it.

Some of these parties recoiled from the formal split which such a conference would inevitably seal. The South African CP stated that no useful purpose would be served by such a meeting.[7] It argued that ' everything must be done to call a halt to this sterile and destructive dispute before it deepens into a complete break ', and added [8]:

> Once a disagreement takes on a factional character the real issues at stake become incredibly oversimplified, crude and false. Distortion and misrepresentation replace the give-and-take of reasoned argument. The object is no longer to prove one's opponent to be mistaken, but to depict him as an enemy to be destroyed. Irreparable harm follows. Dear comrades-in-arms are suddenly ' transformed ' into traitors and spies. Leaders of rival factions are depicted either as enemy agents or as infallible super-men, demigods. Factionalism in a revolutionary movement is like a cancer.

Some parties did not like the idea of excommunication. Gomulka objected to ' any form of excommunication, such as our movement had so painfully experienced in the past '.[9] The Yugoslav deputy Foreign Minister, Mladen Ivekovic, expressed the same sentiments: ' Our own Yugoslav experience with the policy of " excommunication " in 1948 gives us, perhaps, the right to reject any such policy, even in the case of China, although we have our well-known specific reasons to be displeased with Peking '.[10] The London *Daily Worker* (26 May 1964) simply stated that ' there can be no question of " excommunication " '.

The Italian communists rejected the idea of the conference in their resolution of 24 October 1963, saying that it could only produce either a split or an unsatisfactory compromise. They objected to anathemas and excommunications, and Togliatti reiterated this view in his speech of 22 April 1964: ' The method of solemn excommunication contains the danger of a resurgence of authoritarian and sectarian methods of leadership in the individual parties '. The Italians disapproved particularly the implied threat to the autonomy of the parties. Luigi Longo stated that ' the autonomy of the parties in developing their own policy should be maintained ', and Mario Alicata stressed that there must be no return to the ' historically unacceptable centralised form of direction '.

Facing the objections of their reluctant allies, the Russians assured them that ' the meeting will be called not to condemn anybody, or to " excommunicate " anybody from the communist movement ', and they endorsed the Czech opinion that ' central direction, formerly essential, definitely belongs to the past '.[11]

7 *World Marxist Review*, June 1964, p. 41.
8 *The African Communist*, July–Sept. 1964, p. 93.
9 *Trybuna Ludu*, 11 April 1964.
10 *Vjestnik*, 8 May 1964.
11 *Rude Pravo*, 10 September 1964. The article in which it appeared was reprinted in full two days later in the Moscow *Pravda*.

The reasons behind the conference were, however, made abundantly clear by the leaders of the parties giving unqualified support to the CPSU. François Billoux, the French communist leader, said [12]:

> Whether there is a conference or not, the Chinese leaders will continue their splitting and disruptive activity. This they do while pretending that they are the only spokesmen of Marxism-Leninism. This permits them to sow confusion among those who are not on their guard politically. They can do it all the easier if the parties which disapprove of their splitting activities and disagree with their mistaken political and ideological concepts will not say so clearly and solemnly. And at the international conference too. It is normal for communist and workers parties to discuss this, not to 'excommunicate', but to determine a common line of action. We must look at things as they are. We are facing here an attempt at disruption worse than that once made by the Trotskyists, because unfortunately the Chinese leaders use the apparatus of the state for the purpose.

The secretary of the Spanish CP, Santiago Carillo, was even more explicit [13]:

> Comrades, at this very moment the international communist movement is heading towards an international conference; this must be done. There are those who say, 'No! Let's not have the conference, because the conference is the split!' . . . The truth is that the split is already there, comrades, and that it is necessary to stop it in its tracks, that a reply must be made to the splitting manoeuvres. . . .

The irony of the situation was that Soviet attempts to mend the fences in their garden only contributed to their further deterioration. The Chinese may have exaggerated when they warned the Russians that 'the day you call a schismatic meeting will be the day you step into your grave', but it is true that the Soviet insistence on holding the conference instead of consolidating the ranks of their supporters further aggravated the conflict, and led many pro-Soviet parties to take an independent stand.

THE heaviest blow came by one of those accidents which fate does not spare even the most determined historical determinists. When Palmiro Togliatti wrote his memorandum in Yalta he did not expect it to become a public document, much less acquire a sacred status as his 'testament'. It is this, and not anything particularly new or remarkable in it, that immediately put a historical stamp on the document. Master of ambiguity and equivocation to the end, Togliatti expressed in a very restrained form the tendencies often manifested in the Italian party on public occasions and in the press ever since 1956. Yet even in this restrained form the document became an important factor in the failure of the concept of the conference as envisaged by its Soviet

---

[12] *France Nouvelle*, 16 September 1964, p. 17.
[13] Speech on 19 April 1964 published as a pamphlet by the French Communist Party.

sponsors, and in deepening the process of polycentrism. It was already pretty clear that the conference could bring the Russians only a Pyrrhic victory; now there could be no doubt about it. Togliatti's 'testament' crystallised a new, 'European', platform in communism and gave an international status to the 'Italian tendency'.[14]

Contrary to the impression created in the press, Togliatti was not burning any bridges behind him. He declared in his memorandum that the Italian party, despite its doubts and reservations about the conference, would attend the preparatory meeting in Moscow. Togliatti was thus left with two alternatives; either to uphold the October 1963 resolution of his party and wreck the project of the conference at a meeting specifically called by the Russians to prepare it, or, after voicing his doubts and making some compromises, to surrender gracefully by accepting the Soviet proposal, suitably diluted by the guarantees against excommunication, for the autonomy of the parties, etc.

It is, of course, fruitless to assert that Togliatti would have done this or that. Judging by his past performance, it was not his style to make a frontal challenge; it was his death which transformed a diplomatic document into a challenge.

The posthumous publication of the memorandum created a new situation and had a negative effect on Soviet efforts. It became a platform for critical communist attitudes about the conference, focusing reservations and reinforcing doubts among the undecided. The dramatic circumstances added weight to what in itself is a pretty weak and often inconsistent piece of reasoning. Yet even in this form it became more than, as its author undoubtedly intended, a starting point for negotiations. Its three main points: criticism of the Soviet handling of the Chinese tactics, dissatisfaction with the slowness of destalinisation in the Soviet Union and Eastern Europe, and the emphasis on the autonomy of the parties, were a direct blow to the Soviet attempts to rally their supporters. It undermined the position of the 'centralists' who argued that 'it is obvious that the international communist movement is not suffering at the moment from the lack of autonomy of its constituent parties'.[15]

It was ironical that the obituary on the idea of the communist international should be written by its former secretary under Stalin, in what became his own 'testament'. Because this is in effect the role of this document, this is what it amounts to historically.

This was far from his intentions. He thought that the conference might result in 'a declared break within the movement, with the formation of an international Chinese centre which would set up sections in all countries'.[16] He admitted that 'the factionist efforts of the

[14] It was welcomed by one of its followers as the beginning of the 'communist Reformation' (Giles Martinet, 'Un Nouvel Age Politique', *France Observateur*, 10 September 1964). Only Togliatti never thought of nailing his theses to the Kremlin door and was the last person to say: *Hier stehe ich. Ich kann nicht anders.* He was too devious for such public demonstrations.

[15] *l'Humanité*, 6 October 1964.

[16] *Rinascita*, 5 September 1964, p. 3.

Chinese are already in full swing in almost all countries ', yet insisted, without indicating how it could be done, that 'we must prevent the quantity of these efforts from becoming quality '.

In this he was less dialectical than the Chinese and more cautious than the Russians. For the Chinese, it seemed part of a historical process that their brand of ' revolutionary Marxism ' would replace the ' counter-revolutionary, anti-scientific, revisionist Marxism ' of the Soviet Union. Dialectic itself points that way. ' Everything tends to divide itself into two ', and now the Chinese were the wave of the future:

> Those who are seemingly isolated in the beginning are sure to be victorious in the end. So it was with Lenin and the Third International. On the contrary, the celebrities and big battalions are bound to decline and to dwindle and putrefy when they lose possession of the truth and therefore lose the support of the masses. So it was with Bernstein and the Second International. Under particular conditions, things are bound to change into their opposites. There is inevitably a realignment in the forces of revolution in the course of the struggle between the proletariat and the revolutionary people on the one hand and the forces of reaction on the other, and in the course of the struggle between Marxism on the one hand and opportunism and revisionism on the other.[17]

The Russians summarised the Chinese position as aiming to replace Soviet leadership of the world movement:

> The anti-Leninist position of the Chinese leaders is manifested particularly clearly in their utterly shameless claim to hegemony in the Communist movement. . . . A solid front of Communist parties, their active struggle against the petty bourgeois nationalist position of the CPC leaders, will deprive these leaders of opportunities to sow dissension among Communists and will ensure unity on a Marxist-Leninist basis.[18]

Into this bi-polar world of dialectical ' struggle of opposites ', Togliatti injected a polycentric note of ' unity in diversity ':

> The autonomy of the parties, which we champion decisively, is not just an internal necessity of our movement, but an essential condition of our development in the present conditions. We will therefore be opposed to any proposal to create once again a centralised international organisation.

But the growing autonomy of the parties can hardly contribute in practice to their unity. Togliatti's memorandum is in fact concerned with communist independence and not with communist unity. It has as much in common with the idea of the international in the present circumstances as the plan for a tower of Babel. It gives even less hope of concerted action, not just because of different languages, but because of different interpretations of doctrine by the autonomous communist parties.

[17] Chou Yang, *Peking Review*, No. 1, 1964, p. 14.
[18] B. Ponomarov, *World Marxist Review*, No. 6, 1964, pp. 64–8.

The immediate political effect of the publication of Togliatti's memorandum was to reveal the relative weakness of the Soviet position. They had already lost the support of most Asian parties; now a European party, second numerically only to the Indonesian CP among the non-ruling parties, had conspicuously failed to give the CPSU effective support in its conflict with the Chinese. (The only other party which matters politically among the non-ruling parties and which gave the Russians unqualified support, was the French.) Yugoslav and Cuban opposition to the conference, as well as the reluctance of some West and East European parties, must have been stiffened by the publication of this polycentric document.

It is not surprising that the Chinese, for all their disdain for Togliatti's 'reformism', received it with glee. They realised that the purpose of its publication by the Italian party was to assert its independence and it suited them well that this should disconcert their rivals at a particularly crucial moment. For those who are bound to inherit the earth and the international, the disarray in the 'revisionist' camp could only hasten the process.[19]

Doctrinally, Togliatti's testament contained little new. In 1962 and 1963 the Chinese had accused the Italian party of taking up Bernstein's ideas, of using the concept of ' " structural reform " as a substitute for proletarian revolution'.[20] Now Togliatti had spelled it out:

> The question arises of the possibility of the working class capturing the positions of power within a state that has not changed its bourgeois nature, and therefore of the possibility of fighting for its progressive transformation from inside.

This, like the Soviet discovery that a 'peaceful transition' to socialism may be possible in some countries, is indeed a revision of Lenin, who stressed that the 'bourgeois state' must be smashed from outside. The Chinese pointed this out, using all the appropriate quotations from *The Proletarian Revolution and the Renegade Kautsky,* and on this basis they accused Khrushchev of 'revisionism', just as previously they had accused Togliatti of 'reformism'.

However, the parallel with Lenin's rejection of Bernstein and Kautsky, often uncritically accepted by Western observers, was overdone in Chinese polemics. When Pietro Nenni argued (in an editorial in *Avanti*) that Togliatti's testament stops half-way, and it is the Italian socialists who carry the logic through, taking part in the government

---

19 The pro-Chinese *Voix du Peuple* (25 September 1964) referred to Togliatti's testament as ' a reflection of the growing contradictions among the revisionists ', and declared that Togliatti tried to establish a facade of unity ' à la manière de " l'Internationale " socialiste '. It also pointed out that its rival, *Le Drapeau Rouge,* the organ of the pro-Soviet Communist Party of Belgium, had censored the text of Togliatti's memorandum. The Trotskyist *l'Internationale* (September 1964) in Paris, referred to it as ' an opening of the second front in the crisis of the international communist movement '.

20 *Peking Review,* No. 1 & No. 10/11, 1963.

to implement reforms from inside the bourgeois state, *Rinascita* (12 September 1964) replied that 'one should not confuse governmental positions with positions of power'.

It was not Khrushchev who revised Lenin's doctrine on the impossibilty of taking over the bourgeois state from inside, but Stalin. After the war, communists everywhere were taking part in 'bourgeois governments', and where they were in 'positions of power' they could take them over, as in Czechoslovakia, and where they were not, as in France and Italy, they could not. There was a dialectical sophistry in the Chinese rejection of the Soviet argument that the February 1948 coup in Czechoslovakia was a case of 'peaceful transition to socialism':

> During World War II, the Communist Party . . . established a national coalition government. This government was in essence a people's democratic dictatorship under the leadership of the proletariat, i.e. a form of the dictatorship of the proletariat. . . . The February event was not a 'peaceful' seizure of political power by the working class from the bourgeoisie, but a suppression of a counter-revolutionary bourgeois *coup d'état* by the working class through its own state apparatus and mainly through its own armed forces (*Peking Review,* 3 April 1964).

Behind the doctrinal veil, the argument was of course concerned with the strategy and tactics of the struggle for power, and here Togliatti's 'pessimism' was incomparably better grounded in reality than the Chinese denunciations of it based on the Leninist precepts for a proletarian revolution which are clearly inapplicable to the Italian scene.

Whether, in revising the Leninist theory of revolution, the PCI will eventually come to a revision of the Leninist concept of the party, and thus take a step towards a social-democratic transformation, is another question. The evolution of German social-democracy from revolution to reform did not have as its starting point a Leninist type of party, so that there is here no real parallel, despite the fact that Chinese ideological functionaries and superficial Western commentators invoke it so often. The possibility exists, but the problem is different. Robert Michels diagnosed in the German social-democratic party, as in all other parties, oligarchic tendencies, but it was a democratic party with no Leninist structure and Stalinist tradition. The Italian CP also operates in a context of competition with other parties and faces the *embourgeoisement* of the proletariat, but it has a totalitarian character which it will have to shed before one can begin to talk about its social-democratic evolution on lines parallel to Bernstein's 'revisionism'. So far, on their own testimony, it is a matter of means and not of ends, of adaptation to local conditions in the struggle for power, and not of a real acceptance of the democratic framework. In time, however, the change of means may affect the ends, and tactical requirements may affect the structure of the party. This is not yet the case and there is an intellectual (and political) advantage in being clear about what constitutes such a transformation. The criterion here is undoubtedly the abandonment of the Leninist model of the party.

THE same argument applies to the parallel between Mao's dispute with Khrushchev and that of Lenin with Kautsky. Here there is the additional obstacle to a similar development, for the Soviet party does not operate in competition with other parties but is in possession of a state. It can run it less autocratically, but that offers little parallel with the social-democratic revisionism of Bernstein or the Marxist orthodoxy of Kautsky.

The third argument which hinges on the interpretation of the Marxist theory of revolution and the Leninist theory of the state is concerned with strategy and tactics in the underdeveloped countries. The Soviet concept of 'national democracy' and a recent dispensation even of this half-way house to power were rejected by the Chinese fundamentalists. It is really quite foolish to generalise here and to maintain that one doctrinal position offers a better chance of gaining power than the other. It clearly depends on the circumstances in a given country. No less foolish is the acceptance of the Maoist claim to Marxist or even Marxist-Leninist orthodoxy. The simple truth is that in their doctrinal polemics, and in their political practice, both sides revise Marx and Lenin. The Chinese, for instance, were quite right when they said that the Khrushchevian concept of 'the state of the whole people' is un-Marxist, and his concept of the party as 'a political organisation of the whole people' un-Leninist.[21] (They were of course perverting the truth when they attributed the origin of such concepts to Trotsky and Bukharin.) But the Russians were also right when they demonstrated that Mao's concept of 'people's dictatorship' was a deviation from Marxist and Leninist orthodoxy.[22]

More important than the theological arguments by which each party justifies its position is the fact of the emergence of national Marxisms, as a corollary to national communisms and a polycentric proliferation of 'national roads to socialism'. The content of these dialectical exercises may be intellectually blunt, but they indicate the political tendencies of each party; what is more important, the fact that each of them may create its own system of interpretation of the sacred texts gives it a chance to manipulate its own legitimacy. In short, doctrinal autonomy is a necessary concomitant of political autonomy for the communist parties in the era of polycentrism.

This creates not only multiplication but confusion, as political and

---

[21] *Peking Review*, 17 July 1964. Characteristically, a Yugoslav theoretician also stated that 'regarded as a whole, the theory of the state of the whole people is in obvious contradiction with the Marxist theory of the state, which never looked on the state as an organ protecting common social interests', *Pregled* (Sarajevo), No. 1–2, 1964, pp. 51–70.

[22] O. V. Kuusinen, speech at February 1964 plenary session of the central committee of the CPSU, *Pravda*, 19 May 1964.

doctrinal tendencies do not always coincide. For instance the Indonesian party participates in the 'national bourgeois' government of Sukarno's 'guided democracy', but reproaches the 'rightist clique of Dange' for 'collaborating' with the Indian Congress. For local reasons it accepts the slogan of NASAKOM (nationalism, religion, communism) as an expression of what for an orthodox Marxist revolutionary would be the *union sacrée*; Aidit even addresses the Bankers Association to tell them of his support for ' the forces of the national capitalists in economic construction' and is tender towards religion. But when Togliatti advocates a soft approach to religion in Catholic Italy this is revisionism. Clearly what is an orthodox sauce for an Indonesian gander is a reformist poison for an Indian or an Italian goose.

Yet this is only one instance of the ideological confusion resulting from the adaptation of a universalist doctrine to local conditions and political requirements. Under the impact of polycentrism, the communist movement loses its unity, and Marxist theory and Leninist strategy lose their universality. The two processes reinforce each other and in turn add to the polycentric momentum.

For Marx and Engels it was an elementary axiom that socialism emerges out of the class struggle between bourgeoisie and proletariat, and that it cannot be built in the absence of these classes. Lenin's ' voluntarism' diluted the theoretical element of the Marxist theory of revolution, but did not dispense with its proletarian character altogether. This has happened, as even schoolboys know by now, with a further shift of Marxism to yet more underdeveloped countries. It is interesting to see the implications of this in communist polemics.

An American communist, Gus Hall, uses a respectable Marxist argument to condemn the Chinese heterodoxy:

> Any attempt to see other, non-working class elements as a replacement for the role the working class is destined to play is like placing round pegs in square holes. . . . The mistaken views of the leaders of the Communist Party of China can fundamentally be explained as resulting from the weakening of the working-class concept, of working-class ideology, and the increase of non-working class influences. . . . It is also evident that they do not see the rise of socialism as an extension of the class struggle. . . .[23]

The British Marxist, Idris Cox, uses relatively Leninist reasoning:

> The advance to socialism is possible only if the working class advances to leadership in the national united front . . . [but] the fact [is] that the working class is not yet in the leadership of the independent African states.[24]

But the late Professor Potekhin explained in a most un-Marxist way that

> Marxism represents, in particular, a teaching of the most general laws of the development of any society, including a pre-capitalist

---

[23] *World Marxist Review*, No. 8, August 1964, p. 35.
[24] *Marxism Today*, February 1964, p. 44.

one. It includes the conception of a non-capitalist road, that is to say a development which can lead to socialism by-passing the capitalist stage, particularly for those countries where the classes of bourgeoisie and proletariat have not had time to form.[25]

The pro-Chinese *Revolution* (Vol. 1, No. 9), in an article on ' The Class Struggle in Africa ' manages to be even less orthodox:

> A century ago Marx formulated the theory of the evolution of societies, analysing the genesis of European capitalism and demonstrating the possibilities of this society. . . . However, the present societies of West Africa are not essentially similar to the ' classical ' description of class societies: based on slavery, the feudal system, or capitalism . . . [Marx] chose a new term for certain pre-capitalist societies which he felt were not based on either slavery or the feudal system: ' Asiatic society '. But since the appearance of Black Africa on the scene of contemporary history, the problem has been posed of societies until now even less known. Dogmatism in this domain consists in giving a particular historical formula a universal significance. . . . The fact is that the social class begotten by colonialism which had the mission of liquidating its domination was not the proletariat, but the class of minor functionaries. . . . The political consciousness of the workers was not—and could not be— more advanced than that of the minor officials.

Although this article is quite remarkable in the current Marxist ideological output for its relative lack of doctrinal cant, it is a far cry indeed from Marx's own idea of socialism being born out of the womb of capitalism. A Polish poet summarised the position in a striking image[26]:

> *Congo*
> *I welcome your totems*
> *Calling together in the darkness*
> *The naked warriors.*
>
> *Congo*
> *Revolution the witch-doctor*
> *In tiger skins*
> *Marches through the bush*
> *And dances.*
>
> *Congo*

Poor Marx, whose revolution is now symbolised by a witch-doctor in tiger skins! This then is the outcome of his attempt to build a proletarian international with a revolutionary ideology. It has broken down in every respect, and the only remaining question is what will happen to the fragments of what used to be a unitary movement.

25 *Kommunist*, No. 1, 1964, p. 112.
26 *Polityka*, 19 September 1964.

IT is a long time since Marx's slogan, 'Workers of all countries, unite!', was adopted by the First International; the intervening changes in the interpretation of internationalism illuminate the distance traversed. In the twenties Lenin coined a new slogan: 'Workers and oppressed peoples of all countries, unite!'. In 1927 Stalin gave his own authoritative re-definition of internationalism: 'An internationalist is one who unreservedly, without hesitation, without conditions, is ready to defend the Soviet Union'. In their 14 June 1963 letter, the Chinese pointed out that with the emergence of other communist countries 'the touchstone of proletarian internationalism for every communist party is whether or not it resolutely defends the whole of the socialist camp'. The definition still hangs fire and there have been many occasions when it was insisted that, as Kadar put it, ' the attitude towards the Soviet Union and its communist party is still today the touchstone of internationalism ' (*Pravda,* 21 August 1962). On the centennial of the First International the definition was reformulated in the theses published by the Institute of Marxism-Leninism: 'The touchstone of internationalism is the attitude to the world socialist system and its unity' (*Pravda,* 11 September 1964). This, however, as the director of the Institute explained, still means that 'if anyone is a communist . . . then he is at one with and on the side of the Soviet Union, the chief bastion of all socialist countries, of the entire international workers movement' (*Kommunist,* No. 13, 1964).

The hundredth anniversary of the First International provided the antagonists with an occasion to draw some contemporary lessons. The Soviet *Theses* maintained that the Chinese ' are largely copying the tactical postulates and splitting methods of the enemies of Marxism who operated within the First International'. The pro-Chinese *Voix du Peuple* (2 October 1964) asserted that 'like Bakunin one hundred years ago, the modern revisionists . . . [engage] in a diversionist manoeuvre: they denounce an alleged personality cult, of Marx then, of Stalin today '.

Current internationalist feelings were expressed most intransigently by the Albanians, who declared that ' any attempt, any hope, any illusion about the possibility of finding a middle way, a common ground, acceptable to both Marxists and revisionists, must remain futile ' (*Zeri i Popullit,* 6 October 1964).

On their side the Russians continued to press their allies. Their *Theses* proclaimed:

> The present-day communist movement does not have, as it once did, a guiding centre. But it is inconceivable as a single whole without certain organisational principles, strengthening the political solidarity of the various national detachments of the working class of which it is composed.

The rejection of 'Togliattism' was even more explicitly stressed in a speech by Ponomarev at the meeting in Moscow commemorating the centenary (*Pravda,* 29 September 1964):

> Now that the situation in the communist movement has become especially complicated, it is all the more necessary to act as Marx, Engels, and Lenin taught. The organisational forms of the international links have changed. There is no basis now for the existence of a centralised organisation of the International's type. But international solidarity is vitally necessary and it must develop in forms corresponding to the new stage of the communist movement. . . . Any attempt to interpret the independence of the parties as the abandonment of common internationalist tasks, as some form of 'neutrality', cannot be regarded as a sign either of independence or of maturity.

At a similar commemorative meeting in Berlin, another secretary of the CC of the CPSU, Andropov, also made an indirect reply to Togliatti's testament (*Neues Deutschland*, 27 September 1964):

> Recently voices have been heard saying that the party, in order to exist as a national force, must remain aloof from the international movement, must show no consideration for common tasks, in order to demonstrate to the masses that it is acting solely as the representative of national interests. . . . But can we consider it correct that we should for this reason deny international responsibilities and play down common resolution and united action? [27]

But how was united action to be achieved? The Soviets provided a veiled answer in the *Theses*. They declared that the First International was 'the expression of the most important organisational principles of proletarian internationalism', and emphasised that two of them—the prohibition of factional and schismatic activities and the subordination of the minority to the will of the majority—' retain their significance even in our time'.

The centennial provided an occasion to demonstrate again the irreconcilability of the Russian and Chinese positions regarding the internationalist 'rules of the game'. The anniversary editorial in *People's Daily* (30 September 1964), reiterated that 'the solution of common problems can be achieved only by unanimous agreement'. But the majority rule and the principle of unanimity are of course incompatible. In effect, like the Russians in 1945 vis-à-vis the United Nations, the Chinese insisted on having a veto in the international, socialist internationalism notwithstanding.

An article in *Mezhdunarodnaya Zhizn* (No. 8, 1964, p. 17), ridiculing 'those Western gentlemen who imply that "Marx's faith in international proletarian solidarity" has not justified itself', provided figures which in a flash explain the background of the problem. It gave the figure of 50 millions as the total present membership of all the communist parties in the world. Out of this, the ruling parties constitute almost 90 per cent; with the two big non-ruling parties, the Indonesian and the

---

[27] The first part of this paragraph was omitted from the version of Andropov's speech subsequently published in *Kommunist* (1964, No. 14).

Italian, the figure would be 97 per cent. Thus the logical implication of the Soviet attachment to majority rule is that the 70 parties or so which constitute less than 3 per cent of total communist membership would theoretically have a decisive voice. This surely would put a strain on proletarian solidarity; not only the Chinese, but the Russians too would reject the principle if they did not expect to control the (arithmetic) majority vote. They would also reject the principle of proportional representation, as there is nothing simpler for the Chinese party than to arrive at a position in which it alone would constitute the majority of all organised communist forces, by, say, increasing CCP membership by 50 per cent. That would still represent a smaller percentage of the Chinese population than the present membership of the Soviet party represents vis-à-vis the Soviet population.

It is clear, therefore, that as unanimity is utopian in a polycentric communism, majority rule impractical, proportional representation inadmissible for any but the Chinese party, and the hegemony of a single party no longer possible, the chances of reconstituting some form of a communist international may be regarded as nil.

Once again, the hope of Engels that ' the simple feeling of solidarity based on the understanding of the identity of [their] class position suffices to create and to hold together . . . the parties of the proletariat ' proved vain. The communist parties in their majority are neither proletarian, nor holding together.

In this situation the old phrases sounded particularly hollow:

> The principles of socialist internationalism rest on a solid scientific foundation—knowledge of the objective tendencies in the epoch of socialism (*Fundamentals of Marxism-Leninism*, ed. O. Kuusinen, London, 1961, p. 768).

or

> Since the foundation of the First International . . . Marxism has withstood all the tests of time. Its immutable principles have been confirmed by the course of world history (*Pravda*, 11 September 1964)

IF anything might have appeared as inevitable at this moment, it was rather that history seemed to have set the two rival parties on a collision course, with the December 1964 conference in Moscow marking their formal split, whatever verbal concessions were going to be made to satisfy the anti-centralist parties. But things did not look too bright for the Russians: of the 26 parties only a half accepted their invitation, six (pro-Chinese) parties rejected it, and the rest failed to reply.

It was at this point that Khrushchev was removed from the stage of history. Whether the Chinese problem was among the precipitating or contributory factors in his fall is not necessarily a paramount consideration for analysing the post-Khrushchev situation. Whatever they might have been, the new leaders had less freedom of manoeuvre than was generally realised. The dismissal of Khrushchev has not removed the causes of the Sino-Soviet conflict, it has only strengthened the Chinese position in it. Their prestige was also bound to be increased by the explosion of their atom bomb on the very next day. It was in this situation that the new Soviet leaders had to make their actions appear legitimate and to consolidate their authority. In the circumstances, playing for time may appear the only possibility, and, indeed, in their first moves they seemed to evade rather than face the issues, to procrastinate rather than take a definite stand on any problem, to use diplomacy as a substitute for, rather than a complement of, policy. Unpleasant choices were being avoided, hopes maintained or raised in opposite quarters, both internally and externally.

This cannot be done indefinitely, but it can be done for some time, creating the impression that things are simultaneously moving and standing still. At one and the same time, the new leaders were saying that Soviet policy would remain unchanged and implying that it would change to a new course, assuring the Americans about 'peaceful coexistence' and making friendly gestures to the Chinese. The removal of Khrushchev made possible the attempt to avoid the immediate consequences of the collision course by lowering the temperature of the Sino-Soviet dispute, without however giving up any fundamental interest or the doctrinal positions reflecting them. But these are the real issues in the Sino-Soviet conflict. Khrushchev also initially tried to avoid the conflict on two fronts, but failed. His successors may consider that the dilemma can be resolved by more flexible or skilful tactics, but they have only succeeded in weakening the Soviet position in the international communist movement still further.

Predictably, the 'retirement' of Khrushchev embarrassed many parties. They reacted more sharply to this than to any other issue; the subsequent talks between the Russians and Chinese provided another occasion to demonstrate their attitudes. With few exceptions they reacted according to the pattern established before.

The Chinese were discreet and cautious, ready to exploit politically and diplomatically their symbolic (but only symbolic) triumph. The pro-Chinese parties and faction-parties were more explicit. They immediately proclaimed that Khrushchev's fall signified the bankruptcy of Soviet revisionist policy and said the preparatory conference of the 26 parties in Moscow should be called off. They made their approval of the new Soviet leadership conditional upon its abandonment not just of Khrushchev but of the Soviet stand on all contentious issues. In effect, although some of them, like the secretary-general of the Japanese CP, Kenji Miyamoto, showed concern about the Soviet need to save face, what they wanted was complete Soviet capitulation in the conflict with the Chinese and pro-Chinese parties.

A comment in *Akahata* (25 October 1964) was fairly typical: it expressed the hope that 'the leaders of the CPSU would thoroughly re-examine their revisionist line in both its international and domestic aspects and return to the genuine Marxist-Leninist position', and added that 'modern revisionism is bound to be repudiated and smashed by the people'. The same idea was expressed, with minor variations, by other pro-Chinese parties and tendencies, most cautiously by the national communist, Aidit, ex-neutralist in the dispute, and most vociferously by the obscure pro-Chinese American group which demanded in its Bulletin, *Hammer & Steel Newsletter* (October 1964) that the CPSU should be 'self-critical [in its] approach and talks with the Albanian and Chinese parties' and should 're-establish the truth that Stalin was an outstanding Marxist-Leninist leader'. Another American pro-Chinese paper, *Workers World* (29 October 1964) said that there was a 'strong possibility that the Brezhnev-Kosygin leadership will even deepen the retrogressive tendency evident in the Khrushchev regime'.

The Albanians were of course the most vitriolic in their demand for the condemnation of 'the perfidious line of the 20th and the 22nd congresses' and of 'Yugoslav revisionism'. In their public reply to the Soviet invitation to the 26-parties conference (published in *Zeri i Popullit* on 6 October 1964) they announced that they 'will have nothing further to do with the renegade group of Nikita Khrushchev'. Now, not surprisingly, Stiro Koleka, member of the Albanian politburo, declared in his speech of 23 October that 'the disappearance of Nikita Khrushchev from the political scene is a great victory for our party', but added that 'it will continue the struggle until the complete extermination of the revisionist traitors'. *Zeri i Popullit* (2 November 1964) explained that 'the fall of Khrushchev has not eliminated revisionism in the USSR', and in its issue of 9 November requested a *restitutio ad integrum* of Stalin:

> One of the most important measures [in the struggle for the liquidation of the deviations from Marxism-Leninism] will be to bring back to his due place the figure and the work of Stalin and to reject the Khrushchevian calumnies against him.

There was of course consternation in Belgrade and hints against 'rotten compromises' in the Yugoslav press, which uttered warnings against China's 'hegemonistic policy'. On 13 November, the Belgian *La Voix du Peuple* reproduced a declaration (adopted in June) by 'the revolutionary communists of Yugoslavia' calling for the overthrow of the Tito regime and the creation of a new party 'under the banner of Marx-Engels-Lenin-Stalin'.

Even if the idea of rehabilitating Stalin and taking the road to Canossa (in Albania) was not taken too seriously in Moscow, the new leaders had good reasons for anxiety about some less symbolic consequences of their actions. One of the immediate results was the undermining of the Soviet position in the split parties. The Asian parties were already largely lost and now Moscow itself seemed to give the *coup de grâce* to its own last footholds there. The pro-Chinese elements used the occasion to attempt to destroy politically their still surviving opponents. Immediately after Khrushchev's fall, Miyamoto said ' this is an extremely heavy blow ' to the pro-Soviet Shiga-Suzuki group. He added (*Akahata*, 17 October 1964): ' The group of anti-party revisionists who betrayed our Japanese Communist Party and engaged in factional activities staked their " future " entirely on Khrushchev '.

Similar voices were raised everywhere by other pro-Chinese parties, not only in Asia. The pro-Chinese Belgian faction-party declared in *La Voix du Peuple* (6 November 1964) that Khrushchev's fall was a prelude to the political disappearance of their pro-Soviet rivals. It compared what they wrote before and after ' the ouster of their leader ', and indeed, *Le Drapeau Rouge*, the organ of their opponents, found it difficult to swallow and was also most unhappy about a possible Sino-Soviet détente. In its issue of 4 November 1964, it declared that it would continue to defend the line of the 20th congress even ' if the departure of Khrushchev should mark the break with the policy adopted at that congress ', although it finally accepted the original Soviet version of Khrushchev's dismissal as due to ' fatigue and old age '. The *Voix du peuple* (13 November 1964) promptly called this ' completely Jesuitical '.

But the most telling proof that the struggle was continued and the prospects of unity disregarded was provided by the action of the Indian ' leftist communists ' who proclaimed a rival party, ironically enough on the same day (7 November 1964) that Chou En-lai was participating in the Moscow celebrations of the 47th anniversary of the October revolution. It is against this background that the unhappy journey to Moscow of the ' rightist ' leader of the official party, Dange, can be seen in its proper political perspective. Even though the request of the ' leftists ' to be recognised by the Soviet Union as the party eligible to participate in the international communist conference is not likely to be granted, the fall of Khrushchev weakened the pro-Soviet communists in India, undermined their claim to be the only legitimate party, and generally took the wind out of their sails at a time when they were locked in combat with their opponents and were preparing their own congress. It was held in December 1964 and was attended by a Soviet delegation headed by Ponomarev.

The Moscow events had a similarly harmful effect on the prospects of the pro-Soviet Japanese communists. Party secretary Miyamoto said at the 9th congress of the Japanese CP that they were ' utterly discredited by their blind obedience to the leadership of the CPSU ', and dismissed them as ' a handful of parasites who have no basis whatsoever among the Japanese people ' (*Akahata*, 25 November 1964). When, after the failure of the Chou En-lai talks, Moscow finally gave Shiga the green light for the formation of a pro-Soviet communist party in Japan, its proclamation on 2 December 1964 came as an anti-climax. The pro-Soviet group had by then lost whatever small momentum it possessed, and could hope to produce even less of a band-wagon effect in the near future than they could under Khrushchev.

The French CP, which found so difficult the shift from the Stalinist to the Khrushchevian mould, was only slightly less unhappy. According to the Paris *l'Express* (9–15 November 1964), its delegation to Moscow declared that 'Khrushchev's dismissal signifies for the French CP an immediate loss of 15 per cent of its members and 20 per cent of its electoral votes'. Even if exaggerated, *se non e vero e ben trovato.*

It is not surprising that, immediately after the event, *l'Humanité* stressed that 'the major preoccupation of the French communists, even if they are passionately interested in the decisions of their Soviet comrades, is to put into practice their own decisions', and that the reluctant diehard heirs of Thorez felt it necessary to emphasise in their resolution of 6 November 1964 that 'dogmatism is today the main danger'.

The French Union of Communist Students, for a long time in a state of rebellion against the party, went much further in its resolution of 24 October 1964. It announced that the 'practices which led to the dismissal of Khrushchev bring into question the value of the example given by the socialist countries in the struggle for socialism'. It requested 'immediate publication of the full text of the verbatim report of the CPSU central committee meeting of 14 October, including of course the speech by Khrushchev'.

The leader of the Italian communist delegation to Moscow, Berlinguer, stated in *l'Unita* (4 November 1964) that they were not satisfied with the explanations received, and the party resolution published two days later again mentioned its 'reservations'. The reactions of many other West European parties were similar. The Norwegian CP stated that the official reason given for Khrushchev's resignation was 'incorrect', and the British, Swiss, Danish, and Austrian parties sent delegations to Moscow in search of an explanation.

The leaders of the East European parties expressed their dissatisfaction in a more veiled form, but they were clearly taken by surprise, and even Ulbricht referred at the beginning to his 'emotion'. Gomulka and Kadar reasserted their relatively autonomous position vis-à-vis the Soviet change, and so did Novotny. The Czechs immediately published a most unorthodox plan for the structural reform of their economy. Only Zhivkov made no gesture to assert an autonomous stand. The Rumanians simply ignored the affair and published nothing except the official Soviet communiqué. Their ostentatious unconcern emphasised their attachment, newly acquired, to the principle of non-interference in another party's affairs, and being non-aligned they were not embarrassed by the Sino-Soviet talks for which they had pressed earlier, realising that, whatever their outcome, it would still leave them room for manoeuvre.

Another non-aligned party, the Cuban, also largely ignored these events about which they had no particular reason to feel unhappy, except perhaps in respect to uncertainty about the Soviet commitment to Cuba. But this, they may have felt, was no less precarious under Khrushchev, against whom their feelings ran high at the time of the Cuban affair in 1962. On the other hand the Sino-Soviet détente made it easier for them to avoid the choice which so sharply divided the state and party interests of the *fidelistas*.

No such dilemmas existed for the pro-Chinese faction-parties, all of which continued their struggle against their 'revisionist' opponents during the post-Khrushchevian lull in the Sino-Soviet feud. The Chinese themselves eventually abandoned their original reserved attitude and resumed veiled attacks by publishing an editorial in *Red Flag* (21 November 1964) on 'Why Khrushchev Fell', which implicitly criticised the post-Khrushchev leadership. Novotny, in Moscow, complained on 3 December about the 'new unjustified attacks', and the Yugoslavs referred to it as 'starting a new campaign against Soviet policy . . . [in] the absolute conviction that only the Chinese side is in the right, while the Soviet side must change its general line down to the very foundations'. Finally, *Pravda* (12 December 1964) announced that the meeting of the drafting commission to prepare the International Communist Conference will take place on 1 March 1965. The fall of Khrushchev resulted only in a short postponement of the conference. The new Soviet leaders, who were trying to avoid their historical dilemmas, crossed the Rubicon again.

The character of these dilemmas was plain and the choice as painful as before. The difference between the state and the party, which until the death of Stalin was a theologico-diplomatic fiction, has now acquired some significance, at least in the short run. In this perspective a rapprochement with China may improve the Soviet position in the balance of power with the capitalist world, but in the long run it may also improve the relative position of China vis-à-vis Russia. In historical perspective, the alternation of conflict and détente is bound to undermine the position of the CPSU in the international communist movement, whatever tactical advantages it may see in the one or the other at this moment, at the beginning of the polycentric era. But this does not make the immediate choice unreal. In accordance with Marx's own dictum, the consciousness of the actors on the historical stage lags behind the historical realities of the epoch. The paradoxical thing is that while their particular dilemmas now acquire a general significance, they cannot be analysed in this general perspective otherwise than through the individual histories.

GENERAL answers are no longer sufficient; each case must now be studied separately in the process of its adaptation (or lack of it) to the local situation and to the realities of the polycentric communist age.

The present volume is devoted to such studies, within a more or less comprehensive framework. Without basic factual knowledge of the differentiation in what once was international communism no intelligent political judgment is possible in the new historical situation marked by the breakdown of the idea of organised revolutionary solidarity. The complexity of the situation is already fantastic, and this is only an early stage of the process. No doubt the diversification will proceed further, and after German, Russian, Chinese, Italian, Indonesian, and other 'Marxisms', still other doctrinal positions will emerge within the general formula of 'applying the universal truth of Marxism-Leninism to the concrete situation' in a given country. But ideological veils and dialectical acrobatics can no longer hide the fact that, just as there is no longer a unitary movement, so there is really no longer a unitary ideology. The homely truths of the believers are no longer safely anchored in the certitudes of the Inevitable March of History (too many vanguards are marching in too many directions); of the mission of the party to accelerate the 'historical process' and to bring about its predetermined outcome (too many interpretations of what is necessary to achieve it are competing); and of the validity of continuous amalgamation of the original Marxist and the original Leninist components in the Bolshevik formula (the discrepancy between the two has become politically explosive).

Yet the effect of the blows to ideology will be different in different countries; revolutionary attitudes and millennial hopes will not disappear. On the other hand, the erosion of the universal Marxist-Leninist truths will not be without some advantages to the individual parties; like their growing autonomy, national or regional, it may make their activity more, rather than less, effective, not only because it will remove a foreign stain on their image and may help them to break out of their political isolation, but also because they will be able to decide on their own strategy and tactics, and to adjust themselves to the political situation through local leadership and with local doctrinal blinkers only.

Here, too, the effects will be diverse, and it is impossible to draw up balance sheets of each party's potential assets and liabilities following the advent of polycentrism. Undoubtedly they are different in small and big parties, in industrial and in underdeveloped countries, in the ruling and the non-ruling parties. Polycentrism can make both the 'guerrilla' revolutionaries and the 'structural' reformists more successful by making them more flexible in exploiting local conditions, but in practice it is unlikely that it will in many cases, because of the disadvantages which it also carries. In short, no general reasoning can replace a concrete political analysis, either for optimists or for pessimists; now, more than ever before, it must be done case by case.

Some negative generalisations can however be ventured, as they are in fact implicit in the idea of the polycentric era itself.

One is that none of the three main tendencies in communism at present, the Chinese drive for hegemony and the creation of the new international, the Soviet struggle to preserve its domination in a diluted form, and the polycentric tendency of the parties who resist bi-polarisation and aim at communist solidarity based on the autonomy of the parties, is likely to succeed in its major premise. It is difficult to imagine the Chinese achieving a position of domination similar to that once enjoyed by the Russians, because the forces of nationalism are now too strong and the authority of the centre (and its mystique) no longer exist. By contributing to the undermining of Moscow's authority, the maximum they can achieve is a sort of very limited and temporary bi-polarity, one end of which will have a heavy Asiatic emphasis and will amount in practice to a regional grouping of the Asian parties around China. The Russians, as we have seen, can preserve their position only by sacrificing substance to shadow, and by contributing still further to the polycentric divisions and therefore to the inevitable undermining of their own authority. The autonomists may achieve their aim of autonomy or independence, but it will not contribute to international communist solidarity, but to its erosion. Faced with this situation and its likely effects on the national communist parties, they may show a tendency, already visible, to regional groupings to strengthen their position and to counteract the worst effects of polycentric fragmentation on national lines. The communist parties are, to use Weber's classification of parties, not just ideological communities, but also communities of interest, and in the age of polycentrism they are bound to be less of the former and more of the latter; but here again the result is likely to be different in different cases: the parties in the underdeveloped countries will, of course, retain a more ideological posture than those in the industrial countries. Cutting across this division is the difference between the ruling and the non-ruling parties, as one of the results of polycentrism is that party interest and *raison d'état*, where it rules, no longer necessarily coincide. Therefore the effect of polycentrism on party relations is to be distinguished from that on communist state relations.

The logic of polycentrism, carried to its extreme, is of course national communism, and its side effect is factionalism within the parties. But it is unlikely to be carried to its logical conclusion; it will remain a tendency producing different effects in different degree in different cases. Internationally, the communist parties will continue to pay lip-service to the idea of unity. The less it is a reality, the more they will stress their devotion to it. But in practice they will try to safeguard their own interests, which was certainly not the case under Stalin, and not quite yet the case in Khrushchev's time. These interests, needless to say, do not necessarily coincide with the interests of their countries.

The idea of internationalism will thus in effect be abandoned by communists, just as earlier they abandoned the libertarian elements of 19th-century Marxism. Perhaps, just as the idea of liberty was preserved by others, so will the idea of internationalism be preserved in the epoch when communism will have lost it.

SCHISM AND SECESSION

Kevin Devlin

IN the drama of disintegration which we misleadingly call the Sino-Soviet conflict, it is impossible to discern a single point of no return. But there does seem to have been a year of no return—the year between the autumn of 1962 and the autumn of 1963.[1]

This period opened with a watershed in post-war history: the double Caribbean-Himalayan crisis of October-November 1962, which set Soviet foreign policy on a new course more clearly antagonistic to Chinese interests, and strengthened the Chinese claim that the revisionist CPSU had forfeited its position as leader of the international revolutionary movement. There followed an intensification of Sino-Soviet polemics, which now spread to other parties; systematic Chinese attempts to shake Soviet control of the international front organisations and later to set up rival regional organisations; a series of grave Sino-Soviet frontier incidents; and the 25-point Chinese manifesto of 14 June 1963, which represented an explicit challenge to Soviet authority in the world movement. The complete failure of the subsequent bilateral talks in Moscow came as no surprise; and as the twelve-month period ended in the autumn of 1963 the Russians were busy whipping up support among fraternal parties and publishing the first 'trial balloon' calls for an early international conference to put Mao Tse-tung in his heretical place.

The original Russian decision to press for a showdown with the Chinese must have been in large measure due to another major development during that year, the intensification of the Chinese campaign to win supporters throughout the world movement. This global offensive was marked by the growth of old and the emergence of new pro-Chinese factions in Western Europe, the Americas, and Afro-Asia, and by mounting evidence that many of them were receiving not only encouragement but aid from Peking. The flow of expenses-paid visitors to China increased, while a torrent of multilingual pamphlets and papers at uneconomic prices [2] brought the revolutionary gospel to the most unlikely corners of the earth. A significant development here was the appearance, in the spring of 1963, of French and Spanish editions (entitled *Pékin Information* and *Pekin Informa* respectively) of the main Chinese propaganda organ, *Peking Review*.

The New China News Agency (NCNA) played an important part in this campaign, establishing new offices abroad at a rate that no commercial agency could match; by mid-1964 there were thirteen in Latin America alone. These offices served other ends beside those of a

---

[1] Even Khrushchev's fall can produce only lulls in the complex clash of interests.
[2] According to the *New York Times*, 4 April 1964, *Pékin Information* was available in Central Africa for 7½ U.S. cents a year—airmail delivery.

news service. Their links with local pro-Chinese factions were particularly obvious in Belgium and in Chile. In March 1963—a few weeks
after the first number of *Pekin Informa* appeared—a group of dissident
Chilean communists went into business as the firm of *Espartaco
Editores Ltda.* (Spartacus Publishers Ltd.), with an office in the same
Santiago building as the local NCNA bureau. This firm handled the
distribution of Chinese propaganda material not only in Chile but in
other Latin American countries; and any remaining doubts about its
function were dispelled at a public rally in September 1963, when the
Spartacus group came out into the open as an unconditionally pro-
Chinese faction.[3]

One particularly striking feature of this period was the proliferation
of pro-Chinese factionalist publications, which continues to this day.
A survey—which is almost certainly incomplete—shows that the eleven
months following August 1963 saw the appearance of 27 such publications in fifteen countries.[4] Some of these were mimeographed sheets
clandestinely circulated; others were openly distributed and well-produced—so well-produced as to suggest there there were external
resources behind them.

By far the most important of these publications is the international
monthly *Révolution,* edited by Jacques Vergès, which plays such a central
role in the global campaign that it deserves more detailed discussion.
As the newly-appointed director of the Algerian review, *Révolution
Africaine,* Vergès visited Peking in March 1963 at the expense of the
All-China Union of Journalists. On his return his increasing emphasis
on the 'Chinese model' brought him into conflict with the Algerian
regime, and in May he was dismissed. He promptly—so promptly
that it could only have been the result of ripened plans—moved to
Lausanne, Switzerland, where he began issuing his own version of the
English edition of *Révolution Africaine,* which in July was significantly
retitled *Africa Latin America Asia—Revolution.* This was printed in
the same building by the publishing firm run by a young Marxist of
Swedish origin, Nils Anderson, later to become an authorised distributor
of Chinese polemical literature. Then, in September 1963, came the first
issue of the French edition,[5] and with it a new development in the
ideological conflict.

---

³ See Ernst Halperin, *Sino-Cuban Trends: The Case of Chile* (M.I.T. Press, 1964),
pp. 71–72, 83–86 and 147–151.
⁴ The principal ones were *La Voix du Peuple, La Vérité,* and *De Waarheid* (Belgium);
Vanguard and *The Australian Communist* (Australia); *Die Rote Fahne* (Austria);
El Obrero (Argentina); *L'Etincelle* and *Octobre* (Switzerland); *Orientering* (Den-
mark); *Bulletin d'Information Marxiste-Léniniste* (France); *Vanguard* (Britain);
Proletario, El Comunista, and *Mundo Obrero Revolucionario* (Spain); *Principios
Marxista-Leninistas* and *Combate* (Chile); *Nuova Unità* (Italy); *Bandera Roja* and
Peru Juvenil (Peru); *Rode Vlag* (Holland); and *Révolution* (international, Paris-based).
To these must be added at least five vernacular papers in India and two in Ceylon.
⁵ The print-run of the French edition grew in the first year from 10,000 to 20,000,
but sale never exceeded 7,500, and later dropped to 3,000–7,000 copies. The English
edition (about 10,000 copies, of which less than 7,000 sold) suffered from intramural
trouble. In March 1964 it temporarily ceased to appear, and later a cryptic note in

The formidable scope and purpose of this venture were summed up frankly by Vergès in an interview with a non-communist journalist:

> *Révolution* has two aims. One aim is to ensure contact on a political level—and a perfectly legal one—between all revolutionary movements in the world. Two—to fight, within the socialist movement, modern revisionist tendencies which sacrifice revolution to collaboration with imperialism.[6]

WITHIN this framework of world-wide factionalism, Chinese strategy took a new and fateful turn in the summer of 1963. The change was heralded by a pregnant passage in the Chinese letter of 14 June: 'If the leading group in any party adopt a non-revolutionary line and convert it into a reformist party, then Marxist-Leninists inside and outside the party will replace them' (*People's Daily*, 17 June 1963). Within a few months it became clear that the Chinese had gone beyond encouraging factional groups; they were now, in chosen instances, intervening to promote the formation of secessionist parties, as distinct from anti-party factions.

The rival, pro-Chinese parties which have been formed since then present a scene of great diversity. In some countries they are numerically insignificant; in others (India, Ceylon, and Peru, for example) they pose a serious threat to the pro-Soviet party. Again, some use legalistic processes to justify the split—alleged violations of the statutes, a national conference, a refounding congress, and so on—while others simply break with the established party in the name of Marxism-Leninism and announce the formation of a rival body. Some retain the title of the pro-Soviet party in order to strengthen their claim to legitimacy; others emphasise their challenge by choosing a new title. In some instances there is clear evidence of Chinese intervention; in others (as in Switzerland and probably in a few clandestine communist movements, such as the Paraguayan one) the split seems to have been due to local initiative. In short, these secessionist parties cannot be lumped together and labelled with a convenient generalisation: to appreciate their significance and the important part they play in the ideological conflict, we must examine them one by one.

the French edition (July-August 1964) revealed that the American editor, Richard Gibson, had been dismissed, having ' abused his position as former Secretary of the " Fair Play for Cuba Committee " to try to penetrate the ranks of the international revolutionary movement '. In October 1964 the magazine became a bimonthly; the English edition reappeared, and the first number of a Spanish edition for Latin America was to be produced in Bogota, Colombia.

6 *Newsweek*, 9 March 1964. This article claimed that *Révolution* was ' reportedly subsidised by a $75,000 grant from the Red Chinese Embassy in Bern last summer '. The mysterious resources of the project were, indeed, in keeping with its ambitious programme. Vergès was assisted by an eight-nation editorial board. The headquarters office was in the heart of Paris, with subsidiary bureaus in Lausanne, London, New York, Dar-es-Salaam, Havana, and Peking. Given its circulation, high standard of production, and lack of commercial advertising, the economics of *Révolution* could only be explained in terms of politics, though the situation may be more complicated than it appears on the surface.

It should be noted that we are concerned here only with pro-Chinese secession; and it is not the only kind. Thus, an earlier stage of the process of fragmentation which followed Stalin's death has left in Western Europe a number of revisionist splinter-parties which still form a significant feature of the regional communist scene. By a more arbitrary choice, I shall also exclude the complex situation in Mexico. As far as secessionist parties are concerned, Mexican Marxism offers an *embarras de richesses,* but the result cannot be neatly pigeon-holed in Sino-Soviet categories. Chinese influence is certainly at work, but so are Castroist and Trotskyist tendencies, and all of them have their mingled effect upon an earlier patchwork of Soviet-tolerated disunity which produced three rival 'communist' parties,[7] all on good terms with Moscow. Two of the latest splinter-groups in Mexico—the Spartacus League (*Liga Espartaco*) and the Bolshevik Communist Party of Mexico (PCBM)—have adopted revolutionary positions which can be broadly described as Chinese (or Cuban); but, lacking further evidence, neither can be identified as a pro-Chinese party in the terms of this study.

The Forerunners

THE OLDEST OF THE SECESSIONIST, pro-Chinese parties is the Communist Party of Brazil, formed in February 1962. The Brazilian split thus came a year and a half before the wave of carefully prepared pro-Chinese secession in Ceylon, Belgium, Australia, and elsewhere; and in fact it appears to be a special case.

Its origins go back to 1956–57—before the Sino-Soviet conflict came into the open—when a dispute over national strategy divided the party leadership. One faction urged a policy of peaceful infiltration and struggle for the full legalisation of the party; the other emphasised the possibilities of agitation and clandestine violence in such areas as northeast Brazil. The veteran Secretary-General, Luiz Carlos Prestes, gave his decisive backing to the peaceful way, and in August 1957 four 'hard-line' militants were expelled from the central committee. In the organisational battle which followed, leading up to the party's fifth congress in 1960, the rebels had no chance of success. The congress reaffirmed the Prestes line, and its opponents were dropped from the central committee.

The Sino-Soviet conflict with its polarising influence had not yet reached the stage of open polemics and proselytising factionalism in 1960; if it had, a formal split might well have occurred in Brazil at that point. As it was, the internal struggle continued, aggravated by further disciplinary measures, and only gradually found its place in the wider context. In August 1961 the embittered rebels found a pretext for action in the leadership's decision to change the party's name from

---

[7] The Mexican CP (PCM), founded in 1919; the Mexican Workers' and Peasants' Party (POCM), founded in 1940; and the People's Socialist Party (PPS), founded in 1946.

' Communist Party of Brazil ' to ' Brazilian Communist Party '. This was, in fact, merely a device which it was hoped would help the party to regain full legal status; its programme remained substantially the same. But the dissident faction seized upon this as a ' liquidationist ' move, launched a campaign against the central committee, and demanded that a special congress be called to decide the issue. The demand was rejected, and in December 1961 the leading rebels were expelled from the party. Two months later, at an ' extraordinary national representative conference ' in Sao Paulo, they formed the rival ' Communist Party of Brazil '.

Increasingly, the new party aligned itself with the revolutionary positions of the Cubans and Chinese, as opposed to the revisionism represented not only by Prestes but by Khrushchev. Yet for more than a year the Chinese took no public notice of this ally (although there can be little doubt that links had already been established between them). Then, on 31 March 1963, two minor members of the secessionist party's central committee arrived in Peking. Brief NCNA dispatches announced that they had ' a friendly talk ' with three members of the CPC leadership on 4 April and were received by Mao Tse-tung on 19 April. There was no joint communiqué and no mention of the other Brazilian Communist Party; the Chinese were obviously at pains not to draw attention to an historic occasion. For the first time Peking had given official recognition to an anti-Soviet splinter-party. Coming as it did during a lull in Sino-Soviet polemics, the incident gave forewarning of the Chinese intransigence which was to wreck the bilateral talks in Moscow three months later. It also heralded the wave of pro-Chinese secession which followed the collapse of those talks.

In the Soviet ' Open Letter ' of 14 July 1963, replying to the CPC's manifesto issued a month earlier, the Chinese were accused of ' organising and supporting various anti-party groups of renegades ', including the ' Amazonas-Grabois group ' in Brazil.[8] Two weeks later the secessionist central committee drew up a ' Reply to Khrushchev ' in which it rejected this Soviet charge as ' out-and-out slander ', adding that ' the facts have proved to the hilt that internal factors are the main causes of the split, which essentially arose from the penetration of bourgeois ideas into the party '.[9] External influences were, indeed, involved—but they came mainly from the revisionist 20th congress of the CPSU.

From then onwards the Chinese were involved directly in the Brazilian struggle.[10] When Prestes visited Moscow in February 1964 for talks with Khrushchev, the communiqué revealed that the main topic of discussion

---

8 Mauricio Grabois and Joao Amazonas (together with Pedro Pomar, editor of *A Classe Operaria*) are the leading figures of the Brazilian splinter-party.

9 *A Classe Operaria* (Rio de Janeiro), 1–15 August 1963, and NCNA, 4 September 1963.

10 The change from the earlier claim that these secessionists represented the old party to the admission that they had founded a new party reflects their adhesion to the world-wide Chinese campaign of factionalism.

was 'the problems of the fight against factionalist splitting activities in the international communist movement'. By that time the stakes in Brazil had been raised. Under the regime of President Goulart, the pro-Soviet party's hope of full legalisation seemed near to fulfilment: a petition to that effect was before the Supreme Electoral Tribunal, and seemed likely to be approved.[11] Moreover, a popular-front alliance between the communists and the strong Brazilian Labour Party (PTB) was being discussed.

These burgeoning hopes were brutally crushed by the *coup d'état* of 1 April 1964, which sent Goulart and his more radical brother-in-law, Leonel Brizola, to exile in Uruguay, and inflicted a severe set-back on pro-Soviet and pro-Chinese communists alike. All over the country communists and sympathisers were arrested; and, it was claimed, a vast amount of incriminating documents (as well as stores of arms) was found—evidence of communist infiltration, of Soviet and Chinese involvement, and even of plans for an imminent insurrection. The new government's claims were received with a certain scepticism abroad, but this was weakened by the avalanche of documents which the authorities published during the following months. Among these documents were some allegedly found on nine Chinese—two journalists and seven members of a trade mission—arrested after the *coup* and still awaiting trial at the time of writing. According to these reports, the Chinese, heading a network of some 200 compatriots throughout Brazil, maintained close links both with the so-called 'Groups of Eleven', a revolutionary militia formed by Brizola, and with the dissident communists. One letter spoke of their cooperation with Amazonas and Grabois, described as 'the leaders of the true Brazilian Communist Party'.[12]

However objective study may evaluate this mass of documents, it seems clear, first, that the Chinese had intervened directly in the Brazilian ideological battle; second, that the struggle will continue in the changed circumstances; and third, that the pro-Soviet communists have suffered a relatively heavier loss through the *coup* than their rivals, who can point to it as vindication of their revolutionary line and who are better prepared for clandestinity. The Brazilian split is an example of how local communist dissension tends to find expression in Sino-Soviet terms, being sharpened in the process; and it is now an enduring part of that global pattern.

---

11 Although proscribed in 1947, the Brazilian CP had in recent years been able to carry on most forms of political activity, short of entering its own candidates in elections (and in October 1962 communists managed to win some half-dozen Assembly seats by assuming other party labels).

12 A photographic copy of this letter in Chinese ideographs, with a Portuguese translation, was published in *O Globo* (Rio de Janeiro), 9 May 1964. Dated 20 March 1963, it had been sent from 'Comrade Cheng, Bern, Switzerland', to Wang-Chih, one of the arrested men.

Takeover Bid

ACROSS THE ANDES IN PERU we find another split with unusual features: not pro-Chinese secession, strictly speaking, but what might be called a pro-Chinese takeover bid. The result is much the same—a factional battle, with each side claiming to represent the national communist movement. Since its foundation in 1929 the Peruvian Communist Party had been plagued by frequent bouts of factionalism, and during 1963 disunity over policy hardened along Sino-Soviet lines. The 'violent-way' faction was strengthened not only by the increasing circulation inside Peru of *Pekin Informa*, but by the fact that the Secretary-General Raul Acosta Salas, and other pro-Soviet leaders, spent the first six months of 1963 in prison.[13] On 28 August the party daily, *Unidad*, revealed something of the struggle going on by announcing that the 'national leadership' was preparing a detailed report on the ideological dispute for the next central committee plenum—adding the warning that, until the central committee had made known its stand, 'no debates should be undertaken, nor should any statements be made on this matter'.

However, this eighteenth plenum of the central committee produced no agreed stand; instead, it confirmed the split in the party. As the pro-Soviet faction later put it: 'When it was evident that they did not have a majority at the meeting . . . the splitters tried to prevent the decisions from being endorsed and carried out, and to secure the expulsion from the central committee of its best members. When they failed to achieve their ends, they broke with the party—they left the meeting and refused to recognise its resolutions'.[14]

Led by two central committee members, Sotomayor and Paredes, the opposition planned its counter-attack. This took the form of a so-called 'Fourth National Conference' of the PCP, held on 18–19 January 1964, and convened (it was claimed) by 'the majority of the central committee members and representatives from 13 out of 17 regional committees'.[15] With no members of the other faction present, the conference of 'more than 70' delegates unanimously 'expelled' Acosta and eight other pro-Soviet leaders, replaced them with a new anti-revisionist leadership, and adopted a pro-Chinese policy line.

13 Several leaders of the pro-Chinese faction were also arrested in the police action of 5 January 1963, but were released several months earlier than Acosta and his organising secretary, Jorge Del Prado. The latter later claimed, in his *World Marxist Review* article of May 1964, that the police freed the pro-Chinese leaders because they ' knew of their factional activities and evidently decided to turn them to account '.

14 Jorge Del Prado, ' Mass Struggle—the Key to Victory ', *World Marxist Review*, May 1964. A different version of presecession developments was given later by the Italian communist correspondent, Renato Sandri. ' In October 1963 ', he reported, ' a conference was held in which eight of the 35 members of the central committee participated, in addition to some lower-level representatives, and the assembly expelled from the party the majority of the central committee. These then met and proceeded to expel the dissident minority, which came to constitute a second communist party (*L'Unita*, 13 August 1964).

15 NCNA dispatch from Lima, 29 January 1964.

According to the NCNA report issued ten days later, Acosta and his followers were expelled because of ' their betrayal of Marxism-Leninism, their political degeneration, their misuse of party funds, and their recourse to splittism, creating parallel organisations '. However, the political report adopted by the conference also admitted (or boasted) that ' the revolutionary group in the central committee . . . and the leftists in the party have been rallying together swiftly and have started to set up parallel organisations in all possible places '.[16]

The bitter organisational struggle revealed by this phrase found dramatic expression a week after the conference, when pro-Chinese militants stormed and wrecked the Lima office of the now ill-named *Unidad*. Having thus attempted to silence the party organ controlled by the ' expelled ' leaders, they proceeded to found their own rival publication, *Bandera Roja* (*Red Flag*) as well as the weekly *Peru Juvenil* (*Young Peru*). The pro-Soviet leadership, having formally expelled the ' splitters ' at a Lima regional conference, enlisted Soviet aid through a polemical article by Acosta, published in *Pravda* of 22 May and extensively reported in Radio Moscow's Latin American broadcasts. The article described the rebels as a small group ' with no support in party organisations '—although it had mysterious ' financial resources '— but betrayed concern about their challenge.

The concern was justified. In the basic policy clash over revolutionary violence as opposed to political agitation—which in Peru as elsewhere has become linked with the Sino-Soviet conflict—the pro-Chinese faction has valuable allies in what has been called the ' Jacobin Left ' of Latin America.[17] The most important of these extremist organisations in Peru is the Movement of the Revolutionary Left (MIR), which joins the Paredes faction in condemning the ' opportunist ' line of the pro-Soviet communist leadership.[18] The defensive attitude which this *de facto* alliance has forced upon that leadership emerges from the article which Jorge Del Prado contributed to the May 1964 issue of *World Marxist Review*. Admitting that the ' material preconditions ' for violent revolution existed in Peru, he argued that the ' subjective ' conditions were not ripe, since the masses were not yet ready for armed insurrection. However, he emphasised, ' our line of gathering strength contributes in equal measure to the success of either of the two paths '.

The concession implied by this claim touches upon one possible and portentous result of splits in Latin American communist parties. Finding

16 NCNA dispatch from Peking, 14 May 1964.
17 The phrase is that of Dr Robert J. Alexander in his book *Today's Latin America* (New York, 1962).
18 *Révolution* (Paris), December 1963. On the other hand, a smaller Peruvian ultra-left organisation, the National Liberation Front (FLN), decided in May 1964 to expel communist members supporting either faction, on the ground that they were causing ' internal conflicts ' in the FLN.

themselves 'outbidden' by pro-Chinese factions in countries 'object-
ively' ripe for revolution, party leaders may be tempted to raise their
own bids—even if it means abandoning what remains of their former
subservience to the ends of Soviet foreign policy.

European Bridgehead

IN CONTRAST TO LATIN AMERICA, most of Western Europe today is
inhospitable territory for any brand of communism, and particularly
for Peking's gospel of violence. But even in the welfare-state West, the
ruthless logic of that gospel will always appeal to a minority of frustrated
militants. In fact, there is evidence of pro-Chinese activity, serious or
negligible, in every single West European party except the Northern
Ireland CP and the Irish (Republican) Workers Party—and their
apparent immunity may perhaps be explained by lack of information.

While no opening is neglected, the chosen Chinese bridgehead in
Europe is in Belgium, where the secessionist Belgian Communist Party
was formed in December 1963, after two years of factional ferment
marked by direct Chinese intervention and an interesting sectional
approach to secession. The leader of the anti-revisionist rebellion here
was Jacques Grippa, a fiery veteran who was expelled from the central
committee in December 1962. In the organisational battle that followed,
the symbol and instrument of Chinese intervention was the Brussels
office of the New China News Agency, opened in February 1963.
Fighting back, the party leaders made sure that no rebels were elected
as delegates to the 14th party congress held in April 1963; and this
Antwerp congress dutifully agreed to expel Grippa and three leading
followers from the party for 'factional practices'. Grippa replied by
practising more diligently, and the party countered by expelling or
suspending some 250 other dissidents within two months.

The decisive move came, significantly, a week after the Chinese
letter of 14 June had proclaimed an intensified campaign of global
factionalism. Grippa convened an 'extraordinary congress' of the
party's Brussels Federation (at the official congress of the federation,
in March 1963, his followers had been outvoted by about two to one).
The secessionist local assembly declared the official leadership of the
federation stripped of its powers for 'participation in the revisionist and
splitting policy of the Politburo', put Grippa at the head of a 'new'
leadership—and called on other federations to join it in demanding an
'Extraordinary National Congress'.

The rival Brussels Federation promptly sent fraternal delegations
to Peking and Tirana, and on their return the campaign of secession
by stages proceeded apace. In July 1963 the Federation began publishing
a bilingual monthly paper, La Vérité/De Waarheid, appealing to the
practical grievances of French-speaking and Flemish workers. In
September there appeared the first number of a polemical fortnightly
(later weekly), La Voix du Peuple—published, this time, not as the
organ of the dissident federation, but as the 'Periodical of Belgian

Communists'. In mid-November a secessionist Walloon (French-speaking) Federation of the party was founded in Charleroi. The final break came on 22 December, when 194 delegates to a 'national conference' in Brussels declared the Belgian Communist Party 'reconstituted on the national level, on the basis of Marxism-Leninism'. The new party had a uniquely Belgian structure, being made up of the bilingual Brussels Federation, the Walloon Communist Party (no longer a federation), and a barely-existent Flemish Communist Party. When a secessionist Union of Communist Students was formed in April 1964 the same tripartite structure was adopted.

The pro-Chinese Belgian CP has not been particularly successful in its challenge to its homonymous rival.[19] It is difficult to arrive at even approximate figures for relative membership strengths; but, now that the first wave of defections is over, Belgian political observers generally agree that the original party headed by Chairman Ernest Burnelle still has a numerical superiority of about eight or nine to one. This is for the whole country. In Brussels rebel strength rises to perhaps a quarter of the total, while in Flanders it is probably no more than five per cent. Another pointer is the circulation of *La Voix du Peuple*. About 10,000 copies are printed but, as of July 1964, actual sales were estimated at 3,000 or less; the rest were given away free or returned for repulping.

However, numerical strength is only part of the story, and not the most important part. Burnelle merely exposed himself to ridicule when he spoke, in an article contributed to *Pravda* (6 July 1964), of the 'total failure' of the Belgian secessionists. For the Chinese, the Belgian split has been anything but a failure. In the first place, it offers them a testing-ground in which they can try their chances of subverting or dividing a revisionist and politically insignificant communist party in a Western democracy where the revisionist hope of power through parliament has little or no chance of fulfilment. Moreover, a fully-fledged secessionist party in Western Europe, recognised as such by the pro-Chinese parties, strengthens Peking's claim to offer a global, and not merely regional, alternative to Moscow's diminished leadership of the world movement. In addition, Grippa's party can act as agents for the Chinese in Europe by establishing relations with other anti-revisionist groups.

In fact, the attitude of the Belgian secessionists to other dissident factions is often a useful indication of their status in Chinese eyes.

---

[19] Both parties have exactly the same title, *Parti Communiste de Belgique*—which has been registered in Belgium as a political organisation since 1926, the deeds of title being held by the original, pro-Soviet party. Under Belgian law, secessionist communist candidates had to adopt a different title in order to contest the local elections of October 1964 and the national elections of April 1965. They are solving the problem by going forward as the candidates of the Walloon CP, the Flemish CP, and the Brussels Federation—not of the PCB.

Thus, when *La Voix du Peuple* disowned any connection with the Paris-based publication *L'Etincelle,* that mysterious periodical soon disappeared.[20] And when Grippa's party cold-shouldered the break-away Swiss Communist Party it was a sure sign, later confirmed, that these Swiss rebels did not enjoy the approval of Peking. On the other hand, when Grippa visited Italy for talks in Milan with the staff of the new anti-revisionist monthly *Nuova Unita,* it was confirmation that the nascent organisation behind this publication had been chosen from among several other dissident factions to carry Chinese hopes for Italy, such as they are.

On that visit to Milan, Grippa granted *Nuova Unita* (July–August 1964) an interview, in which he declared: ' The Marxist-Leninists of Western Europe have the grand task of rebuilding proletarian parties on the only possible basis—that of class unity. . . . Such new Marxist-Leninist parties are necessary today.' We recognise the tone: this is the rhetoric of forced optimism. Yet it is not without some foundation. Additional splinter-parties, as distinct from factions, may well be among the marginal gains that the Chinese can still make in Western Europe; and Jacques Grippa's PCB will head the (surely unimpressive) list, among them a comic-opera split in Switzerland.

Struggle in the Dark

MORE THAN A THIRD of the world's communist parties, and more than half of those outside what used to be called the Soviet bloc, are proscribed [21]; but clandestinity has not saved them from the disinteg-rating impact of the struggle to win militants and influence parties. Indeed, one would expect the strategists in Peking to pay particular attention to those harried and frustrated revolutionaries. A clandestine movement—which sees its one, faint hope in the violent overthrow of the existing order but is officially loyal to Moscow's ' softer ' line, and is perhaps weakened still further by the frequent opportunism of Soviet foreign policy—offers fertile soil for the seed of pro-Chinese factionalism. Of course, clandestinity makes the sowing a difficult, if rewarding, operation. It also makes it unusually difficult for an outside observer to find out what is happening within an illegal party thus caught in the Sino-Soviet cross-fire.

One example better documented than most is provided by the Spanish communist movement—although ' better documented ' is a very relative term here. It is known that the pro-Soviet party now has a rival in what its leaders describe as the ' self-styled Communist Party of Spain '. But the pattern of the split, or splits, is uncertain. What is certain is that the Chinese and some of their Europeon allies are involved.

20 See the *mise en garde* published in *La Voix du Peuple* of 4–20 December 1963. *L'Etincelle* had claimed to speak for the ' Marxist-Leninists of Belgium and France '.
21 It is estimated that the communist party is proscribed in 41 countries.

In an editorial article, which was given the stamp of Soviet approval by republication in *Pravda* (30 June 1964), the Spanish CP organ *Mundo Obrero* has accused the Chinese of trying to split the party by supporting secessionist factions and financing anti-party publications. Some time previously, the article said, the central committee of the Spanish CP has sent its Chinese counterpart a letter complaining of ' the manoeuvres to which certain adventurist elements resort' in the Spanish movement; but the only reply the Chinese made was to ' increase their subsidies for the publication of anti-party journals '. Two factions were mentioned in the article—the ' self-styled Communist Party of Spain ' and ' the imaginary " revolutionary opposition of the Communist Party of Spain ".' Their challenge was, of course, minimised:

> The so-called ' Communist Party of Spain ' and the ' revolutionary opposition ' have now announced that they are being merged. Altogether, this is a matter of not more than a dozen persons, some of whom have never been members of our party.

As a description of the confused anti-revisionist ferment in the Spanish communist movement at home and abroad, this was a good deal less than adequate; but it did mark an advance on the party leadership's attempts a few months earlier to claim that no such ferment existed, and that indications to the contrary were the Machiavellian work of the Spanish police. This had been their line when, in December 1963, a rival version of *Mundo Obrero* began making the furtive rounds inside Spain. It carried the same hammer-and-sickle masthead as the official monthly of the central committee, except that the subtitle was ' Organ of the Political Commission of the Spanish Communist Party ', and it bore the supplementary slogan, ' For the Purity of Marxism-Leninism in the International Communist Movement '. The rival paper charged the leadership with ' liquidating the party ', and called for the creation of ' a revolutionary Marxist-Leninist party '. The call was soon followed by secessionist action.

In March 1964 leaflets distributed in Madrid and Paris announced that the ' first extraordinary national conference ' of the Communist Party of Spain (PCE) had been held in an undisclosed place on 15–16 February. The unnamed and unnumbered delegates were said to have ' deposed ' the exiled party leadership and replaced them with a new, anonymous executive. A few weeks later the rival clandestine journal, now retitled *Mundo Obrero Revolucionario,* added more details, including the report that the ' extraordinary national conference ' had annulled the existing party programme and statutes, and had decided to convene an ' extraordinary national congress ', at which the party would be formally reconstituted.[22] In its reply to this challenge the PCE leadership did not deny that the conference had taken place. But, it claimed,

22 *Le Monde* (Paris), 6 March, 9 April, 1964.

No member of our party participated in this alleged conference, which was promoted by strangers trying to introduce division and discord into the ranks of the Communist Party of Spain.[23]

Meanwhile, other pro-Chinese strands were being woven into the factional pattern. In February 1964 there appeared the first number of *Proletario,* described as the 'Organ of Spanish Marxist-Leninists'. Its introductory editorial explained that its purpose was to promote the formation of a Marxist-Leninist party of revolutionary violence to replace the PCE. The promptness with which this editorial was reprinted in the Belgian secessionist organ, *La Voix du Peuple* (14 February), and *Révolution* (March 1964); both of which are pledged to the Chinese cause, suggests that this mysterious publication had the approval and support of Peking. Indeed, according to the Spanish CP leaders, the link is one of more than sympathy. The *Mundo Obrero* statement reprinted in the *Pravda* article declared:

> In the same Paris printing-house which produces the luxurious pro-Chinese magazine *Révolution* there is also printed *Proletario,* edited . . . by a man who, with Chinese money, is obviously striving to create another splinter-party in order to unite with the splitters [of the 'self-styled Communist Party of Spain'], after which there will be not twelve of them but thirteen.[24]

In the summer of 1964 came news of another mosaic to be fitted into the pattern of disunity—the distribution inside Spain of a new anti-party publication, *El Comunista.* Again, details were helpfully provided by *Révolution* (July-August 1964), which described this newcomer as 'the organ of the *Federacion Centro de los comunistas marxistas-leninistas*', and added rather obscurely that 'these comrades of the Communist Party of Spain have coordinated their efforts through their central organ, *Proletario*'. The editorial from the first number of *El Comunista,* as reproduced by *Révolution,* did not clear up the obscurity:

> In Spain, nuclei of Marxist-Leninist Communists have been formed and are forming. Our periodical . . . is the organ of the nuclei of the Centre Federation. . . . In the present circumstances, the duty of Spanish Marxist-Leninists is to move towards the break with the anti-party, liquidationist and revisionist group headed by [Secretary-General] D. Santiago Carrillo.

This indicated that attempts were being made to bring together the scattered groups of 'anti-revisionists' inside Spain, and to link them

---

23 *Mundo Obrero,* March 1964, as quoted by a *Radio España Independiente* broadcast of 19 March 1964. (This station is the main propaganda medium of the PCE; it identifies itself as a clandestine transmitter situated in the Pyrenees, but in fact it is known to operate from Czechoslovakia, as do several other clandestine communist broadcasting stations, such as ' Radio Free Portugal ').

24 This jibe cannot be taken as a fair estimate of pro-Chinese strength in the Spanish communist movement. In June 1964 the Spanish security police arrested nearly 100 communists in the southern and eastern provinces, and the authorities later let it be known that almost all of them were pro-Chinese. An earlier wave of arrests in April had brought in fewer than a dozen pro-Soviet communists.

organisationally with the exile factions represented by *Proletario*.[25]
The next, decisive step was reported by *La Voix du Peuple* (16 October
1964), which announced that a merger of three factions had taken place
at a meeting on 4 October. The three were identified as 'Communist
Party of Spain', 'Proletario', and 'Communist Revolutionary Opposition of Spain', which edit the journals *Mundo Obrero Revolucionario,
Proletario,* and *La Chispa* (The Spark). Their joint communiqué added
that they had 'proceeded to rebuild the Communist Party of Spain on
the basis of . . . Marxism-Leninism', and that their joint organ would
be entitled *Vanguardia Obrera*.

But this is a struggle in the dark, so to speak; and while the observer
tries to balance conflicting, partial, and partisan accounts, he can only
guess at the fortunes of battle. What is sure is that the ideological
conflict has given a new and pregnant meaning to the pledge Mao
Tse-tung gave to Spaniards nearly three decades ago: 'We do not
believe that the struggle of the Chinese people can be separated from
your struggle in Spain.'[26]

Trotskyists, Too

THE PATTERN OF MARXIST disunity in Ceylon is probably the most
complex in the world. To start with, the communist split is complete,
as a result of rival versions of the seventh congress of the Ceylon Communist Party (CCP) held in January and April 1964. In addition, however, Trotskyists are involved here to an extent not found elsewhere—
there are no fewer than four rival Trotskyist parties. For good measure,
the island also supports rival communist trade union organisations,
rival communist youth organisations, and rival Afro-Asian bodies.

The roots of this 'supersplit' go back to 1962, when the CCP
opened negotiations on a 'United Left Front' alliance with the LSSP
(Lanka Sama Samaja Party—the largest Trotskyist party in the world
and the only one which has taken the parliamentary path), and the
MEP (People's United Front), a smaller offshoot of the LSSP. Communist opposition to this move was led by two Politburo members,
Sanmugathasan and Kumarasiri. A month before the United Left
Front agreement was finally signed in August 1963, Sanmugathasan,
secretary of the communist-controlled Ceylon Trade Union Federation,
returned from a lengthy visit to Peking and began to organise anti-
revisionist rallies.

When the two were expelled from the party in late October 1963

---

25 It should be noted that the party leadership also has to contend with a revisionist
challenge. An article in the January 1964 issue of *Mundo Obrero*, as reprinted in
part in the French CP weekly *France Nouvelle* (22–28 April 1964) referred vaguely
to 'the new right-wing opposition inside Spain'. It appears that this revisionist
disaffection finds its main expression among the communist students at Madrid
University, many of whom have been influenced by Italian communist thought (see
J.-A. Novais, 'Crise au sein du parti communiste', *Le Monde*, 14–15 June, 1964).
26 Letter to the 'People of Spain, Comrades-in-arms', dated 15 May 1937; quoted by
Stuart R. Schram, *The Political Thought of Mao Tse-tung* (New York, 1964), p. 290.

they took nine others of the 35 central committee members with them. Three weeks later they launched their counter-offensive at a ' national conference of Marxist-Leninists '. A 12-point indictment of the party leaders adopted at this meeting included the charge that they had failed to hold the seventh party congress, due in December 1962, although ' more than half of the membership' had asked that it be convened. This was the legalistic pretext for secession: the rebels, virtuously loyal to the statutes, would convene the congress themselves. At this congress of secession 400 delegates duly ' replaced ' the pro-Soviet leaders (who were later ' expelled ') and repudiated their revisionist policies. The ritual of denunciation was repeated in reverse at the pro-Soviet seventh party congress in April 1964.

Meanwhile the rebels had advanced on another front, exploiting Sanmugathasan's organisational control of the Ceylon Trade Union Federation. At the CTUF congress in December 1963 the pro-Soviet delegates, led by the president, M. G. Mendis, were heavily out-numbered, and walked out of the opening session. Turning the secessionist tables, they proceeded to form a rival Ceylon Federation of Trade Unions (CFTU), which held a congress in March 1964. On that occasion Mendis claimed that ' by the end of February . . . between 70 and 80 per cent of the workers formerly organised by the CTUF [had] joined the CFTU '.[27] More objective estimates give the pro-Soviet communist trade unions about 50,000 members and the pro-Chinese about 60,000. Numbers matter here: the trade union movement is the main battle-front of the factional struggle in Ceylon.

The situation was complicated in June 1964 by a turn in Ceylonese politics which dealt a heavy blow to the pro-Soviet communists. The ruling Sri Lanka (Freedom) Party, with an eye to the 1965 elections and its own slender majority, reached a coalition agreement with the Trotskyist LSSP, by which the latter received three Cabinet seats in exchange for its twelve parliamentary votes. The decision had been approved three to one at an LSSP conference, but at the cost of a split: the anti-coalition minority broke away and formed its own ' LSSP (Revolutionary Section) '.[28] The smaller party, the MEP, also split on its attitude to the coalition, with the dissidents forming a new party, the ' Leftist Fighting Front '.

Thus, the United Left Front, on which the pro-Soviet communists had based their revisionist hopes, had collapsed after only ten months. To make matters worse, one of the four communist deputies resigned from the party in protest against the decision to give only selective support to the coalition, and joined the government parliamentary group. The

---

27 See the report by the Indian observer delegate, Pravathi Krishnan, in *New Age* (Indian CP weekly), 12 April 1964.

28 The Fourth International in Paris subsequently recognised this group as the official affiliate, expelled those LSSP members who joined the coalition government and suspended those who supported it.

gainers were the pro-Chinese communists: events had justified their political line, and they were in a stronger position to carry on the factional struggle, with Chinese aid.[29]

Three-Way Split

IN BURMA SINO-SOVIET polarisation has been imposed on an existing pattern of complex disunity, involving not just two but three communist parties. These are the Burma Communist Party (BCP, known as the 'White Flag' Communists), the Communist Party of Burma (CPB—'Red Flag'), and the United Workers Party of Burma (UWP).[30] The first two are in clandestine insurgency and the third is illegal.

The 'White Flag' insurgents—holding the title of the original party founded in 1939—became firmly pro-Chinese in 1962–63, following earlier signs of disagreement within the leadership.[31] The 'Red Flag' fanatics, uncompromisingly committed to revolutionary violence, also support Chinese ideological positions, but are not allied with the Chinese as the 'White Flag' party is. Only the United Workers Party, still cherishing the hope of a peaceful advance to power despite its illegal status, supports the Russians in the ideological conflict.

The roots of this three-way division go back to the immediate post-war years, when the Burmese communist movement split into two diverging groups—the White Flag moderates (as they were then) under Than Tun, who for several years remained in the coalition government, and the Red Flag extremist splinter-party under Thakin Soe, which took the road to clandestine violence in 1946 and was proscribed early in 1947. In the spring of 1948 the White Flag leaders also gave the order for a nation-wide insurrection. But, even while both factions were fighting the same enemy, the split persisted. It is interesting to note that in October 1949, only a few weeks after the People's Republic had been proclaimed in Peking, the Chinese intervened in a vain attempt to end the rift; a message from the CPC Politburo to the White Flag leaders put forward plans for a united struggle and coordinated political action. Three years later both factions did join in a temporary alliance with a third left-wing insurgent organisation. But by then it was too late: in 1950 the tide of civil war turned decisively against the rebels, and in the following years they defected in increasing numbers in response to amnesty offers. At this point emerged the third element in

[29] A Russian delegate to the (pro-Soviet) seventh congress of the Ceylon CP told *Pravda* readers: 'The Chinese splitters openly and generously finance the " work " of the local splitters . . . We were told that the splitters spend up to 200,000 rupees [about 40,000 dollars] every month on the publication and distribution of their journals and propaganda literature in Ceylon' (V. Stepanov, 'Communists of Ceylon', *Pravda*, 31 May 1964).

[30] To compound confusion still further, the 'White Flag' BCP changed its title late in 1963 to Communist Party of Burma (CPB), already held by the 'Red Flag' party. In the interests of clarity, we may be excused for continuing to refer to it as the BCP.

[31] See Brian Crozier, 'The Communist struggle for power in Burma', *The World Today* (London), March 1964.

the tripartite division, with the formation in 1950 of the Burmese Workers Party, in which many of the ex-rebels found a political home, and which became the dominant party in the left-wing National United Front opposition.

During the nineteen fifties the BWP pursued its tactics of peaceful infiltration and political bargaining with varying success, while the White Flag leaders consolidated their links with Peking (where a group of them lived), and the Red Flag faction dwindled towards insignificance. But the pattern changed dramatically with the coup d'etat of March 1962, in which General Ne Win's Revolutionary Council ousted the government of U Nu. The new regime's 'Burmese way to socialism' disarmed the 'above-ground' Marxists of the BWP as much as it dismayed foreign investors, and at the end of 1962 they tried to strengthen their position by merging with the left-wing People's Comrade Party to form the United Workers Party. Meanwhile, Ne Win had been combining vigorous military action against the rebels with peace moves, and in June 1963 he offered unconditional cease-fire talks to all insurgents, political and ethnic. The fanatical Red Flag leader Thakin Soe emerged from hiding for talks which soon ended in deadlock. He was followed by the White Flag leaders, some of them flown from Peking for the occasion, and the subsequent negotiations dragged on until mid-November 1963, when they, too, were broken off. Scrupulously, General Ne Win let the guerrilla leaders leave under safe-conduct pledges—but he vented his feelings by ordering widespread arrests of the 'above-ground' communists in the United Workers Party: upwards of 700 were rounded up.

This heavy blow to the waning 'peaceful-way' hopes of the UWP was followed by another in March 1964, when Ne Win banned all parties except his own Socialist Programme Party. The Red Flag guerrillas, on the other hand, had been strengthened by the five-months breathing-spell during the peace talks.

As things stand, both the Red Flag and the White Flag parties are supported by Peking. The United Workers Party would cast its vote with the Russians if it got the chance. Soviet commentators have in the past indicated their approval of the UWP's gradualist approach,[32] and in September 1963 Chit Maung, chairman of the UWP central committee, visited Moscow on the invitation of the CPSU for a vacation (and, doubtless, talks).

The splits in the Indian and Australian Communist movements need no more than a brief mention here, since they are discussed in detail by other contributors. The Indian split—numerically and politically the most important of all—was made final and formal by the left-wing version of the seventh party congress, held in Calcutta in November 1964, six weeks before the pro-Soviet version was to take place in Bombay. The Communist Party of Australia (Marxist-Leninist)

[32] See, for example, the article, ' Burma on a New Road ', *Pravda*, 15 March 1963.

had already been formed at a secessionist congress in Melbourne in March 1964.

Finally, we may briefly note three minor splits—in the Lebanon, Nepal, and Paraguay. Little is known as yet about the Lebanese Party of the Socialist Revolution, formed at the beginning of September 1964, except that its leading founder, Youssef Moubarek, had previously spent several months in Peking; but the comparative political freedom in Beirut makes it a useful bridgehead for pro-Chinese influence in the Arab world. The existence of a splinter-party in Nepal was revealed in April 1964 by the pro-Soviet party leader, Raimajhi, who attacked the 'splitters' for holding a secessionist party congress; he had earlier accused them of working closely with the Chinese Embassy in Katmandu. Similarly, Oscar Creydt, Secretary-General of the Paraguayan CP, has admitted in a *Pravda* article that his clandestine organisation is being challenged by a 'Leninist Communist Party'.

*　　　*　　　*

BY THE AUTUMN OF 1963 the Russians were complaining bitterly of the Chinese attempt to 'knock together an international bloc out of . . . factional groups and coteries, consisting largely of people who have been expelled from the communist parties—all sorts of unprincipled and corrupt elements'.[33] In such a bloc the secessionist parties which had already begun to appear at that time would obviously play an extremely important part; but in fact what pro-Chinese factionalism has created is a rival movement only in a looser sense of the word, and not a bloc. The events of the past few years have made one prediction safe: no International of the disciplined Stalinist type will be re-created on either side of the ideological frontier. If the CPSU has lost much, or most, of its former organisational control over pro-Soviet parties, the CPC has little or no prospect of establishing such control over pro-Chinese parties, secessionist or otherwise. The PKI's insistence on 'Indonesianised' communism (and its combination of internal revisionism with external anti-revisionism) is a case in point; the secessionist Swiss Communist Party's quarrel with China's local representatives is another.

On the other hand, the links which bind these secessionist parties to the CPC are real and strong; they are the links of mutual self-interest. Because of the stature of the two protagonists, the Sino-Soviet conflict has had a catalytic effect on a world movement in the process of post-Stalinist evolution, releasing and strengthening disruptive forces within individual parties. As we have seen, these local antagonisms tend to resolve themselves along Sino-Soviet lines, and that for obvious reasons. The essential difference between the present wave of factionalism and the Trotskyist rebellions of the thirties is that dissident groups and breakaway parties can now appeal to the authority of the world's largest communist party, presenting itself as the guardian of doctrinal purity and with the resources of a major state at its disposal.

---

[33] *Kommunist*, No. 15, 1963.

However, there is another side to this picture of an ' anti-revisionist ' alliance. If local issues lie at the roots of secession, they will reassert themselves. ' Anti-revisionist ' communism is no more immune to the disease of polycentrism than is the ' revisionist ' variety. What is more, local factionalism and local secession have a momentum of their own, which would persist even if the Russians and Chinese managed, somehow, to settle their differences. Thus, the Belgian secessionists, exulting over the downfall of the ' traitor ' Khrushchev in *La Voix du Peuple* (23 October 1964), took the occasion to intensify their attack on the ' cynical renegades ' of the official Belgian CP. Jacques Grippa has his own scores to settle, and his splinter-party is not under the control of the Chinese.

Here one must distinguish between the short-term and long-term prospects for the secessionist parties. In the short term they will tend to support the Chinese unconditionally, in their own interests. In the long term those same interests will lead them to put local needs and opportunities first, if necessary at the expense of Chinese policy, and to make their own anti-revisionist contribution to the emergence of national and regional communism. Again, in the long run they will lose much of the purely ideological significance which they have today, and find their true place in the political spectrum, their true weight in the political balance. Some will thrive, while others will wither in the stony soil of non-revolutionary situations, or edge back towards revisionism in practice.[34]

In time, too, the secessionist parties will be subject to another danger: splits in the ranks of the splitters. There is a rift in the secessionist Swiss Communist Party, and disruptive forces are at work within the leftist Indian party. The pro-Chinese faction in Britain has just provided another example, with a split breaking up the former duumvirate of the Old Etonian Michael McCreery and the veteran Stalinist Arthur Evans, until September 1964 editor of the faction's monthly organ, *Vanguard*.

These splits within splits should not surprise any Marxist. Once the process of dialectical division has reached the first, fateful stage, there is no reason why it should stop there. Here the secessionist parties, much more than the pro-Chinese factions, have a direct bearing on a central issue: the crisis of authority in the world movement and inside individual parties. At the roots of Marxism-Leninism lies what has been called ' the myth of the communist party '—both the ' world party ' and the national party—and secession is an axe-blow against those roots.

---

34 It is interesting to note that even in its zealously Sinophile early days, the secessionist Swiss Communist Party adopted (at its conference in November 1963) a programme which consisted entirely of demands for what the revisionist Italian communists call structural reforms. It opened with a call for a 10 per cent wage increase all round and ended limply with a proposal for more ' libraries and other institutions '; in between, there was no word of revolutionary violence.

Such ideological questions are important: it is the 'universal' doctrinal basis of communism which has led the Chinese, in their conflict with the Russians, to embark on a global campaign, first of factionalism and then also of schism; and it is this doctrine which has so bitterly aggravated clashes of interest which pragmatic 'bourgeois politicians' could resolve reasonably through 'unprincipled' compromises. The Chinese, therefore, had to find ideological justification for the intensified organisational offensive which got under way in mid-1963, and which produced the major secessionist parties. This justification was first advanced in a lecture which Chou Yang, deputy director of the propaganda section of the CPC central committee, delivered on 26 October 1963 (although it was not published until two months later). Communism itself, Chou declared, was not exempt from the iron law of the dialectic, the law that 'everything tends to divide itself into two'; and with remorseless logic he outlined the practical consequences for the world movement:

> Where there is revisionism, there will be Marxism-Leninism fighting against it; and where Marxist-Leninists are expelled from the party and other measures taken to create splits, new outstanding Marxist-Leninists and strong revolutionary parties are bound to emerge. . . . This is an inexorable law.[35]

Chou's arguments were repeated, often verbatim, in the polemical *People's Daily/Red Flag* article of 4 February 1964, issued as the latest instalment of the CPC's reply to the Soviet 'Open Letter' of 14 July 1963. His teaching on the inevitability of splits and secessionist parties was thereby officially adopted by the Chinese party leadership. With that, the die was cast: the Chinese were committed. In communism, of all political philosophies, the polemics of yesterday can determine the policies of tomorrow. Even if there were any tactical moves towards rapprochement by the new leadership in Moscow, the Chinese would find it difficult to withdraw from the involvements of this world-wide struggle.

Moreover, the encouragement of secession is a game that two can play. The CPSU has been on the defensive not only because it stood for the *status quo* (in this restricted context) but because the leaderships of almost all non-ruling parties—the only ones seriously subject to factionalist challenge—were on its side to begin with. However, in a number of pro-Chinese non-ruling parties the Russians have a chance to counter-attack; and they are beginning to do so. Pro-Soviet factionalism has emerged in the pro-Chinese parties of Japan, Indonesia, and New Zealand, and in the first case at least there is clear evidence of Soviet intervention with secessionist overtones. The subsidiary conflict between the Japanese and Soviet parties, which had been obvious for some time, came into the open in July 1964, when both sides (starting with the Russians), began publishing the increasingly polemical letters exchanged over more than a year. The JCP accused

[35] *People's Daily*, 27 December 1963.

the CPSU of promoting anti-party factionalism in Japan, asserting that since October 1963 members of the Soviet Embassy staff had been attending meetings 'organised by the anti-party elements'. When Shiga and Suzuki, two communist parliamentarians expelled from the JCP for voting to ratify the test-ban treaty, formed a rival 'Society of Friends of *The Voice of Japan*' and began publishing an anti-party weekly organ with that title, *Pravda* (16 July 1964) welcomed its aim of rallying 'all the comrades unjustly expelled from the JCP and those who, while remaining in the party, uphold the correct line'. A few weeks before Khrushchev's fall *Pravda* (28 September) published an article by Shiga attacking 'those renegades who call themselves communists' and who had 'usurped the leadership of our party'. This counter-pressure has now eased, at least temporarily, but three revisionist factions are still active in Japan. The Indonesian CP leader Aidit may yet have to repeat his warning, given in September 1964 on the occasion of inter-party talks with Secretary-General Miyamoto of the JCP, that 'the modern revisionists are . . . resorting to the establishment of new and phony [communist] parties not only in Japan but elsewhere in the world'.[36]

Even without such a development, the formation of secessionist parties has reduced to vanishing-point any possibility that the vast complex of differences and hostilities can be settled through an all-party conference. The Chinese, with an eye on Brazil, India, and Australia, have already indicated that they will insist on these countries being represented by their 'Marxist-Leninist communist parties' at the preparatory meeting.[37] Their Albanian allies have gone a step farther by declaring that all 'new Marxist-Leninist parties' already formed or to be formed in the intervening period must take part in an international conference.[38] This demand the Soviet side flatly rejected, standing by its contention that 'in no country can there be more than one Communist Party'.[39] Khrushchev may be blamed for his resolve to press for an early showdown, but these realities remain. A month after Khrushchev's fall the Albanians declared that the new Soviet leadership was continuing 'the revisionist line of the 20th, 21st, and 22nd CPSU congresses' (*Zeri i Popullit*, 13 November 1964). The secretary of the Japanese CP announced that 'certain people in the leading organs of the fraternal parties of some socialist countries have fallen into the mire of revisionism, and it can be assumed that it is inevitable that this struggle will be protracted and complicated in the days to come' (*Akahata*, 25 November 1964). The phenomenon of secession has justified Suslov's prediction that a 'grim and apparently long struggle' lies ahead for the world movement which Stalin left in precariously monolithic unity.

---

[36] NCNA, 12 September 1964.
[37] Letter of the central committee, CPC, to the central committee, CPSU, 7 May 1964 (NCNA, 8 May).
[38] *Zeri i Popullit*, editorial, 17 May 1964.   [39] *World Marxist Review*, January 1964.

WESTERN EUROPE

Eric Willenz and Pio Uliassi

THE Sino-Soviet dispute has not seriously weakened the West
European communist parties, but it has involved their leaders in
a half-hearted defiance of Moscow which became more pronounced
after Khrushchev's fall. It led most European communists to reaffirm
publicly their support for the basic policies of the deposed leader—if
only to warn the new Soviet rulers against radical changes in policy.
This effort to commit Khrushchev's successors to positions favoured by
the Western parties was unprecedented, as was their equally emphatic
and almost universal criticism of the manner of Khrushchev's removal.
These developments illustrate the rapidly changing relationship between
Moscow and the West European parties. Their position may be
characterised as continued opposition to the principal ideological
arguments of Peking combined with an increasing unwillingness to
accept subordination to Moscow.

Reactions in Western Europe to the dispute have come from the
party leaders at all levels, but hardly at all from the rank and file, let
alone from communist voters. In fact, despite the seriousness of the
crisis in the movement, many communist parties are in a better condition than they have been in a long time, at least in terms of certain
kinds of popular support. The Italian communists gained about one
million votes in the last national elections in 1963, the French communists have made small but steady gains since 1962, the Swedish
communists did well in the recent elections, and the British CP has
enjoyed a steady rise in membership for about three years. The present
crisis, then, is one affecting the inner core of the party, but it is no
less serious for that; in fact, it may well be more serious than membership
or electoral setbacks, since it is an ideological crisis which can be
expected, in time, to bring major changes in the very nature of the
communist parties and in the roles they are able to play in their countries.

Although there is increasing diversity in the West European parties,
some common features do emerge. All of them have supported most of
the Soviet Union's positions on international issues, but agreement on
these basic matters no longer suffices to ensure compliance with Moscow's
tactics within the communist movement or to spare the Soviet system
from cautious but explicit criticism—as the Italian communists have
shown. Thus their pro-Soviet orientation is hedged with reservations; it is no longer the traditional relationship of almost complete and
unquestioning subordination to Moscow. Their qualified support may
be explained partly by habit and partly by genuine agreement on fundamental issues. Chinese ideological and political pronouncements
have little bearing on the problems faced by the Western parties
operating in relatively affluent democratic societies. But how can the

divergence from Moscow be explained? Size alone is no longer a reliable criterion for estimating a party's independence of or subservience to the traditional centre of authority and control. Only the Italian, French, and Finnish parties have any real political importance in their respective countries. Yet among these, the French party, which has deep domestic roots and might be expected to grasp at opportunities for asserting its autonomy, has been reluctant to do so. Conversely, some of the smaller European parties, like the Swedish or the Norwegian, which because of their weakness might be thought more dependent on Moscow for psychological and material sustenance, have asserted their independence far more vigorously than the French. The reasons for such behaviour are many and complex, and in the final analysis the attitude of each must be explained in terms of its own unique historical experience and present circumstances.

IT should be noted that the smaller communist parties have generally been more seriously affected by the Sino-Soviet dispute than the larger ones, mainly, perhaps, because their organisations are more vulnerable to attacks from militant minorities. The three proscribed parties—the Portuguese, Spanish, and West German—stand as a special case of small-party vulnerability. Since their leaders are safely domiciled in Moscow (or elsewhere in Eastern Europe), there is the danger of a breakdown of communication between militants within a country, working at times under conditions of extreme danger and deprivation (as in Portugal and Spain), and exiled leaders who, in counselling patience and moderation, seem to the militants to have lost touch with political realities. In the following more detailed treatment of the smaller parties, analysis is confined mainly to those countries where pro-Chinese rival parties actually exist.

Of these the small dissident Belgian Communist Party is the star. Founded in late 1963, it is led by some prominent former members of the still existing and much larger Moscow-oriented Belgian party (PCB). They are Jacques Grippa, former member of the old party's politburo and long its principal liaison man with foreign communist parties, and several of his associates from the Brussels area. In addition, the rival party has also attracted Senator Henri Glineur, one of the founders of the old Belgian CP, and a number of other distinguished figures, notably the daughter of the venerable socialist leader Carl Huysmans. It has also made considerable inroads into the membership of the Brussels federation of the old party and the communist university student organisation.

Spurred on by their success in winning some notable supporters and riding on the crest of a presumed wave of new revolutionary consciousness among Belgian workers, Grippa and his associates have been blasting away at ' the Soviet betrayal of Marxism-Leninism ' and its support of an organisation ' which pursues an anti-communist policy and makes fraudulent use of the name of the Communist Party.'[1] But after its initial successes, the fortunes of this new party ebbed, although its leaders continued to fulminate in their weekly, *La Voix du Peuple*, against Khrushchev and to praise China for having wiped out ' century-old backwardness and eliminated the evils of colonialism which the people had so cruelly suffered until their liberation.'[2]

It is difficult to reach firm conclusions about this party and its leaders. Its formation obviously was not due to any sudden revolutionary upsurge among Belgian workers, nor has its reception thus far augured well for its efforts among the Belgian working class; its tactics are not likely to win it many new recruits. It affects a revolutionary stridency that is out of tune with the times; it bristles with verbal violence while professing its devotion to peace; and it praises a cause and a people that are barely known to its domestic audience. Grippa and his group seem to belong to that band of people—and they have sprung up in a number of other parties—who are not only part of the traditional militant left that can be found in any communist party but an extreme variant of it. He represents that breed of Western Marxists whom one observer has described as driven by anger and resentment for having been rebuffed by their own working class and who consequently look to another class, another people, to carry forward the historic mission of communism.[3]

THE dissident Communist Party of Switzerland is rather different. Although it too started in one of the few areas where the parent party was still relatively strong (the French-speaking canton of Vaud), its leaders seem to be more neatly cast than is Grippa's group in the mould of the traditional communist left. Its condemnation of the old Swiss party (PdT—*Parti du Travail*) for its ' glorification ' of Kennedy and ' evil Tito ', and its rejection of the condemnation of the Chinese and Albanian theses, are much more in the nature of a crude and old-fashioned leftist critique.

The party's efforts to hold to a middle course as a radical communist party, looking neither to Moscow nor to Peking, emerged more clearly in the spring of 1964. Its periodical rejected the old party's charge that the new Swiss party was Trotskyist, and its May Day declaration sharply denied that the new party was pro-Chinese, claiming that it was, in fact, a ' genuinely Swiss party ' which took orders from nobody and whose members wanted only to be sincere Marxist-Leninists. To a potential member who reproached the party for not concentrating enough on backing the Chinese and Albanians, the party answered that it saw the value of its work on this subject more in the struggle it carried on in Switzerland.[4] But it greeted Khrushchev's fall with enthusiasm.

[1] NCNA, 9 January 1964.   [2] Ibid. 11 July 1964.
[3] Lewis S. Feuer, ' Marxisms . . . How Many? ' in *Problems of Communism*, March-April 1964.
[4] *L'Etincelle*, January, April, and May 1964.

The situation in a number of other Western European communist parties where there are groups, tendencies, and currents allegedly favouring the Chinese is even more nebulous. Traditional left-right divisions, personal rivalries, and all kinds of long-suppressed friction have surfaced and promptly been labelled 'pro-Chinese' because they all challenge the existing Moscow-oriented leadership. However, such a label grossly oversimplifies the situation.

In Finland, for example, the initial reluctance to join in the condemnation of the Chinese after the 22nd CPSU congress probably reflected concern with the internal repercussions of destalinisation rather than sympathy for Peking's position. Moreover, left-wing sentiment in Finland is hardly in general agreement with Peking, although the radical Marxist nationalist group around the magazine *Tilanen* is undoubtedly in favour of reducing Moscow's sway.

Austria presents a similar picture. A recently expelled member of the Austrian party's central committee, Franz Strobl, publishes a semi-monthly journal, *Rote Fahne,* which fumes against the iniquities of that party and lauds the impressive achievements of China. Although the Austrian party had some difficulties immediately after the 22nd CPSU congress, when some of its leaders objected to the further destruction of the Stalin image, its recent troubles have arisen largely from the right rather than the left.

The alliance—however temporary—between a party's more radical elements and embittered Stalinists is not an uncommon phenomenon. Such a combination may have existed until recently in the British party, which was rather slow in joining the attack on the Chinese. The lines were cleared with the expulsion of a group of relatively unknown intellectuals led by Michael McCreery (whose distinction lies more in his background as the son of a distinguished British General than in his former position in the party). It is more than doubtful, however, that McCreery's group, now in its turn split into two factions, speaks with any degree of success to most of the old party's members, let alone the British working class. In the Norwegian party, on the other hand, the rival factions do seem to have stalemated each other. Here the alliance between the two discontented groups is embodied in the party's chairman, Emil Loevlien, whose ostensible advocacy of non-alignment in the dispute is very different from that of his neighbour, C. H. Hermansson in Sweden.

Hermansson, though superficially on the same side as Loevlien in opposing the Soviet call for a world conference, comes closest to the position of the Italians among the small Western European communist parties. Instead of representing an alliance of militant leftists and Stalinists, Hermansson heads a combination of revisionists and Moscow-oriented old-line communists. Perched uneasily on top of this somewhat unstable coalition, the new chairman—he has only been in office since January 1964—is rapidly moving to consolidate his position in the party and to give it respectability by a policy of reformism at home and freedom from foreign domination. To demonstrate this, Hermansson has not only balked at Soviet demands for a world conference—even though he agrees with Moscow's basic position—but has also criticised certain aspects of Soviet foreign policy, notably the existence of the Berlin Wall.[5] In other ways, too, Hermansson represents a new face in the communist movement, for his relative youth and his background have spared him the historical experience which served in former times to establish a close relationship between Moscow and every European party leader.

IT is characteristic of the French Communist Party (PCF) that the Sino-Soviet dispute has left its internal cohesion apparently untouched. At a time when many communist parties found themselves increasingly affected by the disarray in the movement, and therefore fearful of the consequences of a world conference, the French party was still in favour of such a meeting. It was only Khrushchev's dismissal which produced an independent PCF initiative; a delegation was promptly sent to Moscow to discuss the affair, which French communists found highly embarrassing.

The marked anti-revisionism of the PCF is the result of historical, organisational, and political circumstances. The party is led by rigidly doctrinaire men whose loyalty to Moscow has been tested. Second, these leaders are surrounded by docile followers who seem content to accept the party's revolutionary mission as mere phrase-mongering. Third, the PCF attracts a powerful bloc of voters, testifying to its continued ability to act as the principal spokesman for a large part of the discontented French working class, both in the political arena and in the trade union field. Finally, the PCF's self-proclaimed role as the inheritor of France's revolutionary tradition still enables it to exploit that heritage whenever the French left feels that its common values are threatened.

Precisely because these conditions appear to the Chinese full of revolutionary opportunities, they despise what they regard as the opportunism of the PCF leaders. And this contempt is easily translated into the hope that the PCF's policy, coupled with its firm control of party militants, will create tensions leading sooner or later to a showdown within the party. Peking may well feel encouraged by certain rumblings on the fringes of the PCF that the Chinese communists regard as confirmation of their assessment of the French situation. However, a closer reading of critical statements about the PCF's official policies made by dissident communist spokesmen suggests that they are widely at variance with each other and also that they are far from agreeing with many of the Chinese positions.

An illustrative case is provided by the reaction to the formation, in late 1963, of a group calling itself the French-Chinese Peoples Asso-

[5] *Stockholm-Tidningen*, 6 January 1964.

ciation. The new organisation naturally competed with the already-existing French-Chinese Friendship Society controlled by the PCF. Since the PCF leaders prevented the distribution of what Peking or some of its sympathisers regarded as unbiased information on China, the chief aim of the new group was ' to let France know the truth about People's China ', in the words of one of the new group's chief supporters, *La Voie Communiste* (December 1963), the organ of a group of disaffected communist intellectuals who had broken with the party over its Algerian policy. *La Voie Communiste* was attempting to deflate what it called ' the reactionary myths which try to make China look like an aggressive power scheming to establish communism on earth by unleashing a world war '. At the same time, it disavowed any intention of forming a pro-Chinese faction or a dissident communist party in France. These efforts were naturally derided by the PCF; more to the point here is the fact that *La Voie Communiste's* policy was attacked by another splinter group that might have been expected to endorse it.

These ultra-leftists have been publishing a paper, *Le Communiste,* for over 10 years. In December 1963 they launched a violent attack on the sponsors of the new friendship organisation and announced that ' the true friends of the People's Republic of China take a strong stand against the plan to create a French-Chinese Peoples Association '. Claiming that the new group did not have the approval of Peking, they invited ' the true friends of the People's Republic of China to support the French-Chinese Friendship Society . . . by forming local committees which operate efficiently and without restriction, to present a correct picture of current Chinese problems '.

There is no direct way of ascertaining Peking's reaction to the fact that the number of its adherents in France is so small; whether the Chinese are trying to expand the area of dissidence by financial support is a matter of conjecture. The fact remains that the increasingly bitter tone of the Sino-Soviet dispute throughout 1963–64 generated an air of detachment among dissident French communists. The tendency has been to weigh the merits of the arguments advanced by both sides without giving either Moscow or Peking unqualified backing. This development runs all the way from the Trotskyists, who have noted bitterly China's abuse of them, to the various oppositionists who still claim to have some following in the PCF.

In fact, the French dissidents have rejected the Chinese thesis that puts the defence of Marxist-Leninist principles above the preservation of unity in the movement, and have chided the Chinese for reviving the old Soviet tactics of trying to assert ideological and organisational control of the French revolutionary movement.[6] Subordination to the Chinese in any new international would be no more satisfactory than the earlier relationship to the Soviets. In any such relationship, they say, incompatibilities are bound to arise between the needs of a communist

[6] *La Voie Communiste,* February 1964.

state pursuing its foreign policy objectives and the exigencies of the revolutionary process itself. In discarding the illusion that Soviet foreign policy has always served the interests of the international proletariat, the dissidents have at last recognised that Moscow had subordinated the hopes of communists in other countries to the interests of Soviet foreign policy; the familiar zigs and zags in the behaviour of communist parties, ' so numerous and often so abrupt, were not inspired by social or political changes in the country itself, but by modifications in the Soviet Union's policy '.[7]

The dissidents have also noted a more general problem affecting the creation of new revolutionary organisations in countries with powerful working-class parties solidly rooted in the masses. Efforts to establish a new revolutionary organisation to take over from a degenerate French Communist Party have been made, unsuccessfully, several times in France. The principal reason why they failed was that the masses could not be lured away from an established party which, despite its ideological degeneration, benefited from the inertia of the proletariat, which continued to identify itself with the old party.

THE main opposition in the PCF has arisen not over policy but as a result of resentment about the stifling atmosphere in the party organisation. In this connection, the relationship between the party and its student union (UEC) is noteworthy. The differences which the students have had with the party involve both ideological and organisational questions. The ideological differences, which emerged mainly during the Algerian war, have however been gradually overshadowed by the UEC's resentment of the party tutelage. The students' quest for greater autonomy was reflected in all the three principal factions in the UEC: the so-called Italians who sympathise with the positions of the Italian Communist Party, the pro-Chinese group, and even those who have remained loyal to the PCF leaders. The pro-Chinese are a distinct minority in the UEC and it is not, therefore, the threat of ultra-leftism that has brought the students into sharp conflict with the party, but resistance to party interference.

This interference by the PCF leaders in the affairs of the student organisation has provoked a unified attack by all the students, and this in turn has led to increasingly severe sanctions by the party, prompted in part by their fear of losing control over the situation, but also by their traditional contempt for intellectuals.

At the recent 17th PCF congress, the President of the UEC was not permitted to address the delegates, a courtesy normally extended to the holder of that office. Instead, the floor was given to an obedient member who promptly disavowed the actions of his organisation. The principal speakers at the congress addressed warning words to the students, accusing them of ideological disorientation and asserting the party's

[7] Ibid. March 1964.

right, even duty, to enforce unity among all its parts. Even more sinister was the threat by Roland Leroy, chief party spokesman on youth affairs, that the party was seriously considering the merger of all its youth groups into one organisation under a joint leadership.[8] (It was Leroy who led the PCF delegation to Moscow after Khrushchev's fall.)

What has been said so far suggests that the Sino-Soviet dispute has done little to advance the cause of left-wing communism in France. If anything, the ideological debate has tended to sharpen the differences among French dissident communist groups. This is not to say that the party is invulnerable or that its leaders can continue to resist indefinitely the ravages of time and changing circumstances.

It is widely agreed that the domestic advance of many West European communist parties was seriously handicapped by their subservience to Moscow. While there is much truth in this assertion, it ignores the continued appeal that communist parties have for large masses in certain European countries. A recognition of this is crucial for understanding the failure of the Chinese communists to exploit successfully the dissatisfactions in a party like the PCF. To be sure, the PCF leaders have given little publicity to the Chinese case against themselves and the Soviet Union, but Peking and the French news media have done a comprehensive job on this, and it is hardly likely that the party has been able to prevent its followers, let alone close to four million communist voters, from getting a full view. Nevertheless, the strength of the party has been unaffected.

This is not the place for an extended socio-political analysis of the PCF's ability to exploit the resentment of large numbers of Frenchmen who are still alienated from their society, and to remain an important, though tarnished, symbol for many French intellectuals. It is entirely possible that the profound socio-economic changes that have taken place in France since the war will ultimately lead to a more harmonious integration of the French working class into the French body politic. However, this process has only begun. At the same time, it would be erroneous to look upon the statements of French communist leaders as the sole criteria by which the party is judged by most of its supporters. Conversely, to regard the communist voter who shows little readiness to participate in the immediate revolutionary transformation of his society as a defector from the ranks of the party's supporters at election time is equally misleading. The real situation is considerably more complex.

In the final analysis, the French Communist Party's strength comes from its ability to exacerbate the resentments of the disaffected elements in French society. Its policy, ironically, has served contradictory ends. On the one hand, it has spurred efforts to undertake long overdue

8 *L'Humanité*, 15, 16, 18, 19 May 1964. The decision to merge all youth groups has been taken by the PCF central committee and agreed to by other youth organisations, but the UEC is still holding out pending a congress scheduled for the end of 1964. Technically, only a congress can take such a decision. See *Le Monde*, 23 June 1964.

reforms; on the other, by withholding communist support from, and at times even opposing, particular reforms, ostensibly because they did not go far enough, the PCF has not only retained its ideological strangle-hold on large parts of the working class but has also left the process of social transformation to those forces that are least inclined to promote it. In one sense, therefore, the PCF has really become conservative, convinced that its own weakness prevents it from reshaping French society but still powerful enough to perpetuate conditions that serve its purposes. This was essentially the policy of the late Thorez, who led the party for 34 years, and it is not likely to change soon unless the power relations in French domestic politics are drastically altered.

THE Italian case is quite different. Years before the Sino-Soviet dispute erupted, Italian communists were struggling to win greater autonomy for their party (they became more explicit and insistent in pursuing this goal after 1956), to develop their own strategy of power, and (more important) to 'domesticate' their political objectives. They were obviously intent on travelling their own road to socialism, but at the same time they wished to avoid disruptive conflicts with the USSR, since the Soviet revolutionary myth was and still is an important source of authority within the party and a factor in its appeal to members and voters. The Sino-Soviet dispute has forced a quickening of the PCI's evolutionary pace. It has, of course, enabled the party to assert its independence more vigorously and safely than it might otherwise have done; and it has permitted—even compelled—the PCI to move more rapidly and freely in search of its distinctive identity.

The central question for the PCI, as for the other parties, has been how to react to the dispute. Once Soviet authority began to crumble, how much support would Italian communists give the Soviets or the Chinese on the issues that divided them and plagued the international movement? For a time in 1962 and 1963 it seemed that the Chinese might win a certain number of sympathisers in Italy, although there was never any doubt about where the majority party sentiment lay; but the pro-Chinese leaders and groups have proved extremely weak. The Sino-Soviet dispute reactivated old but usually latent divisions within the Italian party between the unreconstructed revo-lutionaries on the extreme left and the cautious moderates and impatient revisionists of the centre and right. Left-wing dissent is hardly new in the PCI, but the current crop of rebels, unlike their predecessors, find hope for their cause in the power and prestige of China, and even more in the breakup of traditional patterns of authority resulting from the dispute.

It is difficult to formulate a typology of the dissident left in Italy. Some of its leaders are activists who cut their political teeth in the wartime resistance, but most of them are relatively young intellectuals who are disillusioned with the Soviet Union's present leaders and repelled by the unavowed reformism of the PCI, and who find some response to their revolutionary appeals among untutored workers and peasants who flock to the PCI and to the communist-dominated trade unions. Togliatti himself, in his posthumously published Yalta memorandum or testament, specifically noted that 'the Chinese revolution had become popular as a peasant revolution' among some of the PCI's rural supporters. Togliatti's comment notwithstanding, the mass appeal of the pro-Chinese groups in Italy has so far been very limited, though it is probably true, as the dissidents themselves claim, that the PCI's moderation is viewed suspiciously by some party members.

Ever since the end of the war, radical critics of the Italian Communist Party, within and outside its ranks, have accused it of being stodgily conservative and opportunist.[9] The new rebels simply add their voices to an old chorus. A certain number of disgruntled communists of middle and low rank (no top-flight Italian leader can be identified as pro-Chinese) have used the occasion to launch an open attack on the centre forces controlled by Togliatti until his death, and against the more aggressively revisionist right-wing in the party (who lived in uneasy alliance with the late party secretary).[10] Some dissidents have been expelled on various grounds or pretexts and others have resigned to form the numerous splinter groups now scattered around the country. But the rebel groups are small, and there is no evidence that they can fuse into a national organisation of any importance.[11]

The general West European rule holds for Italy: the dissident communist left has no chance of playing any significant role, either in the labour movement or in local or national politics and government. It simply is not in tune with the moderate temper of the overwhelming majority of Italian communist leaders, members, and voters. (A reshuffling of the Italian left involving all three of the main parties in the Marxist tradition—the communists, Nenni socialists (PSI), and dissident socialists (PSIUP)—*might* result in the creation of a small but perhaps significant party to the left of the present PCI, but it is difficult to see how such a realignment could take place in the foreseeable future.) The dissident groups, however, and the radicals still remaining in the PCI, do perform one important task: they press the party constantly towards a more open internal debate on fundamental issues and thus, somewhat paradoxically, add their weight to that of the

9 The charge, with appropriate variations, is also made by some non-communists. See, for example, Giorgio Galli, *Storia del Partito Comunista Italiano* (Milan, 1958), especially pp. 344–60.

10 Among the leaders, Togliatti, Giancarlo Pajetta, and Giorgio Amendola (the generally acknowledged leaders of the PCI right) are favourite targets of the dissident press. Pietro Ingrao, who represents a more radical tendency, is usually spared the scathing attacks directed at his colleagues. See, for example, Ugo Duse, in *Nuova Unità* (Milan), April 1964. *Nuova Unità* is now the principal organ of the dissident communists.

11 There is little reliable recent information about these dissident groups. The most useful surveys were published in mid-1963, when Italian press coverage of the subject took on the character of an organised campaign. See Fausto de Luca, in *Il Punto*, 13 July 1963; Giacomo Maugeri, in *Epoca*, 28 July 1963; and Nello Finocchiaro and Gino Bianco, in *Il Mondo*, 30 July 1963.

revisionists on the right who want to give the party a more democratic structure.

THE Sino-Soviet dispute has simply strengthened certain existing trends in Italian communism. Yet for a long time the PCI took no official public notice of it. No doubt there was some discussion in party circles (disciplined silence is not an Italian—or Italian communist— trait). Most members learned the details of the dispute mainly from the suspect 'bourgeois' press and, more convincingly, from the Nenni socialist press. The PCI's long official silence is perhaps not very difficult to explain: people who make a fetish of unity would naturally be reluctant to admit the existence of profound differences between the two largest communist states; and communist leaders no doubt hoped to avoid public involvement in a conflict which might eventually spill over into their own party, with unforeseeable consequences. Once the PCI did become publicly involved in the dispute, however, there was no doubt that, whatever else it might do, it would use the occasion to expand its margin of independence, picking up, and giving more substance to, the theory of polycentrism first formulated by Togliatti in 1956.

The Italian party's positions can be traced in a whole series of public moves, of which Togliatti's 1956 remarks were the first; in 1961, Italian communists reacted sharply and critically to the 22nd CPSU congress. In January 1962 the PCI published documents revealing that the Italian delegation had been far from docile at the 1960 conference of the 81 communist parties.[12] The 10th PCI congress, in late 1962, took an openly anti-Chinese position. And although this could be interpreted as part of a concerted campaign directed by Moscow, in October 1963 the party's central committee published a strong declaration of independence, asserting that 'every party is responsible only to its own people for its policy and for the contribution that it makes to the advancement of the entire movement'.[13] In 1964 a barrage of speeches, articles, and resolutions, capped by Togliatti's 'testament', elaborated the Italian position on all the major issues confronting the international movement, justifying in theory and illustrating in practice the party's growing autonomy.

This tendency is becoming increasingly clear. On most of the issues involved in the Sino-Soviet dispute, the PCI agreed with the Soviet Union. For example: On the question of the 'peaceful transition to socialism', Italian communists unequivocally opposed the Chinese position (however, in this general area the PCI doctrinal positions and policies differentiate it even from the CPSU). On problems of national liberation movements, the Italians castigated the Chinese as

<hr />

[12] Italian Communist Party, Press and Propaganda Section (ed.), *Interventi della delegazione del P.C.I. alla Conferenza degli 81 Partiti Comunisti e Operai (Mosco, novembre 1960)* (Rome, January 1962).
[13] *l'Unità*, 26 October 1963.

provincial sectarians who fail to distinguish between ' struggles ' and
' wars '—a failure which, according to the Italians, might well isolate the
communist ' vanguard ' in the former colonial areas and/or in the
developing countries. On East-West relations, the PCI's position is
again close to that of the Soviet Union: the official stands on imperialism
and the balance of power, the nature and consequences of nuclear war,
revealed differences of emphasis between Rome and Moscow but no
important conflicts.[14]

Equally noteworthy has been the PCI's strong stand against an
international conference that would, in its view, deal another blow to the
myth of communist unity on which they have lived and even thrived
politically. They also feared that, by reviving the principle of a centrally
defined orthodoxy, it would create new barriers to their own
independence.

How has the Sino-Soviet dispute and Khrushchev's fall affected the
PCI's domestic political prospects? Did they help the party or harm it?
As has already been noted, the dispute obviously has not loosened the
party's hold on its members or its electorate; in fact, both membership
and electoral strength have increased recently.[15] This alone makes the
PCI a major political force on the Italian scene: with the possible
exception of the PCF, the PCI is the only communist party in Western
Europe strong enough to be a serious contender for national power,
or at least strong and influential enough to be an important factor
in determining, directly or indirectly, who will rule and on what terms.
This has not made the PCI's isolation at the national level any less real;
but some groups and leaders of the democratic left in Italy look forward
to the day when a ' nationalised ' and ' democratised ' PCI will play
an active part in governing coalitions. The Sino-Soviet dispute
permitted (and even forced) the PCI to assert its autonomy with growing
determination. It has also—but far more slowly—been helping the party
to shed some of the authoritarian features of its doctrine and practices.
The elimination of Khrushchev, and its manner, deeply embarrassed the
party, which was shortly facing local elections. It had to stress its
independent attitude, and has therefore been trying to dissociate itself
from the Soviet goings on. The head of the party delegation to Moscow,
Berlinguer, declared on his return that the explanations received from
the new leaders were insufficient to dispel Italian reservations ' about the
methods they used in informing public opinion '. The Italian party
was particularly concerned about the possibility that some of its members
and many voters might switch to the socialist party. In the Sicilian
elections the Khrushchev affair became a local electoral issue. The
local CP leader, Napoleone Calojanni, declared that ' we communists

---

[14] See ' Noi e i compagni cinesi ', supplement to *l'Unita*, 29 September 1963.
[15] According to party claims, PCI membership increased for the first time in years in
1964 and reached 1,632,000 in mid-June 1964: *Rinascita*, 11 July 1964; in elections
for the Chamber of Deputies, the PCI received 22·7 per cent of the vote in 1958 and
25·3 per cent of the vote in 1963. In the November 1964 local elections it received
26·1 per cent of the votes.

do not agree with what has happened in Moscow ', but in Catania the whole section of the party joined the Nenni socialists. There was a distinctive shift of emphasis in the Italian party formulations on the post-Khrushchevian Soviet attempts at rapprochement with China. Previously, they had by and large endorsed the Soviet ideological position, while disapproving of the idea of excommunicating the Chinese; now they express their concern about the possibility of ' deals and equivocal compromises which are not founded on the effective over-coming of the causes of disagreements and divisions ' (*l'Unita*, 5 November 1964). In short, the fall of Khrushchev has not slowed down the autonomist tendency of the Italian party; on the contrary, it may have enhanced it. These developments suggest that, in time, the party (or what remains of it, if its evolution should be marked by divisions) may well come to play a different role in Italian politics. In any case, in the short run the real issue will be not whether the PCI has changed but whether the changes are sufficiently great to satisfy its potential allies on the democratic left.

THE Chinese communists' failure to find much ideological support among West European communist parties has not prevented a number of these parties from opposing Moscow's attempts to discipline Peking. The Chinese, therefore, were not at all wrong when they predicted dire consequences for the Soviet party's position in the world communist movement if Moscow continued to press for measures designed to excommunicate them from the movement. The Italians, the Swedes, and the Norwegians had already gone on record as opposing it.[16]

However, the notion that this reflected any Chinese ascendancy squares neither with the observable facts nor with the more elusive underlying reasons that have contributed to this development. There is no denying that the Sino-Soviet dispute has exacerbated the traditional left-right divisions in many parties and has given a fillip not only to those who have chafed at the increasingly revisionist trends in their parties but also to others who have disliked Moscow's treatment of the Chinese and Albanians. This is especially true of the younger communist leaders, who have not been formed by the unique experiences of the past that tied an entire generation of communist leaders to Moscow. Nevertheless, the growth of anti-Moscow sentiment has not been sufficient to align any party with China. Nor does it seem likely that a lengthening of the time scale (the Chinese are obviously a patient lot) will work in Peking's favour.

In resorting to historical explanations for placing the impact of the Sino-Soviet dispute on the West European parties in its proper perspective, it is still useful to note the contrasting approaches to this problem by the two best known communist leaders in Western Europe, the late Maurice Thorez and Palmiro Togliatti. Both were loyal to Moscow,

16 *Ny Dag* (Stockholm), 12 May 1964; *Friheten* (Oslo), 7 September 1964.

and more often than not beyond the call of duty. Yet it is clear that
Thorez's dependence on Moscow was of a very different nature from that
of Togliatti. The French leader excelled in total support of the Soviets
at all times. The Italian leader utilised every opportunity after 1956
to redefine his and his party's position towards Moscow by going from
'polycentrism' to 'unity in diversity and autonomy'.

On balance, the attitude of the Italian party towards the Sino-Soviet
dispute is, *mutatis mutandis*, representative of that of quite a number of
other West European parties. In their eyes, China has in many ways
served as a protector, a reinsurance against the possibility of any
reimposition of Soviet control. That is what these parties feared most
in the event of a formal split, and that is what they fear from the Sino-
Soviet rapprochement which also entails for them a shift towards greater
militancy. Confronted by equally noxious polar alternatives—excommunication of the Chinese or Soviet accommodation of Peking's
positions—the West European communists are pushed by the logic of
polycentrism.

Their increasing impatience with the conventional deference to
Moscow was shown by their overwhelmingly critical reaction to
Khrushchev's expulsion. They openly objected to the suddenness, the
secrecy of procedure, and the questionable explanations of Khrushchev's
'resignation', or lack of them. Many parties were not content with
this, but went on to reflect on the deficiences of the Soviet political
system itself. The Austrian communists, for example, said that the way
he was removed revealed a fundamental lack of socialist democracy
in the USSR, which was 'as important as the continuation of the Soviet
peace policy', and they regretted in their resolution of 4 November that
it was not openly discussed. Various Italian communist leaders expressed
disapproval bordering on contempt for the backwardness of Soviet
political practices. The party secretary, Luigi Longo, said that it was
'worried and critical' about them, indicating as they did the 'resistance
to broad freedom of discussion and debate' in the USSR. Pietro Ingrao
thought that they raised questions about the whole 'problem of
socialist democracy'. The Norwegian party declared that the official
Soviet explanation was 'inexact', and the Swedish communists described
Khrushchev's removal as 'unconstitutional'. Their newspaper, *Ny Dag*
(21 October 1964) commented that it 'leaves a bitter taste in the mouth'
and contrasted it with 'the open debate and intensive election campaigns in Sweden, Denmark, and Britain'. The British, Belgian, and
Swiss parties, and to a lesser extent also the French, took a critical line.
Before Mr Chou En-lai's visit to Moscow, that city was full of Western
communist delegations asking for 'explanations' and not being fully
satisfied with them.

But in their attempts to present themselves in a more independent
and democratic role, the West European parties face the difficult
problem of reconciling their advocacy of greater autonomy in inter-party
relations and their implied criticism of Soviet political behaviour with

their continuing practice of stifling internal party democracy and their rejection of the democratic framework within which they operate. Among the established and emerging leaders of the West European communist parties few are aware of this contradiction, and none as yet is ready to discard the Leninist principles of organisation. The fall of Khrushchev and the Sino-Soviet rapprochement, however temporary and fragile, accentuate the problem, particularly for the parties belonging to the ' Italian ' tendency. Previously, they were against ' excommunications ', now they are against ' unprincipled compromises '. The small parties, like the Belgian, the Swiss, and the Austrian, which face in their countries organised ' anti-revisionist ' splinter groups, have a special reason for concern as the change enhances the position of their rivals.

The Belgian party, in the report of Ernest Burnelle presented at its XV congress (*Le Drapeau Rouge*, 30 November 1964) repeated that it ' proposes to maintain its previous position ' on the question of calling an international communist conference. It is characteristic of the ' symbolic ' difficulties in which the Soviet party finds itself in dealing with the post-Khrushchev situation in the communist movement that, while Brezhnev was still using the ' conciliatory ' formula endorsing the 20th, *21st,* and 22nd Soviet party congresses (*Pravda*, 4 December 1964), the congratulatory telegram sent to the Belgian party congress by the CPSU mentioned only the 20th and the 22nd (anti-Stalin) congresses (*Le Drapeaus Rouge*, 27 November 1964).

The tension between the requirements of ' autonomy ' and ' solidarity ' in the West European parties manifests itself continuously in their pronouncements, whatever their actual position vis-à-vis the Sino-Soviet conflict. A ' conciliatory ' party, like the British, which pointed out that a Sino-Soviet reconciliation ' would involve some changes in the positions previously taken up ', still stressed in its report on the November 1964 talks in Moscow, that it disagreed with the Russians about the treatment of Khrushchev's dismissal (*Daily Worker*, 17 November 1964). The Italians were of course the most explicit. In an interview granted to *Der Spiegel* (11 November 1964), Berlinguer, head of the Italian party delegation to Moscow, said that ' among the problems on which we disagree is the question of how democracy is to be developed within the Soviet system '.

It was not surprising that the pro-Chinese *Le Communiste* (November 1964) should comment ironically on the quandary in which the West European communist parties would find themselves in case of a Sino-Soviet reconciliation: ' Would they, on the pretext of " autonomy " and " independence ", push towards a split . . . [which] would oppose the communist parties of the capitalist countries to the communist parties of the socialist countries? '. Even if the premise of this argument—Sino-Soviet reconciliation—is not very realistic, it points to a very real dilemma which the West European parties are facing.

EASTERN EUROPE

J. F. Brown

THE Stalinist system in Eastern Europe died with Stalin, for without him it had no meaning. Since 1953 it has had no recognisable replacement; there have simply been reactions, dictated and spontaneous, against it. There was the almost immediate realisation that his system could not continue; the national, political, and economic dissatisfaction which found its outlet immediately after his death and its most dramatic expression in Poland and Hungary in 1956; the acceptance by Khrushchev of the fact that more autonomy for each country was necessary if a viable system was to be worked out; the influence on the area of the Yugoslav example—these, together with the Sino-Soviet dispute and the beginnings of a positive Western policy, are perhaps the main factors which have produced the marked diversity which now exists in Eastern Europe.

But did they *produce* this diversity? Did they not rather help to restore it? The dull grey blanket of uniformity which the European satellites have now discarded lasted a very short time indeed. The uniformity began in 1948 and ended early in 1953. Before 1948 it was by no means certain that the communist parties in the different countries of Eastern Europe would slavishly imitate the Soviet Union. Most of their leaders, even Dimitrov and Rakosi—not to mention an outsider like Gomulka—indicated that the policies they would adopt would embody a form of socialism tailored to some extent to the nature and traditions of their own countries. Such statements have often been dismissed as propaganda smokescreens, and to a certain extent they were; but there was an element of sincerity in them. What is certain is that the different communist parties plunged themselves too deeply into the affairs of their own countries for the liking of Stalin, to whom a foreign communist was first and foremost an agent of the Soviet Union. It was the diversity and divergencies caused by this 'domesticism' which in part led to the establishment of the Cominform; the defection of Tito served rather to accelerate this than to cause it.

What Khrushchev did was to give domesticism (or internal autonomy) the green light; the result has been a return, though far from complete, to the diversity which has always characterised Eastern Europe. Khrushchev's concept of autonomy had, however, its strict limits. Though obviously desirous that every country should roughly conform to the Soviet model of Marxism-Leninism, he had been prepared to tolerate glaring deviations, as in the case of Gomulka's agrarian policy. What he insisted upon was that no regime should hold up its deviations as a legitimate example for others to follow, and that in foreign policy and, later when it became relevant, in intra-bloc policy, there should be complete obedience to Moscow. Yugoslavia failed this test on both counts while Albania and, more recently, Rumania, failed on the second, and it is because of this that these three countries have become, in different degrees, the odd men out in Eastern Europe.

THE Sino-Soviet dispute introduced a new element and a new potential in intra-bloc relations which have had their effect on Eastern Europe. As W. E. Griffith has pointed out, it has presented the regimes with three possible courses of action vis-à-vis Moscow: to break away completely; to play off Peking against Moscow; to side completely with Moscow.[1] Albania is a perfect example of the implementation of the first possibility: the emergence of Peking as a threat to Moscow came at a time when Khrushchev was paying court to Tito. Rumania is a very good example of the second. To find an example of the third is not too easy. The GDR, Czechoslovakia, and Bulgaria all gave Khrushchev the staunchest support in his battle with Mao; the support from Hungary was only slightly less staunch. The difficulty arises when one tries to analyse whether this support was given primarily in order to extract concessions from Moscow or for some other reason. In the case of the Ulbricht and Zhivkov regimes it seems to have been due simply to utter dependence on the Soviet Union. But the Hungarian regime has not for some years needed the propping up so essential for the Bulgarian and the East German. Kadar could therefore have been in a position to talk terms with Khrushchev. Yet there were no signs that his loyalty resulted in any tangible concessions to Hungary. The main reason for his support was probably the bond, both political and personal, which united the two men ever since November 1956. Kadar was installed by Khrushchev and in the early years of his regime he certainly did need propping up. Personal gratitude on the part of Kadar, combined with the feeling that his destiny was so closely linked with that of Khrushchev, seem to have been factors stronger than the hesitation he probably felt over pressing the quarrel with China,[2] and at the same time they perhaps precluded his seeking a quid pro quo for his support. Economically, too, Hungary is very dependent on the Soviet Union, especially for raw materials, and in this field her connection with Moscow is actually becoming closer.

It was probably Antonin Novotny's Czechoslovakia which, in some ways, came the closest of any to the implementation of this third possibility. Novotny in the last three years has been faced by the problems of severe economic stagnation, a mounting demand for internal reform, and a resurgence of Slovak national feeling. He at first showed little inclination to try to solve them with a flexible, reformist approach. Whereas to a man like Kadar, the 22nd CPSU congress was the encouragement he needed to press ahead with reform,

---

[1] See *Albania and the Sino-Soviet Rift* (M.I.T. Press, Cambridge, Mass., 1964).

[2] The first Hungarian announcement definitely favouring a world conference of communist parties was published only on 12 April 1964, immediately after Khrushchev's visit.

for Novotny it produced something akin to paralysis. He seemed bent on paying only lip service to destalinisation and then carrying on very much as before. When, early in 1962, the Vice-Premier and Politburo member, Rudolf Barak, sought to put himself at the head of a reform group within the party, Novotny had him jailed for 15 years as a common thief. Although it is too much to consider this an act of open defiance of Khrushchev, it was certainly something of which the Soviet leader, who evidently liked Barak, could not have readily approved. Yet Novotny, whose instinct for survival is of the highest order, realised that what Khrushchev now needed more than anything was implicit loyalty in his struggle with China. This he gave him and, in return, his survival was ensured and he was left to deal with domestic affairs as he thought fit. The relaxation which has come in Czechoslovakia was probably due not so much to Soviet interference as to the strength of the pressure from below and Novotny's slow retreat before it.

IN her relations with the Soviet Union Poland occupies a special position. She has not sought to play off Peking against Moscow, as Rumania has, and she did not give Khrushchev the complete support in his tactics against China which Bulgaria, Czechoslovakia, Hungary, and the GDR did. Gomulka was obviously reluctant to see a conference leading to an excommunication of China.[3] His attitude may be prompted partly by an intense personal dislike of factionalism, whether on a national or international plane, his conception of the communist camp as a very loose commonwealth based on the principle of 'live and let live', and his own awareness that situations can change with bewildering rapidity. An enemy today can be a friend tomorrow and vice-versa. Who could have thought that Tito could have worked himself back into a position of grace and favour? Who would have thought in 1949 that he himself would have been the saviour of his country in 1956? Finally there must have been the fear that, if Khrushchev succeeded in his plan of excommunicating China, then he might have followed this with attempts to restore some degree of unity and cohesiveness in what remained of the camp under his control.[4] It is a measure of the changed situation in the bloc that Gomulka could have held such an attitude and yet remained on very good personal and political terms with Khrushchev.

Some of the motives which have always prompted Gomulka have, of course, prompted Gheorghiu-Dej also. He shared Gomulka's fears, but, unlike Gomulka, Gheorghiu-Dej found himself involved in a very serious dispute with Khrushchev, a dispute which went so far as to force

---

[3] In his speech to the fourth congress of the PUWP on 15 June 1964, Gomulka, while agreeing in principle to a world conference, suggested a procedure which obviously meant delaying it for a long time to come (*Trybuna Ludu*, 16 June 1964). His ideas in this respect were similar to those published in Togliatti's testament, released to the press on 4 September 1964.

[4] The danger of this is, of course, implicit in the whole situation, although specific Soviet statements implying it have been very few.

him into a flirtation with China and an open defiance of the Soviet Union. Gomulka's stand has, in a sense, been rather more disinterested. Much more analogous with the Polish motive has been that of the Yugoslavs. Despite the hatred between Peking and Belgrade, Tito has shown himself extremely hesitant to endorse any move which would formally expel China from the communist camp, mainly on the ground that this would revive the principle of excommunication of which he himself was the first victim.

One finds, therefore, between the Yugoslav, Rumanian, and Polish Communist Parties (and the Italian) a unity of outlook based on a similar concept of what the character of the camp should be. Whereas, however, the Yugoslav party has complete freedom of manoeuvre because of its unique position outside the bloc, and the Rumanian party, carried forward by the dynamic of its quarrel with Moscow, has carved out for itself a great degree of freedom, the room for manoeuvre of the Polish leaders was much more circumscribed.

The Rumanian example has shown the limitations which now exist to the Soviet ability to coerce the Eastern European regimes. Four factors have been mainly responsible for the Rumanian success: a ruthlessly united party in Rumania itself; the Sino-Soviet dispute and the freedom for manoeuvre which it gives; the presence of Yugoslavia; and the beginning of something like an ' activist ' Western policy towards Eastern Europe. The first two factors need not detain us. The last two deserve brief examination.

The question of where Gheorghiu-Dej is going, or would like to go, is one which for a long time Gheorghiu-Dej himself could not answer. It would be a great mistake to see the Rumanian leader (or any leader) coldly setting forth his objectives and marching inexorably towards them. He moved from one brilliant improvisation to another until he found himself at, or close to, the point of no return with Khrushchev. It was then that he probably decided to take Yugoslavia as his model for what his relationship with Moscow and the bloc should be. This does not mean that he is so foolhardy as to want formally to renounce any of Rumania's institutional ties with the bloc—Comecon, the Warsaw Pact, etc.—but that he would simply use them when necessary, at the same time feeling free to follow whatever intra- or extra-bloc policy suited him. It is this which explains his present closeness to Tito and which represents the first success for Yugoslavia's Eastern European policy since 1955 and early 1956. It was a success, however, which must have been rather embarrassing to Tito, for it came at a time when his own relations with Khrushchev were very good. Indeed, Tito may have tried to urge some restraint on Gheorghiu-Dej so as not to endanger his own Moscow connection. He is at present nervously watching the new leadership in Moscow to see what twists in the zig-zag relations with the Soviet Union are on the way.

The change in Western policy towards Eastern Europe has played its small but important part in aiding the Rumanian deviation, and its implications for the other communist countries are obvious. The Gaston Marin visit to Washington, the Maurer visit to France, and the growing series of economic agreements between Rumania and the Western countries represent for the Rumanian regime a political and economic insurance of great present and even greater potential value. The Rumanians have up to now manoeuvred cleverly within the framework of precisely that peaceful coexistence which was one of the main planks of Soviet foreign policy. They have taken the letter (if not the spirit) of this policy and used it for their own ends; they have on occasion even pointed out that they are only doing what the Soviets are both preaching and practising. Hence it was very difficult for Khrushchev to take a public stand against such action, either on the part of Rumania or any other Eastern European country which chose to take advantage of it. The other Eastern European regimes are also, of course, increasing their trade considerably with the West, but up to now this has not had the same political significance which the Rumanian action has had.

Khrushchev also had mainly Rumania to thank for the failure of what might have been a most subtle and powerful unifying instrument in Eastern Europe—the Council for Mutual Economic Assistance (Comecon). The political implications of this body have always been as important as the economic, and although much has been (rightly) made of Rumanian opposition to proposals which would have greatly circumscribed her schemes for economic expansion, the real long-term importance of her victory is that it has contributed to the abandonment of a political unification, through economic means, which would have been far stronger and more lasting than the system associated with Stalin. Economic integration through division of labour would, in itself, have many advantages. But, carried to its conclusion, it would lead to a blurring of national divisions, basically in the interests of the Soviet Union. This Rumania has effectively sabotaged, and the rest of the Eastern European nations have cause to be grateful.

One must, however, end this short introduction on a note of sobriety. The tremendous amount of attention which Rumania has attracted over the last two years has perhaps tended to give the impression that all the Eastern European regimes are, in varying degrees, already asserting their independence from the Soviet Union. The Rumanian example has been generalised; the fever, while rightly diagnosed as highly contagious, is already considered as raging far and wide. A closer examination reveals that, at present, this is a premature conclusion. In the economic sphere, four of the regimes, Hungary, the GDR, Czechoslovakia and Bulgaria, have recently tightened rather than loosened their ties with Moscow,[5] while Poland, special case though it is, must remain at the side of the Soviet Union at least until its

---

[5] For example, the recent establishment between each of these four countries and the Soviet Union of joint governmental commissions for economic, scientific, and technical cooperation. These may be considered by Moscow as substitute measures for the kind of economic integration it would have liked and which Rumania has sabotaged.

Western frontier is guaranteed. But, all the same, what is new is that the conditions had been created, even before the fall of Khrushchev, which made the assertion of more independence by *all* the Eastern European regimes possible and that examples were at hand to show it could be done. What follows is a brief analysis of the more essential features of internal development and intra-bloc attitudes in the countries under review, which have interacted with the Sino-Soviet conflict.

Bulgaria

THE BULGARIAN COMMUNIST PARTY, one with a strong tradition and an impressive Valhalla of its own, finds itself at the end of 1964 a party without inspiration, without real leadership, and with a record of failure unequalled in Eastern Europe. It is still led by Todor Zhivkov, an amiable, well meaning apparatchik who became First Party Secretary as long ago as March 1954 when he was in his early forties.

The BCP has been torn by factionalism ever since it assumed power. There was first the bloody struggle in the late forties between the 'Muscovites' and the 'home communists' which ended in the execution in 1949 of Traicho Kostov; this was followed by the six-year period of ascendancy (1950–1956) of Bulgaria's 'little Stalin', Vulko Chervenkov. Zhivkov replaced Chervenkov as First Party Secretary in 1954, but this was little more than a deferential bow to the campaign against the personality cult which followed Stalin's death. Chervenkov himself was a victim of the 20th CPSU congress and the Soviet rapprochement with Yugoslavia; as such he was forced to step down from the premiership in April 1956. His place was taken by Anton Yugov, a 'home communist' who had been in eclipse during Cherven-kov's period of domination. There followed a six-year period of factional struggle between Yugov and his supporters, the still influential Chervenkov and his group, and the growing faction led by Zhivkov himself, who steadily increased his hold on the party apparatus and prepared for the opportunity to eliminate his rivals. The opportunity came as a result of the 22nd CPSU congress. Zhivkov, whose support for Khrushchev always bordered on the servile and who always had the backing of the Soviet leader, used the destalinisation issue first to oust Chervenkov from his party and government positions and then, in November 1962, to dismiss Premier Yugov at one of the most dramatic communist party congresses held for years.

The period which followed has been one of disappointing anti-climax. Any idea that Bulgaria would become a torchbearer of liberalised communism proved unfounded; liberalisation slowed down and then ground to a halt. An official crackdown submerged the shoots of intellectual freedom and, to cap it all, living standards, rather than improving, at best stagnated and in some sectors actually got worse.

It is not easy to explain why the situation turned out so disappointingly. It may be that Zhivkov was never really interested in liberalisation, that he simply used it as a stick with which to beat his opponents, they being far more vulnerable on the issue of Stalinist crimes than he was. Once he had got rid of his opponents, therefore, he simply dropped the issue. More convincing is the suggestion that Zhivkov, though securing his grip on the leadership of the party, still faced strong opposition among the party apparatchiks, especially in the provinces, who saw any programme of liberalisation as a threat to their authority. But their opposition would not account for the various acts of nervous repression which have recently characterised the Zhivkov regime. The explanation for these is to be seen mainly in the deterioration of Bulgaria's economic situation; the stock response of a weak leader to the discontent which a situation like this creates is repression. Hence the prison sentences for jokes, the boorish outcries against the intellectuals, the warnings against contacts with foreigners, etc.

It is this essential weakness of the Zhivkov regime which has forced it to lean more and more heavily on the Soviet crutch. In 1964 alone Bulgaria has made economic agreements with the Soviet Union involving Soviet loans of 530 million rubles.[6]

Her unconditional support for the Soviet Union in the Sino-Soviet dispute is, therefore, not surprising. It is not a reflection, as is often thought, of the overwhelming sympathy of the Bulgarian people for the great Slav brother and liberator (Russia over the last 20 years has used up much of her spiritual credit in Bulgaria). It is basically due to the weakness and lack of confidence of the Zhivkov regime.

It was shown when the Bulgarian central committee announced its 'ardent approval and unanimous support' of the CPSU central committee proposal for calling an international conference of communist parties. This statement was published in the Bulgarian party daily, *Rabotnichesko Delo,* on 5 April, only two days after *Pravda* had printed the Suslov speech to the Soviet central committee plenum of 14 February which first called for the conference. The Bulgarian endorsement, its prompt and unequivocal character, revealed clearly Bulgaria's attitude in the Sino-Soviet conflict and towards polycentrism in general. The loyalty of the Zhivkov leadership to the Soviet Union has never wavered. In 1964 the character of Soviet-Bulgarian relations is very much the same as it was before Stalin died; the centrifugal forces which have been at work in the bloc have not yet touched Sofia. The Soviet party's proposal for the 26-party preparatory conference in Moscow in December met with equally wholehearted and prompt approval; on 14 August *Rabotnichesko Delo* reported that the BCP 'fully endorses the proposals made by the central committee of the

[6] The first 1964 loan to be announced was for 300 million rubles and was agreed in February, during the visit of a Bulgarian delegation led by Zhivkov. The second, for 165 million, was agreed to in July. On 8 July deputy premier Todorov said in a broadcast over Radio Sofia that an agreement had been signed in January involving a 65 million ruble credit to finance the delivery to Bulgaria of fishing boats.

CPSU and will participate actively both in the preparations for the conference and in its work '.

The official Bulgarian reaction to the downfall of Khrushchev showed perhaps more clearly than anything else could have done the dependence on Moscow. There was not even a parting nod to the fallen leader who, right up to the moment of his eclipse, had been idolised in a manner close to nauseating. Contemptible though this attitude might be deemed, it was understandable, since for Zhivkov, Moscow is the only place where he can go, regardless of who holds the power there. He will, therefore, seek to adapt himself to any change in policy by the Kremlin on, for example, the rift with China. He must, however, reckon with greater insecurity in his position at home. The disappearance of his mentor has further weakened him, and there must be many in his party who feel that this is an excellent time for a change. The new Moscow leaders, for their part, must be anxious to avoid instability in Eastern Europe and may, therefore, support him. But it would not be surprising if he gave up at least one of his posts in the fairly near future.

Czechoslovakia

IN BULLFIGHTING THERE IS ALWAYS a part of the bullring to which the bull seeks to repair, where he feels most at home, where he is most dangerous to the matador who is tormenting him. This part of the ring is called the bull's *querencia*.

In the last two years Czechoslovakia's President and First Party Secretary, Antonin Novotny, has seen his position and his authority undermined in many important sectors. But he has survived and in the course of 1964 actually showed signs of recovering some of the strength he lost. Novotny was driven back onto the ground he knows best, where he was the most dangerous. His *querencia* is the sphere of party control and manipulation. It was in this craft that he progressed from apprentice to journeyman and finally to master, a master with resource, shrewdness, and considerable courage. It was his ability to retain control of the party machine, almost completely in the Czech lands and to a sufficient extent in Slovakia, combined with the support he received from Khrushchev, that has so far kept him in the saddle.

The crisis of the Czechoslovak regime was sparked off by the 22nd CPSU congress, but its real causes preceded that event. One was the failure of the country's economy, the previously smooth performance of which had aways been the regime's trump card. Building on a most efficient and advanced pre-war base, first the Gottwald and then the Novotny regimes had, up to 1960, registered impressive growth rates in industry, and although the socialised agriculture had never been successful, its failures had never reached the danger point. By 1961, however, the results of a far too ambitious policy of over-investment in heavy industry, of a serious labour shortage and a stagnation in labour productivity, of exaggerated commitments for political purposes in the underdeveloped countries, and of an excessive centralisation of the management system, had begun to have their effect.

Unfortunately for Novotny, this crisis blew up at the end of 1961 and the beginning of 1962, i.e. just after the 22nd CPSU congress. Though completely out of sympathy with the spirit of that event, the Czechoslovak leader could not ignore the relaxed atmosphere which followed in its wake, and so gave the Czechs and Slovaks a certain freedom to complain precisely at the time they had something to complain about, thereby creating a dangerous situation. Popular discontent rose to a point it had not reached since 1953.

Together with this discontent came agitation from other, more vocal quarters. The references at the 22nd CPSU congress to the crimes of the Stalin era in the Soviet Union and the rehabilitation of its victims created an impatience in the Czechoslovak party to see its own slate wiped clean. The danger to Novotny of such a thing happening was obvious to no one more than Novotny himself. Though he could plead that he was 'not in the highest leadership at the time', everyone knew that he was high ranking enough to have had a big hand in much of the dirty work that had gone on. Everyone also knew that some of his colleagues were even more directly implicated than he was. Although Novotny contrived to stage-manage the 12th congress of the Czechoslovak party in December 1962 with great skill, so that it passed with scarcely a ripple, he was forced to agree to an inquiry into the trials of the Stalinist period. The full findings of this inquiry were never made public, but in April 1963, immediately after they had been made known to the central committee, Novotny was forced to dismiss two of his senior colleagues.

This sign of weakness was the encouragement the reformists needed. The pent-up forces of frustration and anger burst on the regime. The spirit of rebellion was strongest among the Slovaks impatient with the centralist policy of the Prague regime, conscious of their separate Slovak nationality, and demanding equal status with the Czechs.

Equally important and equally dangerous to Novotny as the nationalism of the Bratislava rebels, was their revisionism (almost all were communists). This was something on which they could be joined by their like-minded brethren in Prague—and joined they were, enthusiastically and with courage. Throughout the second half of 1963 the cultural journals in Bratislava and Prague released a flood of criticism against which Novotny was about as effective as Mrs Partington and her mop. The climax of the rebels' triumph came in September 1963 when Premier Viliam Siroky, a Slovak who had 'sold himself' to Prague centralism and a Stalinist to boot, was dismissed.

During this period gains were made to which Novotny has resigned himself and which will not be lost in the foreseeable future. But where Novotny's opponents have sought to undermine or deny the full authority of the party—where they have tried to invade his *querencia*—

they have met with effective resistance. During 1964 Novotny began
to reassert himself. He has issued sharp warnings to the dissident
intellectuals and in some instances has, as a deterrent, resorted to such
administrative measures as expulsion from the party or the dismissal
of the culprit from his post. The effect has been noticeable. If one
compares the tone of the Czech and Slovak periodicals today with that
of a year ago, the difference is striking; rebellion has been replaced
by the 'constructive criticism' which Novotny, with a brave face, is
now prepared to allow.

Apart from his own considerable exertions, he was aided by
three other factors. First, there was the support from Khrushchev
already referred to. Whatever misgivings the Soviet leader may have
had about Novotny seem to have been counterbalanced by his
realisation that in him he had a stable, loyal ally. The visit which
Khrushchev made to Czechoslovakia in August-September 1964
removed any lingering doubts there may have been about where
Moscow's favour lay. Secondly, the economic situation has somewhat
improved. The shortages which so rattled the population are now less
acute. The trend generally is upwards. Thirdly, there has been no
real alternative to Novotny.

Despite, therefore, all the rumours and the many pointers to the
contrary, he has survived. In November he was re-elected for a further
presidential term of five years and, since it was stressed at his re-election
that the practice of combining the posts of President and First Party
Secretary had proved sound and effective, one may also assume that
he will continue, at least for some time, as Party Leader.

What has been the most surprising of all, however, has been Novotny's
reaction to the fall of Khrushchev. Circumstantial evidence, backed
by unofficial reports, suggest that there is considerable coolness between
Moscow and Prague over the fact and the manner of Khrushchev's
dismissal. Novotny evidently forcefully objected to the treatment of
Khrushchev and the Soviets replied by not answering the protocol
telegram of congratulations which the Czechoslovak party and government sent to the new leaders. Novotny countered by refusing to attend
the 'summit' meeting in Moscow on the occasion of the 47th anniversary
of the October Revolution; instead he sent his number two man in the
party, Jiri Hendrych.

There the matter rests; it may not proceed much further. Both sides
have an interest in resuming normal relations. But it may be a very
long time before this comes about and the new Soviet leaders will have
been served notice that even the Czechoslovak regime is not one to be
trifled with.

Hungary

FROM THE POINT OF VIEW OF internal liberalisation Hungary continues
to present the most encouraging picture of all the communist countries
of Eastern Europe. In certain respects it may still be behind Poland but,

whereas the retrogression from the Polish October has continued slowly but uninterruptedly, the situation in Hungary is steadily becoming relaxed. Without wishing to idealise the situation, one can speak of a vast improvement even since 1961, not to mention since the days of the Rakosi era.

So far, so good. But the situation is not without its gloomier prospects. There are elements in it which must be, or should be, profoundly disturbing to Kadar and his more thoughtful associates. Kadar's aim in embarking on his liberalising policy was to effect a grand reconciliation, to heal the wounds of 1956 and to harness the talents and the good will of all to the task of socialist construction. The whole purpose behind his now familiar slogan of ' Who is not against us is with us ' was to try to establish a contract between the regime and the people. Without such a contract his regime could exist but could not operate constructively. In his own way Kadar has tried to fulfil what he has considered to be his part of the contract—hence the concessions. But for the Hungarian people no such contract exists. They take the concessions gladly but do not consider that they owe anything to Kadar in return. There is no *rapport* with the regime, no give and take. Kadar expects them to put their shoulders to the wheel of socialism; what they expect are more and more concessions which they consider their due.

This is Kadar's central and long term problem. His main short term problem has been that of trying to get his own party, especially the middle and lower level apparatchiks, to accept and implement his whole policy of liberalisation. That it was a difficult and is still an unsolved problem is hardly surprising, since some aspects of this policy represented a threat to the authority and even the positions of many party officials. These men, weak in Budapest but strongly entrenched in the provinces, have all the while been biding their time in the hope that the whole policy would turn out to be so unsuccessful that it would have to be changed and that the party leadership would have to be changed too. They were strongly opposed to Khrushchev because they knew that Kadar was the Soviet leader's protegé and personal favourite, the man who backed Kadar in the policy that was threatening them.

When Khrushchev fell, therefore, Kadar had to do two things and do them quickly. He had to warn the ' dogmatist ' apparatchiks that their hour had not come, that he could stand on his own feet, and that he intended to go full steam ahead with his policy. He also had to assure a very nervous population that the better times would continue. This he did and has gained in stature as a result.

There can be little doubt that this very human person was profoundly affected by the fall of his friend and protector. But the personal loss might well turn out to be a political blessing. In Hungary itself he will now be judged on his own merits and will cease to be regarded as the stooge of the man who destroyed Hungarian independence in 1956.

In intra-bloc and international politics he will no longer feel bound by personal loyalty to follow the wishes of the man in the Kremlin. Kadar would have followed Khrushchev even to the point of excommunicating China, but there was enough evidence to show that it would have been against his better judgment. He has accepted the new regime in the Kremlin as a fact of life but he will never feel as obliged to the new as he did to the old. He is now personally freed to embark on a more independent course if he wishes. If he does so, he will further enhance his prestige among his own countrymen.

Poland

IN JUNE 1964 THE POLISH COMMUNIST PARTY held its fourth congress. It was a congress dominated by Gomulka, responsive to his wishes, reflecting both his personal strength and his mediocrity.

It is a source of considerable displeasure to many Poles, both at home and abroad, that their country has clearly ceased to be the most interesting in Eastern Europe. Czechoslovakia has been in ferment, Hungary has stolen headline after headline, Rumania has become the cynosure of all eyes. Even the GDR has been quietly changing itself. Poland under Gomulka finds itself a companion in the backwater with Zhivkov's Bulgaria. The man responsible for this is Gomulka himself. Perhaps more than any other party leader in Eastern Europe, it is he who sets the pattern and tone of the regime he heads.

The old Western picture of Gomulka as a liberal, national communist leader closer perhaps to Western social-democracy than to bolshevik communism has now been turned to the wall. Gomulka was brought to power in 1956 on a wave of popular enthusiasm of which he was not the initiator, hardly even a participant. Far from responding to or being stimulated by the spontaneity which elevated him, he was profoundly distrustful of it and ever since 1956 he has been steadily chipping away at the flattering monument which the Polish people (and, more especially, Western observers) erected to him.

The 'retreat from October' began in 1958 and has continued ever since. It has affected the economy, where the situation in recent years has gone from bad to worse mainly because an unimaginative system of 'orthodox' planning was preferred to a flexible model which would have made Poland the torchbearer of economic revision. Only now is the old system beginning to be revised. In cultural affairs the extent to which the retrogression has gone could clearly be seen by the Wankowicz trial in November. Church-State relations have seriously worsened over the past year, with the regime mounting an offensive on several fronts against the policy and authority of Cardinal Wyszynski. On the political scene most of the liberals of 1956 have been deprived of all influence and, in general, the population is being subjected to much more interference than in the past eight years. Gomulka managed the fourth party congress with great skill and enjoyed something of a personal triumph, but many members of his party must be quietly aware of the blind alley into which he has led the country. His prestige among the nation has never been so low as it is now.

His prestige, however, in the socialist camp never seems to have been as high as it is today. The very fact that Brezhnev and Kosygin paid him the courtesy of visiting him on Polish territory to explain Khrushchev's dismissal and presumably to reassure him on certain points, is significant indeed. Only Gomulka received such attention. It seemed to indicate that, in the Soviet view, he and his regime were considered as sufficiently independent and influential and yet—and here is the contrast with Gheorghiu-Dej—sufficiently loyal to be worth the trouble of prompt and personal reassurance.

Before Khrushchev fell Gomulka had clearly distanced himself from the Soviet leader's intention to excommunicate China. Though roundly condemning Chinese policy he had constantly stressed the need for patience and perseverance in trying to settle the dispute. He was for a world conference that would restore harmony rather than one that would impose sanctions. At the fourth party congress in June he supported a world conference of communist parties [7] but only after the most careful and complicated preparation. Gomulka's real feelings on the Sino-Soviet dispute were shown after his meeting with Brezhnev and Kosygin in October. He urged both parties to sit down again and negotiate and then, steadily, layer by layer, confidence could be built up which would make a conference worthwhile. His views had become identical with those of the Rumanian regime, with whose attitude on this problem he had always had much sympathy.

That Gomulka spoke so confidently so soon after meeting the new Soviet leaders was probably in itself an indication that there was some agreement on this point. He must also have warned them about the dangers of Khrushchev's policy of rapprochement with West Germany. Here also his undoubted influence may make itself felt.

Rumania

CREEPING INTO THE JARGON of Western students of communist affairs is another handsome word—'desatellisation'. It means, presumably, the process whereby a communist state manoeuvres into a position of complete or partial independence from the Soviet Union. It is often used in juxtaposition to the now respectable 'destalinisation', which means a process of internal liberalising, a relaxation of the tyranny associated with the Stalinist system.

While Hungary is considered at the moment to be the number one example of destalinisation, Rumania certainly takes pride of place for desatellisation; she is still, however, near the bottom in destalinisation.

[7] *Trybuna Ludu*, 16 June 1964. In an advance text released to correspondents there was a passage which stated that any parties which did not take part in a conference prepared along the lines he suggested would 'put themselves beyond the pale of the international movement'. This passage was deleted from his speech as delivered.

It has often been pointed out that the three countries (all Balkan) which have achieved independence from the Soviet Union, Yugoslavia and Albania completely, and Rumania partly, had, at the time they achieved their independence, strongly Stalinist regimes. Yugoslavia in the course of a few years transformed itself radically; Albania has not and shows no signs of doing so. Which course Rumania will take will be watched with very great interest. She will be another test case of whether desatellisation brings destalinisation in its wake.

Gheorghiu-Dej has been the leader of the Rumanian communist regime ever since it was installed. The 22nd CPSU congress in October 1961, with its emphasis on the sins of the Stalinist era, presented him with a very serious problem, one which he overcame, however, with an enviable sang-froid. At a party central committee plenum held in November-December 1961 he indulged in a masterly exercise in diversion. He blamed everything on the Pauker-Luca-Georgescu trio which he himself purged in 1952, i.e. before Stalin died. He claimed, therefore, that he had destalinised before Stalin's death, that the situation since 1952 had been a model of socialist legality and that any further destalinisation was unnecessary and irrelevant. Those who remembered the execution of Patrascanu in 1954, the Ottoman-type measures of intimidation in 1955 and in the two years after the Hungarian revolution, knew how much truth there was in these contentions. But for Gheorghiu-Dej this masquerade was necessary, and the pretence must still be kept up. There is also the important consideration that he has been at the top long enough to realise the danger of too many concessions all at once. He remembers what happened in Poland and Hungary in 1956; he has seen the more recent difficulties of Novotny in Czechoslovakia. He is cautious or prudent enough not to take the same risk in Rumania.

If there is real destalinisation it will come slowly, quietly, and by stages. The amnesty for political prisoners announced in June 1964 and implemented with the minimum of fuss, is probably an example of how the whole process will be carried out. Actually, there seems little reason why it should not be carried out.

The ruling group is strongly united; the secret police are firmly under the control of the political leadership; the population is behind it in its foreign policy. There seems no reason why it should not proceed to strengthen its basis of popular support by granting substantial concessions. Within the limits of the heavy industrialisation policy, the standard of living could be further improved, the rigours of collectivised agriculture could be modified on the Hungarian style, private artisanry could be reintroduced; above all, the security apparatus, already less pervasive than before, could recede further into the background. The Rumanian people naturally find great pleasure in having its nationalist, anti-Russian emotions gratified, but, unless accompanied by more solid benefits, the novelty of such a pleasure can wear off in time. Destalinisation will, therefore, probably follow desatellisation. The pace will be a sedate one but Rumania will probably be the first to join Yugoslavia among the countries which have achieved both.

An interesting comparison could be made between the intra-bloc policies of Gheorghiu-Dej and Gomulka. There are similarities and contrasts. The Rumanian attitude towards the Soviet Union over the past eighteen months has resembled the Polish attitude in 1957 on the basic issue of the position of Moscow in the socialist camp. Despite Gomulka's having made his peace with Moscow, the similarity to some extent remains. The Polish leader, in his quieter way and his different circumstances, is as concerned as Gheorghiu-Dej over the prospect of a strong reassertion of Soviet hegemony. But whereas Gomulka regards some measure of economic integration as being of great advantage, to Gheorghiu-Dej it represented a serious threat to the very future of his country. The Rumanian dispute with the Soviet Union began precisely on this point, since integration, Soviet-style, would have meant the end of the regime's plans to industrialise.

The dispute, of course, always had political overtones and it is the political side which was carried on after the purely economic side seems to have been settled in Bucharest's favour. Rumania will proceed without let or hindrance in her industrialisation campaign but things could never have been the same again between Khrushchev and Gheorghiu-Dej. Gheorghiu-Dej used the Sino-Soviet dispute as an instrument in his dispute with Khrushchev and even went so far as a flirtation with Mao. Even now he still needs Mao or, more correctly, he still needs Mao in the camp since he realises that China is the best guarantee for polycentrism, the best guarantee that Rumania may continue on her course. Moreover, Mao and the whole Sino-Soviet dispute has provided a tremendous boost to the prestige and self-respect of the Rumanian Communist Party. Always considered one of the weakest in the bloc, it has now assumed an importance second only to that of the Soviet and Chinese parties. By its spectacular efforts at mediation it won respect throughout the movement and by its defiance of Moscow it gained considerable admiration. This might also stand the regime in good stead in the future, since it could be another factor protecting it against any move which Moscow might wish to make.

The Rumanian standpoint on intra-bloc affairs was laid down in the famous central committee declaration of April 1964.[8] It followed a plenum called to discuss the mission led by Premier Maurer to Peking the previous month. This document has been aptly called the Rumanian declaration of independence, since it placed on record the regime's opposition to all (Soviet) schemes for supra-state planning and to any forms of economic cooperation which would involve even the most indirect infringement of national sovereignty. It repeatedly stressed the complete independence of all communist parties, pointedly proclaimed that there were no such things as a ' parent ' party or ' son parties ', and

8 *Scinteia*, 26 April 1964.

came down heavily against any attempts at interference by one party in the affairs of another. On the Sino-Soviet dispute it strongly supported the Soviet Union on the issues involved; it criticised China for its splitting proclivities but also made indirect criticisms of the Soviet Union for its part in the public polemics and made it quite clear that the days when parties could be excommunicated from the communist camp were over.

On the question of a conference, the document contained proposals similar in many respects to those which Gomulka suggested at the Polish congress two months later, and identical with those he made after meeting Brezhnev and Kosygin:

> We address a heartfelt call . . . for preparing a conference of the representatives of the communist and workers parties with a view to defending and strengthening the unity of the camp of the socialist countries, of the world communist and working-class movement. The Rumanian Workers Party deems it necessary that immediate consultations should be started between the CPSU, the CCP, and the other fraternal parties with a view to setting up a commission consisting of representatives of a number of parties. This commission should proceed to prepare a conference of representatives of the communist and workers parties. Such a conference should be organised only on the basis of the participation of all communist and workers parties and should be convened only after having been thoroughly prepared. The Rumanian Workers Party central committee considers that a conference with the participation of only part of the communist parties would run counter to the cause of unity, and would lead to an aggravation of the situation, to the isolation of some of the fraternal parties, to the establishing of a split in the world communist and working-class movement.

The April Declaration was both the justification of previous Rumanian policy and the basis for future action. Bucharest continued its attempts at mediation. In August, invitations (all accepted) were sent to *every* ruling party to send representatives to the 20th anniversary celebrations of the country's liberation,[9] and, in September, Premier Maurer went again to Peking to attend the 15th anniversary celebrations of the Chinese People's Republic.[10] Right up to the very end of the Khrushchev era the Rumanians continued on their own road in intra-bloc and international policy.

Their reaction to Khrushchev's fall and to the new leadership has been one of utter detachment, even of indifference. Khrushchev's fall must have pleased them greatly but they have been very careful not to show their hand in any way. The new Soviet leaders will presumably wish to normalise relations but it is difficult to see the Rumanians

---

[9] The delegates from China, North Vietnam and North Korea arrived several days before the festivities and had personal interviews with Gheorghiu-Dej, probably on the issue of the conference.

[10] Maurer was the only premier to attend from Eastern Europe and his delegation also included Politburo member and vice-premier Bodnaras, who had also been a member of the delegation to Peking in March. They talked with Khrushchev during a stop-over in Moscow.

surrendering anything they have gained and it is difficult to see how the Soviets could force them to do so.

East Germany

THE WALL HAS COME TO BE REGARDED as the symbol of both Ulbricht's tyranny and his failure. It is true that he could not have a more appropriate monument. But from the point of view of the East German regime it was an essential and long overdue step. It need not necessarily be identified with Stalinism, since even if Gomulka or Kadar had been governor in Pankow, they too would have had recourse to such a step; either of them would have been the nervous tyrant which Ulbricht is today.

In this artificially created political unit it is impossible for the regime to reflect in any way the nationalism of its population, which is the nationalism of the German nation, expressed by the simple desire for absorption into the German republic of the West.

One need not labour this cliché. But in the context of the Sino-Soviet dispute and polycentrism in general, it is necessary to bear it in mind, since it is the utter dependence of the Pankow regime on the Soviet Union, regardless of the character of the leadership in Moscow, which makes Ulbricht perhaps the most dependent of the East European regimes. The East German regime supported without delay Suslov's call for a world communist conference, and accepted the invitation to the Moscow preparatory conference without demur. Ulbricht himself and other prominent East German leaders have been loudest in criticising China and, for the sake of irony, one should perhaps recall that it was Ulbricht, the dogmatist who, obviously at Soviet orders, broke an Eastern European tradition of 15 years by inviting a representative from revisionist Yugoslavia to the congress of his party in January 1963.

And yet, despite his Muscovite background, Ulbricht is essentially a Hoxha, but without the opportunity and probably without the courage. Many of the circumstances which prompted Hoxha to defect have also faced Ulbricht: the fear of a neighbouring power (Yugoslavia, Federal Germany); the suspicion that the Soviets might do a deal at their expense; the threat to their repressive rule of Khrushchev's liberalising policy. But, unlike Hoxha, Ulbricht has had 20 Soviet divisions in his domain and his geo-political position makes defection impossible. All the same, it is not difficult to detect where his heart lies. This was shown during the period 1958–1960 and even for some time afterwards, when the East German press was full of laudatory articles on China and when relations between Pankow and Peking were very close. When the full gravity of the Sino-Soviet conflict became known to Ulbricht, the attitude, of course, changed. But for what Ulbricht really thought about Khrushchev's foreign policy, one should have read the occasional article in the Chinese or Albanian press. The *People's Daily,* for example, on 8 September 1964 said that ' the Soviet Union was planning to sell the GDR out ', and Radio Tirana four days later accused the Khrushchev clique of ' betraying the interests of the GDR '. This was undoubtedly what Ulbricht himself thought, but such was his unenviable position that his press has even denounced the charges as interference in East German affairs.[11]

But what Ulbricht thought was of little consequence to Khrushchev, or to the other East European states for that matter. The Adjubei visit to Western Germany in July, the conference of several bloc foreign ministers in Prague in early September (excluding the East German), and the announcement of Khrushchev's intended visit to Bonn—these were enough to illustrate the influence of Ulbricht in the Grand Alliance. But even more galling from the East German point of view must have been the trade agreements which Bonn has signed with Bulgaria, Rumania, Poland, and Hungary (Czechoslovakia will shortly follow) involving not only the establishment of West German trade missions in the capitals of these countries, but also stipulating the inclusion of West Berlin in the West German currency area. Over this last insult Pankow openly showed its pique. Politburo candidate Horst Sindermann, during a central committee plenum last February, warned the GDR's communist allies that ' it must never be forgotten that the inclusion of West Berlin in the West German policy of revenge and atomic rearmament endangers the peace of Europe. In any agreement with the West German Federal Republic, no sovereign state can be requested to recognise Bonn's aggressive demand for the inclusion of West Berlin in the Federal Republic '.[12]

From the new leadership in Moscow Ulbricht can probably hope for more restraint in its policy but hardly for any basic change. He cannot hope that Khrushchev's six-year-old pledge to sign a separate peace treaty will ever be honoured. The Soviet government has assured the West (including Bonn) that the old policy of détente will be continued. This bodes ill for Ulbricht's hopes, but he must always remind himself of the painful truth that he will always be a satellite whom Moscow can afford to ignore.

Yugoslavia

YUGOSLAVIA'S FOREIGN POLICY in recent years has increasingly gravitated towards the Soviet-led part of the communist bloc. To account for this one must look in the first place at her domestic situation. This is complex and controversial, a melange of progress, stagnation, retrogression, and nervous uncertainty about the future.

[11] e.g. Horst Dohlus in *Neuer Weg,* No. 32, 1964.
[12] *Neues Deutschland,* 13 February 1964.

Liberalisation in Yugoslav domestic policy began about 1950 and continued up to 1961, probably reaching its height in 1958–1960 with the new programme approved by the seventh party congress in April 1958. This liberalisation, both political and economic, left an impression which will probably never be eradicated. But it had always been opposed by a strong group of conservatives or centralisers, who saw their chance in the economic crisis of 1961 to press for a tightening of the reins, more centralisation, and a curbing of what they considered the 'excesses' of political freedom. It was then that the serious split in the Yugoslav League of Communists came out into the open, with Kardelj and Rankovic, as the leaders of the two warring factions, emerging as the contenders for Tito's throne. For two years the conservatives seemed to be dominant, but this year the liberals have made a strong comeback, especially in the economic sector.

There is a connection between this trend and the course of Soviet-Yugoslav relations. Mainly because of the Soviet rift with China, these relations began to improve in 1960, despite the fact that it was necessary for Moscow occasionally to criticise Belgrade so as not to give Peking (or Tirana) too many debating points about 'selling out' to revisionism.[13] But after the 22nd CPSU congress, Soviet friendliness towards Yugoslavia became more and more marked and Khrushchev cast the veil aside during a trip to Bulgaria in May 1962. This was followed by exchanges of visits on the lower level, culminating in the exchange of visits by Khrushchev and Tito personally and the general rapprochement between Yugoslavia and the Soviet bloc which we see today.

The retrogressive changes in Yugoslav internal policy, beginning in 1961 and continuing well into 1963, should therefore be explained partly by the domestic crisis and partly by Tito's wish to remove obstacles to a rapprochement with Moscow. This did not mean giving up any essential independence; it was a gesture of accommodation. But it was a measure of the decline in Yugoslav self-confidence since 1955 that Tito now thought he should need to do any accommodating at all.

The main reason for this decline in self-confidence has been a fear for the future—particularly of what will happen after Tito's death. If he were younger, the split in his party would certainly not be so serious or open. Now, however, the contending forces are openly grouping themselves and the groupings are in many ways a reflection of the most chronic of Yugoslavia's problems—that of the nationalities.

Nowhere is the problem of nationalism more acute than in the Federation of Yugoslavia. It has several aspects of which the Serb-Croat antipathy is only one. Perhaps more fundamental is the complete

13 Attacks on Yugoslav revisionism continued even at the 22nd CPSU congress, with the obvious aim of trying to make the Soviet position appear a 'centrist' one, and in the new CPSU programme approved at the congress 'Yugoslav revisionism' is still criticised as a 'danger'.

difference in outlook towards the Federation between the 'have' republics (Slovenia, especially, Croatia, and parts of Serbia) and the 'have-not' republics (Bosnia-Herzogovnia, Macedonia, and Montenegro). The decentralisation tendency is strongest in Slovenia because this, as the most prosperous republic, has suffered most from Federation. The 'have-nots' represent the opposite trend since, without the help extracted from the more prosperous republics, they would be even more backward than they are now. Tito, of Croatian descent but a quintessential Yugoslav, is still the one uniting or placating force. Rankovic is a Serb, powerful in Serbia, but with little authority and less prestige elsewhere. It is difficult to see how he (or anybody else) could check the centrifugal forces of the country without a severe tightening of centralist control, which the Slovenes and Croats would find intolerable and which to them would simply be the resurrection of the old Serbian hegemony.[14]

The second half of 1964 was a period of great diplomatic activity on the part of the Yugoslav regime and of Marshal Tito personally. In early June he met Khrushchev in Leningrad; later the same month he met Gheorghiu-Dej in Rumania; at the end of June and the beginning of July he was in Poland; early in September he met Gheorghiu-Dej again, to inaugurate the Iron Gates project; almost immediately afterwards he visited Kadar; later in September he played host to Novotny; finally he entertained Walter Ulbricht when the latter was returning to East Germany from a visit to Bulgaria.

All this diplomatic activity was concentrated on communist Eastern Europe and was a reflection of the growing closeness of Yugoslav-Soviet relations. What did it signify? Was it the end of Yugoslavia's ideological and political independence? Was it the beginning of the gradual but inexorable process of reabsorption in the Soviet bloc? Or, on the other hand, was it the signal for the mounting of a new offensive by Tito who, taking advantage of Khrushchev's predicament, sought again to play a major role in Eastern European affairs? These are important questions, since they concern the future of the state which became the first example of polycentrism in the communist camp.

First, it can be said that, though Tito was prepared to accommodate himself to some extent to Soviet wishes, he was not prepared to abandon his independence. His foreign policy and his approach to the Sino-Soviet dispute were sufficient proof of this. But in one basic factor Tito *has* changed and this change has important repercussions. The essential quality of Tito in intra-bloc relations was not so much that he was a revisionist, as that he considered himself to be an example of revisionism which others should follow. He was the anti-Pope in Belgrade, or at least an ardent proselytiser. Now, however, he no

---

[14] For a most revealing discussion of the present differences in Yugoslavia, see speech by the Croatian Party leader, Vladimir Bakaric, reported in *Vjesnik* (Zagreb), 21 September 1964.

longer has the disruptive potential which he had, say, in 1955 or 1956. Wisely, he realises this and does not attempt to revive it.

Why the change? There are three probable, mutually connected explanations. The first is the deterioration in the domestic situation; this has considerably shaken the confidence of the Yugoslavs, and in consequence the regime has moved closer to its old camp. The decision to enter into association with Comecon, announced in mid-September, was the result of the country's economic difficulties. It can, of course, be argued that Yugoslavia's association will mean a dilution of Comecon, making it more unwieldy and difficult for the Soviet Union to control. But those who expect Yugoslavia to have a disruptive effect within the organisation will probably be disappointed. She has done what she has in order to gain economic advantage and she will not spoil this opportunity by being too awkward.

It was both the policy and the predicament of Khrushchev which enabled the Yugoslavs to draw closer to the Eastern European bloc without giving up the essential aspects of their independence. The Soviet leader was never averse to Yugoslav independence as such. What he objected to was Tito's proselytising and his independent role in foreign policy. One of his first moves when it became obvious that the point of no return with China had been reached was to effect yet another reconciliation with Tito. This was completed in 1962, and it implied tacit concessions on both sides. Tito stopped a proselytising which he was no longer in any position to carry out, while Khrushchev refrained from insisting on a full obedience in foreign or intra-bloc policy which he would never have been able to enforce. No one can say that both sides were satisfied, but the unwritten agreement was acceptable because both sides realised that they were less strong than before.

The third reason why Tito can never again be the disruptive force he was is that much or most of his attractiveness in Eastern Europe has evaporated. His influence began to deteriorate sharply after 1956, when his prestige throughout the area suffered a serious blow. But even if this had not been the case he must realise (his tremendous vanity notwithstanding) that events in the communist bloc have overtaken him and have made his example now largely irrelevant. The Sino-Soviet dispute and the beginnings of an activist policy by the West have themselves created opportunities for independence for the Eastern European countries. Everybody may now get in on an act which at one time he monopolised and, moreover, the Eastern European states realised that Tito was drawing closer to Khrushchev. It is true, of course, that Rumania is probably trying to achieve a status which is essentially similar to what Yugoslavia has now. But this does not invalidate the argument, since Rumania was a special case of a regime in direct dispute with Moscow, and, in any case, times had so changed that Belgrade was trying to pacify rather than aggravate Rumania's relations with Khrushchev.

It is a safe bet that since the downfall of Khrushchev no one has been watching developments in Moscow more closely than the Yugoslavs. Despite all the vicissitudes in his relations with Khrushchev, Tito always regarded the Soviet leader as his man in Moscow. Now his man has gone and been replaced by an unknown quantity. What the Yugoslavs are most concerned about are Moscow's future relations with Peking. Though Tito may have opposed Khrushchev on the question of excommunicating the Chinese, he realised that the Sino-Soviet dispute as such had brought many advantages to him. What he is afraid of now is a genuine détente which could only be at his expense. Even an attempt at a limited détente would adversely affect his favoured position with Moscow. If he himself were younger and the internal position of his country stronger, he might regard the new situation as ripe for a reassertion of his influence and for a policy of complete disregard for Moscow. But the days when he could even contemplate this are over.

Albania

PROBABLY FROM THE BEGINNING of 1961, and certainly since Khrushchev's open attack on Hoxha at the 22nd CPSU congress in October of that year, Albania has been China's bridgehead in Europe. The bridgehead has been maintained but it has not been expanded. It remains an isolated segment of the anti-Soviet alliance, sustained by the stream of slow boats from China which have now completely replaced the quicker vessels from the Soviet Union as the country's lifeblood.

The value of the Hoxha regime to China in its struggle against the Soviet Union is almost entirely of a prestige nature. Hence it still must be supported economically and politically. The visit of Chou En-lai in January 1964 was a political gesture designed to boost Albanian morale and to assure Peking's isolated ally that she was not forgotten. If the Chinese ever hoped that the Albanian alliance would make a positive contribution to spreading their influence in Europe, if they hoped that the bridgehead could be widened, they must be disillusioned by now.

The bridgehead has become a propaganda pocket, and not a very effective one at that. The days when Albanian pronouncements were useful because they mirrored what the Chinese were thinking ceased immediately when the Chinese themselves began to say what they thought. The tirades from Tirana are often still as picturesque as ever, but little notice is taken of them. The Eastern European press practically ignores Albania; politically she has become almost an uncountry.[15]

---

[15] All the East European countries except the Soviet Union maintain some diplomatic representation in Tirana but this is mainly for commercial purposes.

But in one important sphere—that of commerce—Albania has actually increased her ties with the Eastern European communist states, except for the Soviet Union which has comprehensively boycotted her. In 1963, trade treaties concluded for the same year called for substantial increases over 1962 with Rumania, Poland, Czechoslovakia, and Hungary. At the same time the character of the trade with these countries has changed. It is now to the ' mutual benefit ' of both parties. In other words Albania no longer trades on the basis of deficits which would entail credits from her former friends, a healthy improvement which seems to have been effected by increasing the quantity of her exports and by modifying the structure of her imports. The complete industrial products which once constituted the bulk of Albanian imports have partly been replaced by the importation of semi-manufactured materials for conversion into finished products in Albania. (This is in itself a reflection of the development of Albania's economy.)

What is important, however, from the political point of view in the continuing and even developing trade between Albania and the Eastern European states is not its character, but its existence. While the Soviet Union has boycotted Albania, her allies have not. This is not due to economic considerations alone, since, though Albania has important reserves of chrome and nickel which Czechoslovakia, for example, seriously lacks, such deficiencies could be made up from elsewhere. The (Moscow-directed) policy has probably been aimed at preventing Albania going to the West to obtain the vital commodities with which China cannot supply her. This might seem an odd explanation in view of the Chinese alliance and the Hoxha regime's constant anti-Western diatribes. But the Soviets must certainly remember the lesson of Yugoslavia after 1948 and, on the other hand, it is becoming increasingly clear that China herself is not averse to commercial deals with the West if they are necessary. If this has been the Soviet motive, it has been largely successful. Albanian trade with the West *has* increased and it is by no means insignificant that Tirana and Rome have agreed to raise their diplomatic missions to the embassy level.[16] But, generally, commercial and diplomatic contacts with the West have increased far less than might have been expected; over 90 per cent of Albanian trade is still with the communist countries. Soviet policy has evidently been predicated on the assumption that Albania as a Chinese satellite still has a better chance of returning to the fold than an Albania which had fallen again under the commercial and then political influence of one or more of the Western countries.

The chances of Albania returning to the fold in the near future seem remote indeed. Unlike their Chinese allies, the Albanians lost no time in registering their jubilation over the downfall of Khrushchev but they made it quite clear that this was only the first and not the

---

16 Albania maintain diplomatic relations at the legation level with France, Austria, and Finland.

conclusive victory for the true Marxist-Leninist cause. What was needed
now was a renunciation of the whole of Khrushchev's policy, and
Tirana's initial tirades on this subject showed little confidence that
Brezhnev and Kosygin were the men to do this. Moscow, for its part,
has shown much less inclination to be courteous to Albania than it has
to China. Radio Moscow has stopped for the moment its personal
attacks on Hoxha, Shehu and company, but its Albanian transmissions
continue to expound the policy which Tirana insists must be discarded
along with Khrushchev. The most significant snub of all was, of course,
the failure to invite an Albanian representative to Moscow for the
November celebrations.

*   *   *   *

IT WAS SAID AT THE beginning of this essay that the Khrushchev era
had witnessed the steady erosion of Soviet-imposed unity and uniformity
in Eastern Europe. This erosion is still very far from complete but
it is definitely under way. Khrushchev himself contributed to this
process both directly and indirectly. But the Soviet dictator was, nevertheless, through his personality and prestige, a cohesive force, a brake
on the centrifugal forces which were in operation.

His departure means one less brake on the whole process, one more
powerful thrust to the forces of erosion, a further encouragement to
the revival of nationalism. One need not, of course, expect an immediate
or even an early disintegration of the Soviet dominance in Eastern
Europe. In the immediate future one may even have a semblance of
greater unity. But few would deny that in their relations with Moscow
the Eastern European states have greater opportunities to assert their
independence and equality than ever before. Their initial reactions to
the downfall of Khrushchev showed, for the most part, a spontaneity
which evidently surprised the new Soviet leaders. In the post-
Khrushchev era the Soviet Union will, with most of the Eastern
European states, have a problem which cannot be solved by any of the
old prescriptions. It is doubtful, over the long run, whether it can be
solved at all.

ASIA

Donald S. Zagoria *

THE communist parties of Asia are, with few exceptions, firmly on the side of the Chinese in the Sino-Soviet dispute. Of the ruling parties in Mongolia, North Korea, and North Vietnam, only the Mongolians remain faithful to Moscow. In 14 other Asian countries where the CPs are not in power the parties are pro-Peking in eight, and in all remaining six there are strong pro-Peking splinter parties or pro-Peking factions within the party. Qualitatively, the strength of the pro-Chinese communist groups in Asia is even more impressive. The largest and most successful non-ruling communist party in the world, the communist party of Indonesia, is firmly committed to China. So is the Lao Dong party in North Vietnam which controls derivative parties in Laos, South Vietnam, and Cambodia, and also operates in Thailand. In Japan, strategically perhaps the most important country in Asia outside the bloc, the CP is firmly allied to China. Finally in India, the newly formed pro-Peking party, although commanding only less than half of total communist strength, has its membership heavily concentrated in certain key states.

The phenomenon of an Asian communist coalition raises a number of questions for the student of the international communist system. What are the reasons for Peking's success? What effect will this division between European and Asian communist parties have on communist ideology? If the monolithic model of the international communist movement is no longer adequate (if indeed it ever was), what is the proper or the most useful conceptual approach to the communist world today? What are the future relationships between the various parties in Asia and in the international movement as a whole likely to be?

To begin with, three general hypotheses may be advanced. First, there was fertile ground for schism in the international communist movement well before the Sino-Soviet conflict. These schisms might not have occurred so rapidly or at all had it not been for that conflict, but the conditions for them were well established. In this sense, the Sino-Soviet conflict is but one aspect of a larger phenomenon, the crisis of the international communist movement. Second, no schematic explanation is possible for the alignments of the communist parties of Asia. Neither proximity, disgust with Moscow, stages of economic development, race, nor any other single factor can adequately account for them. A variety of factors are at work in each individual case. Third, many Asian communists share similar views on the world scene and on revolutionary strategy. It is their strategic outlook, in which US ' imperialism ' is the main enemy, that binds some of them together.

* The author would like to express his gratitude to the Rockefeller Foundation and to the Research Institute on Communist Affairs at Columbia University for supporting the research connected with the preparation of this article.

India: Regionalism and Nationalism

BEFORE THE DIVISION of Indian communists into two rival parties, their party was a strong and growing force in India. Now, division has already reduced its vote in recent local elections, and it is quite likely to reduce the seriousness of its challenge to the ruling Congress Party in the next general elections in 1967. The division precipitated by the Sino-Soviet split is unquestionably the most critical problem the party has ever had to face.

Before the split, the CPI had approximately 250,000 members and another million and a half members in its trade union and peasant organisations. Through three general elections it had been the principal opposition to the ruling Congress Party, getting more than 11 million votes in the 1962 general elections, 10 per cent of the total vote polled. In the state of Kerala, one of 14 constituent units of the Indian Union, the communists were voted into power in 1957. Although removed by the central government in 1959, a year later they received 1·2 million more votes than they had received in 1957.

As a result of the split, the 29 party representatives in the Lok Sabha (Parliament) are now divided into two groups, a left-wing group of 13 and an 'official' right-wing group of 16. At the state and regional level, too, the CPI is now so deeply divided that it is questionable whether the differences can be ironed out even for waging an electoral struggle. In recent local elections in Andhra, for example, the pro-Peking and pro-Moscow groups sponsored separate candidates to the detriment of both. In Kerala, where elections are to be held in February 1965, the split may inhibit the chance for regaining power which, before the split, appeared good. On the other hand, the prospect of replacing the unpopular Congress government, recently removed from power as a result of a no-confidence vote in the State Assembly, is so good that the rival communist parties in Kerala may yet agree to an electoral alliance.[1]

What is the split in the CPI all about? First of all, it should be noted that division antedates the Sino-Soviet conflict. Since the end of World War II, Indian communists have differed among themselves to a far greater extent than almost any other. There were those who wanted to lead an armed agrarian revolution, and those who placed more emphasis on organising the urban workers. More recently, division has turned on the strategic question of electoral alliances and of the attitude towards Congress.

The right-wing argues that there are significant divisions of opinion in the ruling Congress Party which can be exploited and that the CPI should ally itself with the 'progressive' elements within Congress in an effort to push the balance of power in the ruling party further to the left. This means electoral alliances with approved Congress candidates, less

---

[1] Such an alliance based on a 'minimum programme' has been proposed by the pro-Moscow group in Kerala. *New Age* (Delhi), 6 September 1964.

criticism of Congress foreign and domestic policies, etc. According
to this view, the communists would gradually come to share power with
the left-wing of the ' national bourgeoisie ' in a ' national democracy '
closely aligned with the communist bloc.

The left-wing of the CPI, on the other hand, argues that there are
no important differences of view within Congress, that Congress as a
whole is the main enemy—all the more insidious because it confuses
the Indian public with slogans of ' socialism ' and ' anti-imperialism '.
The left-wing not only opposes broad united fronts with Congress, but
is ready to ally itself even with ' reactionary ' parties, such as the Muslim
League and Swatantra, in order to defeat Congress.

These differences also involve a dispute over the equally hoary
strategic question of whether India must undergo a one or two-stage
revolution. The right-wing aims at a National Democracy in which the
' national bourgeoisie ' retains hegemony, arguing that the anti-
imperialist, bourgeois-democratic phase of the revolution must be completed before India is ripe for socialism. The left, by contrast, contends
that the communists must aim at a ' People's Democracy '—i.e., a
government dominated by the communists in which the ' national
bourgeoisie ' is merely a subsidiary ally.

These questions are, of course, not new to communist parties in
underdeveloped areas. Basically they reflect the dilemma that Lenin
himself sought unsuccessfully to resolve in the 1920s : how far can the
communists go in allying themselves with nationalism and nationalists
without fatally compromising their own programmes and objectives?
To what extent can the interests of the national bourgeoisie be accom-
modated either in the first or the second phase of the revolutionary
process? Traditionally the right-wing of the communist parties has
been willing to enter into comparatively sustained periods of cooperation, while the left-wing has been more suspicious about, and less
willing to cooperate with nationalists.

This is the main question at issue; more interesting are the conditions
which seem to be dictating the differences among Indian communists.
These, I believe, are the differences between the regional and the national
faces of Indian communism.

A mere glance at Indian voting statistics demonstrates the great
divergence between CPI strength in Andhra, West Bengal, and Kerala,
on the one hand, and in the rest of the country on the other. In the
elections to the Legislative Assembly in 1962 the CPI got 19·5 per cent
of the vote in Andhra, 25 per cent in West Bengal, and 43 per cent in
Kerala, but not more than 8 per cent in any other. In short, Indian
communism is a regional phenomenon, not a national one. The CPI
has been unable to provide an all-Indian alternative to Congress; it
remains a loose federation of regional units which have succeeded, when
they have succeeded, only on regional ground by exploiting regional,
caste, and other parochial loyalties.

My hypothesis is that it is the tension between the national and the regional wings of the party which is at the root of the left-right split. It is significant that the left is strongest precisely in those states where the regional CPI party machines are strongest—Andhra, West Bengal, and Kerala—or where strong separatist feelings still exist, as in Madras, while the right is composed more typically of trade union leaders and intellectuals who have no regional basis and who thus operate on a national level.

Thus in West Bengal, the left is in the overwhelming majority. In Andhra, a district-by-district survey conducted by the pro-Moscow group (which certainly exaggerates its own strength) showed that the pro-Peking group had 11,000 out of a state-wide total of 31,000 members. In Kerala, the right-wing had a strong majority in only two of nine district councils,[2] although the left and right seem to be about evenly divided within the state as a whole. The most prominent Kerala communist leaders, however, are on the left. Thus, in all three states where the communists were formerly the major opposition party in the state legislature, the pro-Peking group is very strong.

It is symptomatic that the leaders of the left include Namboodiripad and Gopalan, who run the successful Kerala party machine, while the right is led by S. A. Dange, who has his base not in his own Maharashtra region, where the CPI is weak, but in the communist-led all-Indian trade union organisation which he heads.

The CPI left looks upon Congress as the main enemy because regionally for them it is. They can obtain power only by aligning themselves with other regional and communal parties—no matter how reactionary—against Congress. But such a regional strategy harms the CPI in other provinces. An alliance with the Muslim League in Kerala, for example, greatly harms the CPI in most of Northern India. The right-wing leaders, in short, look at the problem of obtaining power more from a national point of view either because they have no strong regional bases or because their trade union base dictates a national outlook. For the regional CPI leader, regional politics is paramount; for the national CPI leader, regional politics and strategy must be subordinated to national strategy.

We can now appreciate how the left-right struggle in the CPI overlaps with divergent Soviet and Chinese policies towards India. The Chinese, because they are engaged in a border conflict with India and in a contest for hegemony in Asia, are hostile to the Indian government. They would naturally like the Indian communist party to reflect that hostility in its own policies. The Russians, on the other hand, are friendly to India and satisfied with her non-alignment policy. They would like the Indian communists to improve the Soviet position by pursuing moderate policies and, in general, playing the national game. Thus Moscow and the CPI right have a common, if not equally strong, interest in

2 Ibid. 10 May, 26 July 1964.

supporting the Congress government in the short run, while Peking and the CPI left have a common and powerful interest in opposing it. No doubt if the CPI right were to become disillusioned with the national game, they too would fall out with the Russians whose patience with a ' bourgeois-nationalist' government is likely to be greater than their own.

Just as the left-right division within the CPI was crystallised by the Sino-Soviet dispute, so it was intensified by the Sino-Indian border conflict. If it had supported China, the right-wing group in the party would have had to abandon its policy of alliance with Congress. The left, on the other hand, had no such compunctions; indeed, it had an interest in discrediting Congress. Moreover, China had the same negative attitude towards Nehru as the leftists' own, albeit for different reasons. The left could not, of course, take an openly pro-Chinese stand on the border issue, but it wanted to take a much more guarded position than did the right-wing, which completely supported the Indian government.

Thus, after the first Chinese moves on the Himalayan frontier in 1959, the centrifugal forces within the CPI increased. By the end of 1961 the CPI right was openly criticising China and being criticised in return, while the CPI left was publishing statements supporting the Chinese line on Nehru. A shaky compromise between the two factions was achieved in April 1962 when Namboodiripad, a centrist who had gone over to the left, was chosen as Secretary-General to replace Ajoy Ghosh who had died. At the same time a new post of party chairman was created and given to the leader of the right, Dange.[3]

This uneasy compromise blew up after the Chinese attack on the Himalayan border in October 1962. In the heat of the nationalist reaction against China, the right-wing group in the CPI forced through a resolution condemning China; a month later, the right-wing gained control of the CPI leadership, aided in this by the arrest of a large number of the CPI leftists. But the ease with which the right-wing gained control of the central apparatus, and at the same time failed to gain control of a number of regional machines, reinforces the hypothesis advanced earlier.

In trying to predict future developments, it should be noted that the left-wing regional forces are by no means homogeneous and there are greater divisions within their ranks than within the pro-Moscow party. The left convention at Tenali in July did not even consider the differences within the world communist movement, much less adopt a resolution on these differences, because the range of disagreement in their ranks is too broad to achieve a compromise. Some are more or less completely pro-Chinese on the outstanding issues in the international movement while others have reservations about some of the Chinese positions. There are differences within the left over the Sino-Indian border dispute

---

[3] For this and other details on the evolution of the split, see Harry Gelman, ' The Communist Party of India: Sino-Soviet Battleground ', in *Communist Strategies in Asia*, A. Doak Barnett, ed.

and even over basic revolutionary strategy. In fact, the left has developed its own left, right, and centre; the nine-member committee nominated at the Calcutta congress in November reflects the balance between them. The secretary, Sundarayya, is a ' centrist ' in the new context, while Namboodiripad, the ' centrist ' in the old party, represents the right wing of the new one.

JCP: The Road to Disaster

IF THERE IS ONE COUNTRY where the Soviet strategy of peaceful coexistence seems most suited to advance the fortunes of a local communist party, it is Japan. Like the West European countries whose communist parties have almost all opted for Moscow against Peking, Japan is a parliamentary democracy and has a highly developed economy. Moreover, it has a large socialist party, part of which professes orthodox Marxism and—like the communists—oppose rearmament, the Japanese-American Mutual Security Pact, alliances with the West in general, and capitalism and imperialism understood in a narrow Leninist sense. Finally, Japan is unique in having suffered the consequences of a nuclear explosion three times since 1945; pacifism accordingly finds supporters across the political spectrum and particularly on the left.

Nevertheless, the Japanese Communist Party has sided with China. It has even become the first party in the international movement (aside from the Albanian and Chinese) to enter into open polemics with the Russians.[4] The two pro-Soviet members of the central committee who voted in favour of the test ban agreement were expelled by an overwhelming majority.[5]

Nor can it be argued that the adoption of a pro-Chinese position has not hurt the Japanese communists. On the contrary, they have already paid a high political price and the long-range cost is likely to be even greater. By joining China in opposition to the test ban treaty, the JCP has forfeited support from the strong pacifist left in Japan, forced a break with the socialists in Gensuikyo (the Japan Council Against Atomic and Hydrogen Bombs), the largest mass movement, and has given pause to many intellectuals.

Several reasons might be advanced for the JCP position in the Sino-Soviet dispute. First, there is a strategic factor. For much of the past decade there has been a debate within the JCP over the question whether the United States or domestic monopoly capitalism is the main enemy. While both the Russians and the Chinese have agreed in principle with the majority view in the JCP that the communists should concentrate their attack on the American position in Japan, the Chinese advocate a stronger anti-American line, consistent with their more

---

4 For the JCP letters to the CPSU, see *Peking Review*, 31 July 1964.
5 53 of 57 central committee members present approved the expulsion while three opposed and one reserved his attitude. The three opposed were Shiga, Suzuki, and Shigeharu Nakano; Shigeo Kamiyama reserved his attitude. *Mainichi*, 23 May 1964. Nakano and Kamiyama subsequently left the JCP and joined with Shiga and Suzuki to form a new pro-Soviet CP; *New York Times*, 4 October 1964.

pressing interest in removing American power from Asia. The Russians may have advocated a milder line towards the United States in order to make it easier to unite the entire Japanese left. But many Japanese communists feel that the Soviet détente with the United States will inhibit the JCP's anti-American strategy.

Then there are the close personal ties between the Chinese leaders and many of the JCP leaders; moreover, since they came to power in 1949, the Chinese have taken a greater interest in, and promoted closer ties with, the JCP than the Russians who, it seems, have concentrated more on developing diplomatic and economic relations with the Japanese government and on cultivating front organisations.

In the last analysis, however, Peking's capture of the JCP cannot be fully explained on rational grounds. If rational factors alone were operative, the Japanese communists would follow the line of the Italian communists. Japan is in many respects more similar to Italy than to any Asian country. Togliatti's ideas, particularly the theory of structural reform, have had considerable influence on the Japanese Socialist Party, on the 1961 defectors from the JCP, and on many of the radical youth. The fact that the Japanese communists are so overwhelmingly inclined towards China, regardless of the political liabilities and the conditions in their own country, suggests that the powerful cultural and psychological affinities for China which cut across all political parties in Japan, including the most conservative, are particularly strong among the communists.

The test ban treaty brought matters to a head not only because it forced the JCP to choose between Moscow and Peking, but because it exacerbated a division within the Japanese left that had been growing since 1958. Gensuikyo was a broad coalition of left, trade union, pacifist, and communist groups united in opposition to the development and testing of nuclear weapons. As early as 1958, the organisation was divided between the communists and their allies, and a second group which felt that the organisation discriminated against the West. In 1960 a small group sympathetic to the Democratic Socialist Party left Gensuikyo and formed a rival organisation. In 1961, and particularly after the USSR unilaterally resumed tests, a much larger group within Gensuikyo, including the socialists and the most powerful trade union organisation, Sohyo, objected strongly to its one-sided criticism of the West. The issue came to a head in August 1963, the month in which the test ban treaty was signed; at the Hiroshima conference of Gensuikyo, an open split between the communists and the socialists occurred. The socialists argued that Gensuikyo should oppose all nuclear arming and testing, while the communists, under Chinese influence, contended that a distinction should be made between the ' peace forces ' and the ' imperialists ', that nuclear arming and testing by the latter was justified because it is defensive.[6]

6 *Asian Survey*, May 1964, pp. 833–841.

Immediately after the split at Hiroshima, the Russians openly attacked the JCP delegation to the conference for ' not considering the broad masses in Japanese society ', for ' denying the positive signifi- cance . . . of the test ban treaty ', and for ' following the instructions of the Chinese delegation '.[7] Behind the scenes, the Russians strengthened their contact with anti-Peking members of the JCP central committee, particularly Shiga and Suzuki.[8]

The problems of the test ban and of Gensuikyo were discussed at the 7th plenum of the JCP central committee in October 1963. It was agreed to oppose the test ban on grounds similar to those of Peking. This decision made a formal split in Gensuikyo inevitable; it was formally sealed in August 1964, when separate meetings were held by the communists and the socialists, supported by Sohyo and 25 other organisations. The Russians and pro-Russian communist parties from abroad sent delegates to both meetings, but soon walked out of the communist one on the ground that it had been rigged by the JCP and its Chinese allies.

Meanwhile Shiga and Suzuki have formed a new communist political group called Voice of Japan Comrades Society and have proclaimed it a rival party, urging all like-minded party members to join its ranks.[9] The Shiga group appears to have Moscow sanction. It is interesting to note that the Shiga and Kasuga groups include many of the leaders of the pro-Moscow internationalist faction of more than a decade ago. At that time, the opposing faction led by Nosaka was criticised by the Cominform for right-wing deviation. Since then, other divisions within the party have cut across this one, but today the leaders of these two factions still face each other in basic opposition, despite the fact that they have reversed their political positions, with the pro- Moscow group at the more moderate end of the spectrum, and the pro-Chinese tendency—now dominant—representing the militant side.

One explanation of this interesting phenomenon may be their different backgrounds. The Kasuga-Shiga groups are better educated and more internationalist Marxists than the insular and poorly educated members of the Nosaka faction, which is rooted in the rigid and parochial ways of the party bureaucracy. The Shiga group is supported by the prominent party intellectuals and includes such Marxist writers as Shigeharu Nakano and Shigeo Kamiyama who are not dependent on positions in the party apparatus for their livelihood. Thus, com- munism in Japan has for more than a decade shown a division between ' nativist ' and ' internationalist ' tendencies and this has been reactivated by the Sino-Soviet conflict.

While sponsoring the Shiga group, Moscow has moved to strengthen relations with the Japanese Socialist Party, an amorphous coalition of

[7] *Pravda*, 25 August 1963.
[8] Letter from the JCP central committee to the CPSU central committee, dated 15 July 1964, published in *Peking Review*, 31 July 1964.
[9] *Mainichi*, 3 December 1964.

left-wing forces ranging from an extreme pro-Chinese minority group to more moderate factions, some of which are influenced by the Russian and Italian communist parties, and others which look more toward West European socialism as a model. A high-level Socialist Party delegation, led by its secretary, Tomoni Narita, visited Moscow from 29 June to 14 July 1964 and was, according to Narita, ' welcomed even more heartily than we had expected '.[10] *Pravda* carried an article by Narita written during his stay in Moscow in which he supported the nuclear test ban treaty and condemned the JCP for rejecting it. This was apparently the first time that *Pravda* had carried an article by a member of the Japanese Socialist Party.

Russian friendliness to the Japanese socialists is not surprising, since Moscow could be expected to seek new allies in Japan now that the JCP has sided with Peking. Moreover, the left-wing Japanese socialists profess to be orthodox Marxists, contending that they have more to learn from socialism in Eastern Europe than in Western Europe. Finally, the very fact that the socialists are the leading opposition party in Japan with prospects of taking power in the future would in itself help explain Soviet overtures.

The move nonetheless raises thorny ideological problems for Moscow. Will Soviet ideologues now argue that the Japanese socialists, rather than the communists, represent the authentic voice of the Japanese proletariat although they have a large moderate wing which is reformist by communist standards? How can communist goals in Japan be achieved by a non-communist party? More generally, is Moscow, confronted by the Peking challenge throughout the Afro-Asian world, now prepared to give ideological approval as well as political support to any nationalist or left-wing party which will support it against China?

While the JCP itself now appears to be solidly united on its pro-Peking course, there remain differences of emphasis in the pronouncements of its leaders. Sanzo Nosaka, the party chairman, seems to be completely committed to Peking. Secretary-General Miyamoto, on the other hand, one of the few leaders of the old internationalist faction who has remained in the party, seems to favour greater independence from both Moscow and Peking. In a recent speech, he criticised Moscow for supporting Shiga and reaffirmed his opposition to the test ban treaty, but at the same time attacked ' dogmatists ' who ' mechanically adopt the views and policies of other parties ', and do not ' skilfully apply the Marxist-Leninist revolutionary principle to the specific conditions of their own country '.[11]

Despite the fact that the JCP increased its strength at the polls in the most recent general elections in November 1963, its decision to support China is likely to be costly. The anti-bomb movement is now split with the communists in control only of the smaller, sectarian wing

10 *Tokyo Shimbun*, 4 August 1964.
11 NCNA, 3 August 1964.

of the originally powerful Gensuikyo. Moreover, some socialist leaders are calling for a complete break with the communists. Since Sohyo is closely linked to the socialist party, this also means that the communist position in the labour movement will suffer. By adopting a sectarian attitude towards the mainstream of the Japanese left, the JCP is becoming increasingly isolated from any but the most extreme and weak political forces in Japan. In a broader perspective, the position of the JCP looks even less hopeful. The reshaping of Japanese democracy, which has been going on since the end of World War II, challenges the Marxist analysis and puts Marxism on the defensive. All left-wing elements have been affected by this, but while the socialists have been attempting to respond to the challenge, the communists do not seem even to have recognised the problem.[12] Similarly, the extra-ordinary economic development in Japan puts Marxism on the defensive as it is no longer so relevant to Japan's problems, since the country may be said to be moving towards a post-Marxist stage. This may in fact help to explain the frantic reaction of the JCP; in the midst of change it scarcely understands, it resorts to stale Marxist-Leninist maxims.

Finally, although Japanese modernisation pains are likely to continue producing a large protest vote, there is no indication that the communists will benefit from this. The socialists are getting most of the protest vote on the left because they are almost as leftist as the communists without having the stigma of foreign domination. Meanwhile, on the right the protest vote is going to a strange new phenomenon in Japan, Soka Gakkai, a militant Buddhist group which emerged as a powerful third force in the elections to the House of Councillors in 1962 and which is likely to play an increasingly large political role in the future.

PKI: The Road to Power

OF ALL THE COMMUNIST PARTIES IN ASIA, the Indonesian party (PKI) stands alone in having weathered the Sino-Soviet split with no serious sign of factionalism and no weakening of its power within the country. Indeed, it now occupies the strongest position it ever has in the more than 40 years of its history. Until quite recently, the prevailing opinion of informed observers was that President Sukarno was carefully balancing the army against the growing strength of the communists, periodically throwing his weight to one side or the other in order to maintain the balance. But a succession of developments since the middle of 1962, culminating in the recent appointment of a PKI leader to the inner cabinet, have so enhanced communist influence that it is no longer clear whether Sukarno is able or willing to check them. The possibility of Indonesia's becoming an Asian Cuba is no longer remote.

Communist strength can also be measured in terms of prestige. In part because it has successfully played the national game over the past

---

[12] See Robert A. Scalapino, 'The Left Wing in Japan', in *Survey*, August 1962, and 'Japanese Socialism in Crisis', *Foreign Affairs*, January 1960.

decade (it has opposed only two cabinets in that period), and in part because it has been protected by Sukarno, the PKI has acquired great respectability. Sukarno and some members of his cabinet hammer away at the need to eradicate what they call ' communist-phobia '. In general, the communists are regarded not as part of an international revolutionary movement, but as radical Indonesian nationalists. As a result, Indonesia presents the strange spectacle of a head of state inaugurating and addressing a communist party congress and communist leaders regularly lecturing to the officers of the armed services and the staff of the Foreign Ministry.

With the formation of Malaysia in September 1963 and the immediate intensification of Indonesia's confrontation campaign against it, the position of the PKI grew even stronger. The economic stabilisation programme, sponsored by the International Monetary Fund and urged by the American government, collapsed. It had been strongly opposed by the PKI because it would have involved an increase of Western influence in the Indonesian economy. At the same time there was a new series of arrests of the leaders of banned pro-Western parties, the removal of the three-year old ban on several PKI publications, the dismissal of several strongly anti-communist regional officials, the appointment of two PKI men to ambassadorial posts in China and Ceylon, the ending of the American economic aid programme, and finally the inclusion of a PKI leader, Nyoto, in the inner cabinet, a long-sought communist goal.

The PKI position is further reinforced because Sukarno himself has become increasingly anti-Western and has moved closer to the communist world, particularly to China. Doctrinally this movement has been reflected in Sukarno's concept of the ' New Emerging Forces ', which amounts to a declaration that Western ' imperialism ' is Indonesia's principal enemy. On the diplomatic side it has been reflected in Indonesia's recent recognition of North Vietnam.

So far as the PKI itself is concerned, the rapid rise in its fortunes makes the Sino-Soviet dispute almost irrelevant to its major concerns. The sweet smell of success has almost certainly been one of the major reasons for the impressive unity of its ranks in the face of the schism that has rent almost all other major communist parties. It is no doubt for this reason that Aidit speaks detachedly and almost patronisingly of ' all this commotion in the international communist movement. . . . We certainly must not get drowned in endless discussions about the differences of opinion in the international communist movement '; it was more important to oppose imperialism than to know what ' the differences of opinion are between fraternal parties regarding the most effective ways of opposing imperialism '.[13] In personal interviews I conducted in August 1963 with Lukman and Nyoto, the second and

[13] D. N. Aidit, *Dare, Dare and Dare Again*, Peking Foreign Languages Press (Peking, 1963), p. 62.

third most powerful PKI leaders, I gained the impression that they were
largely uninterested in the ideological problems so assiduously debated
in recent years by Russia and China. ' We have our own brains and we
must think for ourselves ', was a running theme in their conversation.
One can look in vain through PKI publications and speeches for the
scholastic analyses of the Sino-Soviet debate to be found, for example,
in Indian communist publications both of the left and right. While it
may be going too far to conclude from this that the Sino-Soviet dispute
is leading to an ' end of ideology ' in the communist world, it is certainly
contributing to its debasement and to an increase in pragmatism. When,
for example, I asked Nyoto who would decide what was true Marxism-
Leninism now that there was no single authority in the communist
movement, he said that future revolutions would decide what was right
or wrong. The essence of Marxism-Leninism, he told me, was creativity
and it was useless to ' tie oneself up with subjective predictions '. They
had only read about 1905 and 1917, he said, and they didn't really
have the feel for it. That was why the PKI emphasised its own
experience. The PKI criticised Yugoslavia, he said, not because it
followed the baton of other parties, but because the Yugoslavs were a
disruptive influence in the Afro-Asian movement, supported Malaysia,
and interfered in the PKI's internal affairs. PKI leaders insist they are
following an independent line in the Sino-Soviet dispute. No one party,
both he and Lukman stressed, can think for all.[14]

The PKI has nevertheless been one of the firmest supporters of the
Chinese since 1960, and particularly since the campaign against Malaysia
began in 1963. Since the beginning of 1963 it has sharply criticised
the pro-Moscow wing of the Communist Party of India, engaged in
veiled polemics with the Russians, who are evidently accusing it of
degenerating into a peasant party,[15] taken Peking's position on all
outstanding issues, including the crucial question of a new international
conference, opposed Soviet representation at a number of Afro-Asian
conferences, and evolved a formula to describe the present state of
the international communist movement which in effect condemns all
parties sympathetic to Moscow and openly encourages pro-Peking
split-offs.[16]

[14] Interestingly, both Lukman and Nyoto, in their interviews with me, frequently quoted
Lenin but neither referred to Mao except Nyoto once in a rather offhand way when I
said that his conception of the united front seemed to be based on Mao. He said
many people had had this idea.
[15] In a New Year's 1964 speech, Aidit said: ' We Indonesian communists should put
aside as far as possible those ideas of the dogmatists and revisionists who hold that a
good communist party cannot possibly exist without a strong proletariat as its basis.
There have been many facts in the world and in Indonesia as well which show that the
peasants plus Marxism-Leninism can become a mighty strength of the proletariat.
But there have also been many facts in the world showing that the proletariat plus
social democracy and the proletariat plus revisionism constitute a mighty strength of
the bourgeoisie '. NCNA, 6 January 1964.
[16] As adopted by a recent PKI plenum, the formula divides the international communist
movement into four types of communist parties: (1) Marxist-Leninist parties; (2)

The Indonesian communists apparently feel that the Russian and European communist parties are naturally more interested in ' peaceful coexistence ' because they have more to preserve, while the communist parties in the underdeveloped countries have a greater interest in fighting ' imperialism '. This seems to be the principal explanation for the PKI's unequivocal support of the Chinese line.

The PKI's success in the past two years has been intimately related to the increasing anti-Western drift of Indonesian domestic and foreign policy which in turn resulted from the Malaysia crisis. The PKI clearly wishes to fan the flames of the Malaysia crisis and there is even good reason to believe that it wants a full-scale war to develop in the Borneo jungles and in Malaya—a war which would involve the British on an even larger scale than they are now involved and eventually bring in the Americans on the side of Malaysia.[17] Such a war would move Indonesia even closer to the communist powers and the PKI closer to power. It would also facilitate the Chinese strategy—supported by most Asian communists—of weakening the United States by forcing it to fight guerrilla wars in several parts of Southeast Asia at once. These communists hope that after a considerable drain on its resources the United States would withdraw completely from Asia.[18]

The Russians, on the other hand, while they have given diplomatic support to the Indonesian government and arms to the Indonesian army, almost certainly do not want to get involved in a war by proxy with the United States and Britain in Southeast Asia, particularly a war in which the chief beneficiary would be a pro-Peking communist party. Such a war would make it difficult for the Russians to pursue their détente

parties whose leadership is controlled by the revisionists but where there is Marxist-Leninist opposition within these parties; (3) parties under the complete control of the revisionists, but Marxist-Leninists expelled by them have set up Marxist-Leninist organisations; and (4) parties whose leadership is under the complete control of the revisionists, but new communist parties have been set up side by side with them. Report of resolution adopted by second plenum of PKI held in Jakarta from 23 to 26 December 1963, NCNA, 27 January 1964. The resolution was published in the PKI daily organ, *Harian Rakjat*, 17 January 1964.

[17] In a recent speech Aidit cited Lenin's comment on *The Junius Pamphlet* in 1916 to the effect that ' national wars against the imperialist powers are not only possible and probable; they are inevitable, progressive, and revolutionary '. In an obvious allusion to Moscow, he said it was the task of revolutionaries ' not to regret the outbreak of such wars or to scare peoples who are waging war against imperialism with the danger of the thermonuclear war '. NCNA, 25 April 1964.

[18] ' Why should we be afraid of the U.S. imperialists? Take what Robert Kennedy said recently, for example. He said that if a cease-fire on the North Kalimantan border was not effective, then war would break out and the war would involve other countries. Apparently he is frightening us. However, what would be more exact is that he himself is afraid; he is afraid that militarily the United States will have to stand openly on the side of Malaysia in hostility to the Republic of Indonesia; he is afraid that the U.S. troops will be dispersed in South Vietnam, Laos, and North Kalimantan, thus unavoidably going to failure. He is afraid that the United States will lose everything in southeast Asia.' NCNA, 4 February 1964, reporting a speech by Nyoto. In the same speech he said that the struggle against America in Japan, South Korea, South Vietnam, Laos, Cambodia, North Kalimantan and Indonesia ' is only a prelude to a great storm, a storm to wipe the United States from the whole of Asia, and a storm which will surely come '.

strategy in Europe and to reach agreements with the United States to lessen the danger of global nuclear war. This is why, particularly since the beginning of the Malaysia crisis, the PKI has not only unequivocally taken the side of the Chinese in the Sino-Soviet dispute, but has in effect urged other Asian communist parties to do the same. In short, like most other Asian communist parties, the PKI shares with Peking a strategic interest in waging a virulent anti-imperialist campaign in Southeast Asia whose ultimate goal is the elimination of American power and influence from the area.

It is the anti-American core of Maoist strategy which also appeals to the North Korean and North Vietnamese communist parties, both of which are now firmly aligned with Peking against Moscow. The overriding interest of both is to unify their countries, an objective which requires the elimination of the American presence in South Korea and South Vietnam. North Korea was from the very beginning of the Sino-Soviet conflict one of Mao's staunchest allies and the North Vietnamese have moved off the fence into the Peking camp since the middle of 1963.

Before that time, a debate had apparently been raging within the Vietnamese party over economic development strategy and over the policy to be followed in South Vietnam and Laos. The economic debate centred on the question of whether North Vietnam should specialise in agriculture and light industry and integrate its economy into the Soviet-led European bloc, or whether it should continue to give priority to heavy industry and seek to develop an independent economy. The Russians naturally favoured the former course. The Chinese just as naturally favoured an independent approach. By July 1963 the independent approach had won, as is evident from a speech made at the time by Secretary-General Le Duan and promptly republished by Peking.

The debate over strategy in South Vietnam probably revolved around the question of how much risk could be accepted in pushing the guerrilla war. By the fall of 1963 the pro-Peking group had evidently won this argument too. In August, the party journal *Hoc Tap* claimed that 'modern revisionists' were distorting Marxist-Leninist theories on the historical role of violence '. . . [which] is the midwife of the new socialist system '. It went on to deny that nuclear weapons change the laws of development of society and, citing the Chinese, Korean, and Algerian wars, as well as the Vietnamese and Cuban revolutions, argued that liberation wars 'do not necessarily lead to world wars '.

Several reasons can be advanced for the triumph of the pro-Peking group. First, the American military built-up in South Vietnam probably played into their hands. Second, the chronic North Vietnamese food shortage may have led to the conclusion that a major economic crisis was ahead if reunification with the South was not achieved soon. Third, a new generation of North Vietnamese leaders, hardened in the revolutionary war against the French, is gradually coming to the fore and replacing the Paris-educated and internationalist-minded elements in the party. This group looks to the Chinese as the leaders of the Asian revolution.

A variety of forces thus seem to be working to solidify the Asian communist parties around Peking. Almost all of them are still in the stormy and heroic days of their revolutions. Emotionally, they identify more with the Chinese than with the second and third generation communists of the Soviet Union. Many of the Asian parties share with Peking a strategic interest in eliminating American influence in Asia. The Chinese cultural impact on Asia is also an important element. Japan, Korea, and Vietnam are part of the Sinitic civilisation; in contrast, the cultural distance between Russia and Asia is vast. There is also a suspicion among many Asian communists that the Chinese are right in charging that Moscow has opted out of the revolutionary game and has a greater interest in stability and long-term peaceful coexistence with the West. Finally, there is undoubtedly much resentment against past Soviet domination of the international communist movement which, in many cases, led to disasters for local parties. Thus the Japanese communists have recently informed Moscow that one of their ' main complaints' against the Russians was the fact that Moscow had ' imposed' upon them ultra-left and adventurist tactics during the Korean war.[19] Many other parties undoubtedly share similar grievances against the Russians. While this anti-Russian resentment can be exploited by the Chinese in the short run, the very fact that many of these parties bitterly resent the costly setbacks suffered because of Russian domination is one reason why they are not likely ever again to submit to a new domination from Peking. This ' national communist' tendency will in the long run be reinforced by Khrushchev's fall, although the immediate effects of Moscow's search for a détente with Peking are likely, to different degrees in the different countries of Asia, to strengthen the position of the Chinese.

In a broader context, the split between the European and Asian branches of the international communist movement signifies the end of Leninism. Lenin forged an alliance between the revolutionary pro-letarian forces in Europe and revolutionary nationalist and communist forces in the underdeveloped areas. This alliance is now broken. The result is to remove the doctrinal and tactical restraints that inter-national unity of action imposed on the Asian communists. As a result, elements which were always latent in Asian communism are now coming to the fore. These include emphasis on Asia and the underdeveloped areas as the decisive revolutionary background in which imperialist contradictions are the sharpest; the great importance of the peasantry and the agrarian revolution; a profound dissatisfaction with the status quo; a virulent, xenophobic anti-Western nationalism with strong racialist overtones; a belief that imperialism, particularly American imperialism, is the basic enemy; and a view that the underdeveloped

[19] *Soviet Documents*, 31 August 1964, p. 14.

countries, as a result of common historical experiences, particularly their subjugation by Western colonial powers, have a number of common problems and obstacles to overcome in their drives toward modernisation and industrialisation which are unlike the problems of the USSR and Europe.

It can be argued that a decisive break with Marxist-Leninist thought is contained in the first of these elements. While it was Lenin and not Mao who first recognised the importance of anti-colonial nationalism, for Lenin the anti-colonial revolutions were still merely a sideshow, to be encouraged in order to weaken the European colonial powers and to exacerbate imperialist contradictions. The main arena of revolutionary struggle, for Lenin, remained in Europe. In short, while Lenin recognised the tactical importance of nationalism and the ' national bourgeoisie ' in Asia as a revolutionary force, he never assigned it a strategic role, and neither he nor his heirs, conceptually imprisoned by their Marxist, internationalist, class view of the world, ever came fully to terms with it. It was Mao's historic role to do so.

The essence of Mao's grand strategy, now openly revealed by the Indonesian communists, is that the world revolution will be a reproduction on a world scale of the Chinese revolution. The underdeveloped countries—the ' external proletariat '—represent the ' villages ' and the advanced, industrialised countries represent the ' cities '. The strategy is to surround the cities by occupying the villages. It is for this reason that Mao places such primary importance on the national liberation movements. A succession of anti-imperialist, communist-led revolutions will drive the United States and its Western allies from Asia, Africa, and Latin America, thereby intensifying the contradictions in the United States and Europe, and ultimately leading to a world-wide victory over imperialism.

The appeal of a strategy which attaches such decisive importance to revolutionary struggle in the underdeveloped countries is of course considerable for both communists and radical nationalists in those areas, for it means that the Soviet Union and the European communist parties should attach primary importance to aiding them in their struggles to obtain or to expand their power.

THE STRATEGIC TRIANGLE:
(1) INDIA

Sathi

SINCE its foundation, the Communist Party of India has passed through several crises. If it was able to survive them, the reasons were partly fortuitous, and partly the cadre nature of its organisation. The Sino-Soviet ideological dispute, engulfing as it does communism throughout the world has, however, thrown the CPI into what may turn out to be a permanent crisis.

The hopes entertained in some of its circles that the CPI would survive the present crisis unharmed were finally dashed with the publication of letters written in 1924 to the British Viceroy by the present CPI chairman, S. A. Dange. These letters, at least to his critics in the CPI, suggest that he was willing to work for British intelligence to secure his release.[1] Certainly the disclosure is not the cause of the split, but it has enabled those Indian communists who were pro-Peking in their leanings to come out on the plausible ground of conscience. In fact, their diametrically opposed assessment of the Indian situation leads them to regard Dange and his supporters as compromisers if not actually renegades.

Until Khrushchev's denigration of Stalin, the CPI had the reputation of being, like communist parties everywhere, a monolithic structure; it had one body and one soul—the latter in Moscow. The 20th CPSU congress destroyed not only the image, but also the intellectual and political cohesion of the party.

The crisis was still simmering when the revolt in Tibet flared up. Though, at that time, both the pro-Russian and pro-Chinese communists were united in denouncing the revolt as a 'feudal counter-revolution in league with imperialism',[2] divisions in the CPI began to take on concrete shape. For allied with the Tibetan revolt was the question of India-China relations. Public opinion in India was shocked that Peking should have gone back on its promise of respect for Tibet's internal autonomy. In defiance of public opinion, the CPI, even after the Dalai Lama's arrival in India in search of asylum, continued to support the Chinese action; it even extended 'warm greetings to the Communist Party of China under whose guidance the People's Government of China is leading the people of Tibet from medieval darkness to prosperity and equality'. P. C. Joshi, who deserves mention because of his present reputation as a moderate pro-Russian communist, went so far as to hint that the Indian town of Kalimpong on the Indo-Tibetan border was the 'commanding centre' of the Tibetan rebels

[1] *Current* (Bombay), 7 March 1964.
[2] *The India-China Border Dispute and the Communist Party of India* (New Delhi, 1963)

Nor did he stop at that. He alleged that the anti-Chinese espionage network 'is fairly widespread and covers not only Kalimpong, but also Calcutta, Bhutan, and Sikkim'.[3]

On 1 September 1959, the late Prime Minister Nehru grudgingly let the Indian people know that the Chinese had occupied nearly 15,000 square miles of Indian territory bordering on Tibet. Now the communists had to make a choice. If they remained lined up behind China, they would lose support at home; if they condemned China, they would be accused of betraying proletarian internationalism in favour of petty-bourgeois nationalism. They first tried a balancing act, appealing to the Governments of the two countries to resolve their differences amicably and to avoid rigid positions.[4]

Ajoy Ghosh took off for Moscow. During his absence, however, the CPI leadership found itself divided. Some of them, like Mr Dange, E. M. S. Namboodiripad, former Chief Minister of Kerala, Dr Z. A. Ahmad and Mr A. K. Gopalan, the then Deputy Leader of the communist group in the Lok Sabha (Lower House of Parliament) felt compelled to criticise the Chinese action. Others regarded this as a deviation from the CPI's international duty, and the Calcutta meeting of the CPI central committee in September 1959, turned out to be extremely stormy. Three different lines emerged. One group pleaded for unreserved condemnation of the Chinese incursions. Opposed to them were men like Mr P. Sundarayya, Mr Jyoti Basu, secretary of the West Bengal section of the CPI, Mr P. C. Joshi and Mr Harkishan Singh Surjeet, secretary of the Punjab section, who maintained not only that India had no case, but was, in effect, the aggressor; the Nehru Government had raised the bogy of Chinese aggression 'to stem the rising tide of the people's offensive'.[5] The third line was associated with Mr Ghosh, who found fault with both India and China.

SOON after this meeting, Mr. Ghosh, with four others, left for Peking to participate in the Chinese National Day and to persuade the Chinese communist leaders to change their policy towards India. For Mr Ghosh the trip proved a disaster. The Chinese did not give him a patient hearing; he was not invited to address a single public function where communist leaders from other countries were much in demand, and Mao Tse-tung refused him an audience. Infuriated, Mr Ghosh flew to Moscow to seek advice; there he was assured that Peking would soon retrace its steps and modify its policy.

His faith in Moscow strengthened, Mr Ghosh returned to New Delhi on 21 October 1959, where he told pressmen that the territorial dispute would soon be settled amicably. Unluckily for him, on the following

---

3 New Age (Delhi), 5 April 1959.

4 The India-China Border Dispute . . . op. cit. pp. 8–11.

Traitors to the Cause, published by the National Marxist Association of India (Delhi, 1960).

day came the news that nine members of the Indian border police had been massacred by the Chinese near Chusul, in Ladakh, a part of Kashmir.

For the first time the party's secretariat openly, though mildly, criticised China. It described the Chinese action as ' unjustified ' and shared ' the feelings of deep resentment and indignation of the Indian people ' over the ' heavy loss of life ' in Ladakh.[6] When the CC met, the pro-Chinese communists turned down the draft resolution prepared by Ghosh for the meeting of the 101-member National Council at Meerut, and adopted instead, by a majority of one, a draft drawn up by P. Ramamurti.

After a week-long discussion in the National Council at Meerut, the original CC resolution was amended to make it more ' nationalistic ' in tone. It described the MacMahon Line as the country's border in the north and north-east, though it insisted on the desirability of adjustments in Ladakh to enable the Chinese unhindered use of the Aksai Chin Road which they had surreptitiously built between 1954 and 1958. In essence, the resolution hardly departed from Premier Chou En-lai's position on the subject. It did not put responsibility for the deterioration of India-China relations squarely on Peking because of opposition by the Bengal group, led by Basu and Somnath Lahiri. To them any criticism of communist China was not only a gross violation of the accepted norms of behaviour between one communist party and another, but would also be the occasion for large-scale resignations from the party. Another significant development was that at the National Council meeting, some of those who were until then thought to be pro-Peking, switched to the ' nationalist ' line, including the head of the Peace Council in India.

Until June 1960 the CPI appeared to remain in a state of suspended animation; then the Sino-Soviet differences erupted into the open at the Rumanian CP congress. According to their own admission, the CPI's two fraternal delegates to the congress were ' stunned ' when they observed—behind closed doors—the clash between the two.

According to circles close to CPI headquarters, when Khrushchev at Bucharest chided the Chinese ' for stabbing the communist movement in the Afro-Asian world in the back in return for a few hundred square miles of Indian territory ', Gupta objected that this was not true. The Soviet leader retorted: ' Go back and convince your own countrymen about the just nature of the Chinese action '.[7]

The CC of the CPI, which met in New Delhi from 4 to 11 September, echoed Khrushchev's sentiments. It passed a resolution which stated that ' China had lost the sympathy of millions of Indians in return for the claim on a few square miles of worthless territory '. But it still took care to add, ' it is an indisputable fact that the first breach in the India-China friendship was created by the attitude and acts of the

---

[6] *The India-China Border Dispute . . .* op. cit. p. 12.   [7] *Link* (Delhi), 16 October 1960

Indian Government towards the counter-revolutionary uprising in Tibet and the aid given to the Dalai Lama to conduct an anti-China propaganda campaign in India '.[8]

Even this resolution did not remain unchallenged for long. A month later, the West Bengal CP came up with a resolution accusing the pro-Russian communists of 'immaturity in Marxist understanding'. It also charged the National Council with 'appeasement' of Indian chauvinism, 'following a liquidationist policy', and 'trailing behind Nehru'. The whole territorial dispute was, in its opinion, irrelevant because 'it was not and it is not an issue in the international controversies'.[9]

This repudiation of the National Council resolution followed the visit of a two-man CPI delegation to the congress of the Communist Party of North Vietnam in September 1960. One of the two was soon to become prominent for his advocacy of the Peking line. Harekrishna Konar told the Calcutta communist conference that he had 'long talks with fraternal Chinese delegates'. It is believed that he went secretly to Peking from Hanoi and met Mao Tse-tung, Chou En-lai, and Liu Shao-chi.[10]

TAKING their cue from West Bengal, the Punjab pro-Chinese communists passed a resolution on 24 October 1960, rejecting the National Council resolution and demanding its withdrawal. In spite of the intransigence of these two sections, the CPI leaders did not take disciplinary action against them, although a letter censuring the West Bengal CP was sent. The charge against it was not that it had challenged the National Council's stand on the territorial dispute, but that it had made its opposition public. It became clear that being almost equally divided, the CPI leadership was unable to take any coercive action against insubordination.

Soon after a five-member delegation left for Moscow to take part in the conference of the 81 communist parties. In addition to Mr Ghosh, the leader, Dange, Gupta, Basavapunniah, and Ramamurti were its members. Ghosh's 8,000-word statement at the conference was published for the first time in July 1963 as an 'inner-party document' entitled *The India-China Border Dispute and the Communist Party of India*. It told the story of how the CPI was let down by the Chinese CP on the border issue: 'We maintain that this question should not be looked at as one of border claims based on history, about which endless arguments over facts may be raised, but we should approach it keeping in view the paramount need to strengthen the democratic forces in India'. But criticism of the Chinese attitude towards the CPI, if made public, would only strengthen the anti-Chinese reaction in India.[11]

8 *The India-China Border Dispute* . . . op cit. p. 22.
9 *Thought* (Delhi), 23 December 1961.
10 *Link*, 16 October 1960.
11 *Questions of Ideology in the International Communist Movement*, No. 6 (Delhi), 1963.

After the Moscow conference, Suslov called the CPI delegation to his office and told its members that the Soviet Union neither supported the Chinese action in India, nor approved of the CPI's 'somewhat critical attitude towards Peking'. If the Chinese action, he said, 'has stabbed the communist movement in Asia in the back', the CPI's attitude would only help reactionary forces in India to isolate the communists from the Indian people. He advised the Indian delegation to follow the Moscow Declaration in letter as well as in spirit.

After the return of the CPI delegation, a meeting of the National Council was held in Bombay in the last week of December 1960. Ostensibly convened for the purpose of explaining the Moscow Declaration to party cadres, it actually called a halt to the anti-Chinese campaign inside the party ranks. Though, following Suslov's advice, no formal resolution was adopted on the territorial conflict, the pro-Chinese communists demanded the repudiation of the Meerut resolution of the National Council. They interpreted Suslov's advice as a vindication of their stand.

The pro-Chinese communists now launched an all-out inner-party campaign in favour of China. At the Burdwan conference of the West Bengal CP in January 1961, one Mr Promode Das-Gupta replaced Basu as secretary. Basu's exit from the office was significant. He had been in full agreement with the pro-Chinese communists on the issue of the India-China frontier, but he was against making that the main plank in the inner-party struggle. This showed that from then on the pro-Chinese communists were prepared to tolerate neither tactical heterodoxy nor silence on this vital issue. They contended that the conclusion to be drawn from the Moscow Declaration's characterisation of the present period as 'the epoch of transition from capitalism to socialism' was a call to the 'progressive forces' to make the final assault on imperialism, capitalism, and other vestiges of reaction.

The pro-Russian communists argued that the statement on the 'general retreat of imperialism' in the Moscow Declaration was the most important; in its light the Indian Government, in spite of its occasional vacillations, had followed an anti-colonial, anti-imperialist, anti-West, and pro-peace foreign policy. Ghosh also laid stress on the Nehru Government's consistent refusal to join any military pact sponsored by the Anglo-American bloc and its unequivocal condemnation of the Anglo-French aggression against Egypt in 1956.[12]

Ghosh's thesis was adopted by the National Council at Bombay, but by so slender a majority and in such a highly charged atmosphere that it was evident that the split would not be long delayed. It was thought prudent to circulate the rejected resolution as one of the documents for the forthcoming CPI congress, but this did not appease the pro-Chinese. Led by Ranadive, they walked out of the meeting.

12 Ajoy Ghosh, *Resolution on the Present Political Situation* (Delhi, 1961).

The Kremlin was deeply disturbed by this situation, and sent Suslov as head of the Soviet delegation to the congress. This was the first time Moscow had sent so high-ranking a member of the CPSU to a communist congress in India.

The proceedings of the congress revealed that the differences between the two factions had become more acute. While the pro-Chinese communists accused the pro-Russian communists of revisionism, the pro-Russian communists contemptuously called them Trotskyites. Throughout their 14-day stay at Vijayawada, members of the two factions did not exchange even the ordinary courtesies. The atmosphere was one of virtual civil war.

Although the pro-Russian communists won in some of the initial skirmishes, the pro-Chinese communists avenged their defeat when they successfully resisted the passage of the Draft Programme jointly prepared by Dange, Joshi, and Dr G. Adhikari. The draft advocated the formation of a 'National Democratic Front' to 'defend and strengthen India's independent foreign policy of peace and anti-colonialism' through the 'elimination of existing foreign capital'.[13] The pro-Chinese communists' draft, prepared by Bhupesh Gupta and Ramamurti, pleaded for the establishment of a 'People's Democratic Front Government— a government in which the working class and the Communist Party will increasingly play a weighty role and pave the way for advance towards socialism'.[14]

Ghosh stole much of the thunder of the pro-Chinese communists by himself taking an extremist stand, sharply criticising the Government's foreign and economic policies. But his concluding recommendation was that the CPI must intensify its efforts ' to unite all patriotic and democratic forces in the country . . . to alter the correlation of forces and lead to a situation when it becomes a practical possibility to raise the slogan of the establishment of a Government of a National Democratic Front '.[15]

Namboodiripad tried to strike a balance between the two warring factions; he too was for a united front of all ' progressive ' forces, both inside and outside the ruling Congress Party, but only to shorten the period of transition from the bourgeois-democratic to the socialist stage of the revolution.

After a prolonged wrangle, the congress adopted a patchwork resolution to preserve the semblance of unity. But it could not be maintained. There were in all five resolutions on the India-China territorial dispute, to which the pro-Chinese Communists moved 450 amendments. After endless wrangling at the congress itself and in a specially appointed sub-committee, it was agreed (probably on Suslov's advice) that this question should be taken up by the new National

13 *Draft Programme of the CPI* (Delhi, 1961).
14 *Draft Programme of the CPI* by Bhupesh Gupta and P. Ramamurti (Delhi, 1961).
15 Ajoy Ghosh, *New Situation and Our Tasks* (Delhi, 1961), pp. 56–68.

Council because ' the congress has no time ' (although it devoted many precious hours to Algeria, Pakistan, West Germany, etc.).

Vijayawada might have witnessed the formal split but for the pro-Russian communists' offer to the pro-Chinese communists of proportional representation at all levels of the party hierarchy.

BY the fall of 1961, with the Sino-Soviet dispute wide open, the pro-Russian communist leader, Mr. Ghosh, who was still General Secretary of the party, felt free to be openly critical of the Chinese action, although until September 1962 the India-China dispute itself remained practically frozen. Even when the Chinese launched their attack on Indian territory and crossed the MacMahon Line, the CC, at its meeting in New Delhi on 18 October did no more than express its ' grave concern at the serious happenings on the NEFA border '.

On 2 November 1962, the National Council again passed a resolution condemning the Chinese as aggressors, but a significant section, criticising the Chinese action, was omitted from the press release (but was later included in the pamphlet on the border dispute already quoted). It reads in part: ' The behaviour of socialist China towards peace-loving India has most grossly violated the common understanding of the communist world arrived at in the 81 Parties' Conference in 1960 in relation to peaceful coexistence and attitudes to newly-liberated countries and the question of war and peace '.

On 20 November 1962, the CPI Secretariat sent a circular letter to other communist parties over the joint signatures of all its members, which, after narrating the history of the India-China territorial dispute and the rebuff the Chinese leaders had given the CPI, referred to the repercussions of Chinese aggression in the country. ' The entire people belonging to all classes, especially the working people—the workers, peasants and employees—have risen in universal indignation. Never since independence has India witnessed such a universal demonstration of patriotic feelings throughout the country as is in evidence today. . . . To view all this as a manifestation of bourgeois nationalism or capitulation to the bourgeoisie will be the greatest imaginable folly '.

Whether in fear of arrest or for tactical reasons, some of the confirmed pro-Chinese communists were vociferous in their demand for throwing out the Chinese. But as soon as the Chinese announced their withdrawal, they turned their guns on the official leaders of the CPI. They had already resigned their party offices in protest against the CPI's approval of the Government of India's acceptance of arms from the West. Namboodiripad, hitherto a centrist communist, requested Dange, the Chairman of the CPI, to relieve him of his post as General Secretary. He also indirectly echoed the Chinese charge that the pro-Russian communist leader had betrayed the pro-Chinese communists to Indian police.

In February 1963 Namboodiripad delivered his long prepared blow. In a 72-page closely typed document addressed to the National Council, under the seemingly impartial title *Revisionism and Dogmatism in the CPI,* he attacked the pro-Russian communists. Officially, the document is still meant ' for party members only '. It is therefore of interest to quote it at some length: ' The stand taken by the majority in the National Council on Chinese aggression was the logical culmination of the revisionist-right-opportunist outlook and attitude referred to above. Not only was the content of the resolution incorrect from the ideological-political standpoint. The way in which it came to be pushed through the National Council, and subsequently sought to be implemented, was highly disruptive from an organisational point of view. The result, as we see today, is that the unity of the party has been completely broken. We are in the midst of the most serious inner-party crisis in history '.

It would not be wrong to say that the Namboodiripad document was avidly seized on by the pro-Chinese communists since it came from a ' sober-minded ' Centrist of great prestige. A leading pro-Russian communist theoretician, Adhikari, published a reply which he called *Communist Party and India's Path of National Regeneration and Socialism.* This 206-page book is also supposed to be ' for members only '.

Thereafter little happened until the publication of the story of the Dange letters. The pro-Chinese communists seized the opportunity to denounce Dange publicly as a traitor and spy, and demanded his resignation. Dange denounced the letters as ' rank forgery ', but he agreed neither to resign nor to sue the Bombay weekly which first came out with the story. At the National Council meeting in April 1964, 32 pro-Chinese communists walked out; they acted as the organising committee of the ' real ' Communist Party of India until July, when they convened a conference of their followers at Tenali, Andhra. The conference witnessed an internal struggle between the different tendencies within the leftist camp. The dialectic of factionalism was manifested in the battle between the pro-Chinese ' ultras ', led by Konar, and the ex-centrist ' vacillators ' like Basu and Namboodiripad. The strongly pro-Chinese Basavapunniah tried to moderate the differences; the resolution adopted was too mild for the ultras, and it was criticised at a meeting of the West Bengal leftists. The strength of their position in that state was great enough to compel Basu to change his position, and to give them his support. The fall of Khrushchev made no difference to their determination to establish a separate party, and its foundation was formally proclaimed at a meeting in Calcutta in early November. The new party elected a committee of nine, reflecting the balance between the three tendencies, with Mr Sundarayya, who holds a middle position, as secretary. It considers itself the only legitimate Communist Party in India, and has asked Moscow for recognition—a request unlikely to be granted. Whatever attempts may be made at a Sino-Soviet rapprochement, the personal antagonisms and rivalries, as well as the political differences which have emerged in the last two years, will remain.

(2) INDONESIA

Ruth McVey

WITH two and a half million members, the Partai Komunis Indonesia (PKI) has supplanted the Communist Party of Italy as the world's largest non-governing communist organisation. It possesses a well-developed system of mass organisations and in some districts, particularly in Central and East Java, it is strong enough to represent the normal political affiliation of the population. It is, in fact, Indonesia's major party; none of the others can boast a comparable apparatus, and none can claim as broad a popular following. Like their Italian colleagues, the PKI leaders explain their party's past success and base its future hopes on its ability to make use of local conditions and opportunities, and like them they face the task of maintaining momentum in a situation where dogmatic opposition to the status quo, let alone efforts at its violent rejection, appears unprofitable. This has given them a common ground in the Sino-Soviet debate, namely, a warm interest in broad autonomy within the international communist movement. The PKI, borrowing from the lexicon of the official national ideology, calls for all decisions in the world movement to be reached by *musjawarah* (consultation) and *mufakat* (consensus) and asserts that each party should be absolutely equal and independent.

Here, however, the similarity of the PCI and PKI positions in the Sino-Soviet debate ends: the Italians have been principal spokesmen of the revisionists while the Indonesians have been supporters of the intransigents. The principal reason for this contrast is the very different backgrounds against which the two movements operate. The Italian environment is highly stable compared to that of Indonesia. The parliamentary path is the only one that seems to hold promise, but, as the PCI is so far unacceptable as a political partner except in areas where it has overwhelming strength, it remains an outsider. Reason is appealed to rather than emotion, enlightened self-interest rather than messianic enthusiasm; proletarian exclusiveness is abandoned for a broader if less militant following. The post-Stalin view of communism fits very well into this approach, and accordingly the PCI has found the evolution of the Soviet-sponsored line a congenial one on issues other than that of central control.

Indonesia's political environment is not at all of this sort; it exists in a sense on a different plane, so that the communist response to it can at once be opposed to and very much the same as the strategy pursued by the Italian party. The parliamentary path does not exist. True, the PKI's potential electoral strength is formidable, and some non-communist politicians consider that it might win an absolute majority. When Khrushchev announced the possibility of parliamentary victory the PKI welcomed the concept and declared it appropriate for Indonesia; but that was in 1956, before the country abandoned its experiment with constitutional democracy. Before the end of the decade the parliamentary system had been rejected as alien and ineffective; no elections have been held since, and if they are it will be under a new law that provides for such a division between appointed and elected seats, and among seats allotted to parties, regions, and functional (corporate) groups, that it is hard to imagine any political group achieving control of parliament through its electoral strength. Moreover, control of parliament no longer implies control of the government, for the system of majority rule has been condemned as the product of divisive, self-seeking ' free-fight liberalism ' and replaced by the principle of *mufakat,* a sense of the meeting to be reached under the guidance of the president. Parliament and the regional representative assemblies have lost most of their influence, for the power they possessed has passed to the bureaucracy or has flowed to such newer political factors as the army and the National Front. The very existence of political parties has been threatened, for they have been held responsible for corruption and discord; their activities have been restricted, and moves towards their replacement by a monolithic political organisation have been launched repeatedly, if thus far unsuccessfully.

In spite of their participation in the campaign against Western-style democracy, the communists have been anything but pleased with these developments; they have urged the restoration of their powers to the representative assemblies and the holding of elections, and have fought for the preservation of independent political parties. The situation is not without its ironies: while accusing the revisionists of favouring liberal principles above revolutionary ones, the PKI is charged with the same offence by its enemies in Indonesia.

The PKI, however, does not base its hopes on a return to parliamentary democracy, nor does it seek to follow the Chinese example of armed struggle against the regime, if this can be avoided. Instead, its policy has been to attempt to integrate the communist movement with the present regime and with society as a whole, on such a grand scale that it becomes identical with the nation's organisational and ideological backbone.[1] It seeks to become indispensable, for indispensability means invulnerability, and invulnerability means power. Communists outside Indonesia have been known to comment sourly, and not without cause, that the compromises required by this strategy, presented by the PKI as the Indonesianisation of Marxism-Leninism and Chairman Aidit's great contribution to communist philosophy, have involved more revision of the doctrine and more collaboration with the powers that be than ever the communists in Europe contemplated. The PKI must endorse, and with enthusiasm, Sukarno's imitation of Mussolini in calling on Indonesia to appreciate the romanticism of the revolution

---

[1] The term used is *integrasi*; it is not unique with the PKI, having been employed by the Chinese communists, from whom it is probably derived, and currently used widely in Indonesian official statements (the integration of the government with the people, and so on).

and to 'live dangerously '.[2] In the end, of course, the essential question
will be not which party remained truer to Marxist doctrine, but which
one was the more successful. It is a game the Indonesian party has
been playing with consummate skill, and in the past year it seems to have
approached measurably closer to success.

IN the charged atmosphere of guided democracy, aims and not
institutions are real. Stability is tantamount to stagnation, motion
to progress. If the economic situation worsens, if foreign relations grow
more tense, the response must be more radical than before, for such
things only indicate how many and how determined Indonesia's enemies
are. The nation's aims cannot be achieved by compromise and calcula-
tion, but only by enthusiasm and faith; the goals themselves expand,
become millenial: the revolution will not be completed until imperialism
has been crushed and the just and prosperous society established over
the entire world. The pragmatic flexibility of Khrushchev's goulash
communism was hardly compatible with this spirit; it appeared self-
seeking, complacent, concerned with the petty problems of adjusting to
the present rather than the monumental task of creating the future. Far
more sympathetic was the Chinese stand, with its crusade against
imperialism, its assertion that the underdeveloped countries are the
world's revolutionary centres, and its assurance that even the poorest
nations need not depend on foreign aid—all themes recurrent in the
rhetoric of guided democracy.

One of the PKI's most important and difficult tasks has been to
persuade Indonesia's leaders that their ' active and independent ' foreign
policy does not preclude but rather requires alignment in the cold war,
and that the country's survival is not dependent on Western friendship
or aid. Its efforts in this direction have been greatly aided by the fact
that Sukarno's outlook, like that of a great number of Indonesian
nationalists, has always been heavily influenced by Lenin's interpretation
of imperialism, and this viewpoint has been reinforced by a decade's
experience in economic frustration, radical domestic politics, and
deteriorating relations with the West. Thus, whereas it was necessary
in 1953 for the PKI to ' Indonesianise ' Marxism-Leninism by declaring
that the Netherlands and not the United States was the country's principal
imperialist enemy, it was possible for it to announce in 1963 that
America had assumed that position. Its domestic opponents have
attacked this stand, particularly during 1964, on the ground that the
PKI is diverting Indonesia's energies from the struggle against its real
main enemy, Britain-Malaysia, and is doing so in the interests of China,
which is America's enemy and Britain's friend. The argument seems

---

2 This was the theme of the President's 17 August 1964 Independence Day speech; the
coming year has been proclaimed the year of ' *vivere pericoloso* '. The theme was
promptly seconded by the PKI and by its peasant organisation, BTI, and labour
federation, SOBSI, both of which held major conferences in September at which the
slogans were elaborated and fitted to communist demands.

unlikely to carry great weight, however, in view of Sukarno's denunciation of the United States in his Independence Day speech of 17 August
1964, in which he charged America, among other things, with aggression
in the Tonkin Bay incident.

The PKI's own stand on Malaysia has been militant; the issue, which
it discovered before the Indonesian government itself decided Malaysia
constituted a threat, offered a welcome opportunity to revive the
xenophobic radicalism that had begun to flag with the settlement of the
West Irian (New Guinea) question. The Malaysia campaign has given
the party an outlet for action by its mass organisations, whose ability
to demonstrate is otherwise severely restricted by the authorities; no one
in power wishes to be accused of obstructing the expression of popular
sentiment in such an issue. Moreover, the army, normally the principal
check on PKI mass agitation, has been attempting to outbid the party
in radicalism on the Malaysia issue, among other reasons because it has
not wished to run second to the communists in appearing as the vanguard of militant nationalism, as it tended to do during the Irian
campaign.

As a result of these circumstances, communist unions were able to
launch a drive to take over British-owned firms in Indonesia at the
beginning of 1964; although it was apparent the authorities had not
desired the move, it was difficult for them to repudiate it, and, except
for the arrest of various local union officials, they accepted the fait
accompli.[3] Similarly the communists were able to initiate a boycott of
American films in mid-1964; the government were not taken with
the action but, having themselves inveighed with increasing vehemence
against Western 'cultural imperialism', they felt unable to repudiate it
outright and instead have sought its end by various indirect manoeuvres.

B Y thus forcing the government to match its radical slogans with
acceptance of radical actions, the PKI has attempted to accelarate
the regime's movement toward complete alienation from the West. It
has not seen universally favourable progress in this during the past year,
in spite of the marked exacerbation of differences with Britain and the
United States, for it has been forced to observe a reconciliation with the
Netherlands which reached honeymoon proportions by mid-1964.
Except for an occasional admonition to Indonesia's leaders to regard
the former number one imperialist enemy with caution, the PKI has
maintained a stony silence on the subject, comforting its followers with
the argument that the Dutch, like the French and West Germans (who
are also currently popular in Indonesia), present only a secondary contradiction and should therefore be ignored. Similarly, the party had to

---

3 The SOBSI unions made it more difficult to retaliate by taking care to gain the
cooperation of non-communist unions at each enterprise before embarking on the
action; representatives of the unions went in a delegation to the office of the local
authority to hand over the enterprise to the state immediately after taking it over.
The communists apparently entertained some hopes that the unions would be allowed
a voice in managing the seized firms, but these were soon dashed.

endure until mid-1964 Indonesia's flirtation with the Philippines and the Maphilindo concept. The PKI could not afford to oppose a project so closely identified with Sukarno, and thus found itself issuing a series of mild cautions, discoveries of a Philippine revolutionary spirit, and reminders that a Maphilindo cooperation must be anti-imperialist. The situation was the more embarrassing for the party in that it gave pro-Moscow communists a chance to return the PKI's charges of opportunism in foreign affairs; the Indonesian party replied testily that its attackers were dogmatists who could not distinguish flexibility from lack of principle, but there is little doubt that the PKI leaders must have been greatly relieved when the need for that particular kind of flexibility ended.

Since the PKI is interested in increasing Indonesia's revolutionary momentum and its alienation from the West, it has little liking for Soviet efforts at a détente in international relations, which it has seen as placing the interests of the established communist powers above those of revolutionaries in the underdeveloped areas. The countries of Asia, Africa, and Latin America, Aidit has declared, are the villages of the world; if the workers in the advanced nations, the world's cities, ignore the rural revolution, they will be unable to consolidate their own gains, for the proletariat cannot achieve victory without peasant support. One cannot talk of building communism in one country, for until imperialism has been completely abolished the need for defence will absorb too great a part of the national income to allow this; moreover, the danger of domestic capitalist resurgence will continue to exist so long as a capitalist example is present.[4]

The PKI's sympathy for the Chinese stand in the Sino-Soviet dispute was long established, and apparently the Russians have given up hope of persuading the Indonesian leaders from their position, to judge from the cool reception they accorded a major PKI mission to Moscow, Peking, and lesser communist capitals in July–September 1963. Returning from the trip, Aidit proclaimed that the international communist movement was undergoing a process of 'selection, crystallisation, and consolidation', and that it was the duty of the true Marxist-Leninist parties to aid this process, if necessary by helping to split revisionist-controlled parties.[5] At the time of writing only the Yugoslav and Indian parties have been placed completely beyond the pale. The PKI never moved in the direction of reconciliation with Tito, whom it has seen as a particularly unfortunate example available for Sukarno's emulation, and it made specific its long-hinted charges that the Yugoslav leader had urged Sukarno not to give the PKI a significant role in his government.

The Indian party has suffered even more than the Yugoslav at PKI hands, perhaps because Indonesian relations with India, and particularly

---

[4] For a statement of this position, see Aidit's report to the December 1963 central committee meeting, in *Harian Rakjat*, 1 January 1964.

[5] Ibid. 4 and 5 October 1963.

Sukarno's with Nehru, have never been truly cordial. For having
supported India's struggle against the Chinese, the Indian party is
referred to as the ' Dange clique '; if its official title is given at all, it is
given in quotation marks to indicate that as ' Malaysia ' is an un-nation,
so the ' CPI ' is an un-party. Relations with the CPSU have become
exceedingly strained, a nadir being reached in April 1964 on the
occasion of a meeting commemorating the ninety-fourth anniversary of
Lenin's birth, at which the Soviet ambassador challenged Aidit and was
roughly treated by the public.[6] In spite of such incidents the PKI has
not gone so far as to abandon all hope of preserving some unity
in the international movement. It has been extremely cautious in
referring to the idea of a conference of communist parties, virtually
its only allusion to it being a joint statement with Japanese Communist
Party leaders, signed on 7 September, reiterating a position long held
by the PKI: a conference should not be held unless there was reason to
believe it would promote unity rather than division. Since Khrushchev's
fall, Aidit has shown a similar caution. In his speech of 24 October
in Bandung, he declared that it ' presents the possibility of a rapprochement between China and the Soviet Union ', but added that there were
difficulties and obstacles because the Soviet CP ' still persists in following
the line of the 20th, 21st, and 22nd congresses, and this line can only be
modified at a future Soviet party congress '. He said that ' only future
developments can show if Khrushchev's departure was a good thing ',
but expressed the hope that it might result in a Sino-Soviet reconciliation
' which may be beneficial to the newly emergent forces in Asia '.

THOUGH the PKI has hinted at Soviet attempts to establish a pro-
Moscow faction in its ranks, there is so far no concrete evidence
of a split within the party regarding its position in the dispute. The
likelihood that this is not just a product of the party's general success
in maintaining an outward appearance of unity seems the greater in that
the Chinese position is shared to a considerable extent by the Indonesian
regime as well. Indonesia has been increasingly involved in efforts
to establish itself as an international political and ideological force.
Partly because of its revolutionary temper and partly because of rivalry
with India for moral leadership of Asian nationalism, it has rejected the
' non-aligned ' group headed by India, Yugoslavia and the UAR in
favour of an Asian-African (and potentially Latin American) alliance
that would include—and needless to say is backed by—Peking.
    Indonesia's bid for leadership of a more radical alliance was made at
the 1961 conference of non-aligned powers in Belgrade, when Sukarno
advanced the proposition that the world was divided into the Old

[6] Aidit's speech, which was published in *Harian Rakjat*, 24 April 1964, took an extreme
pro-Chinese stand. The Soviet ambassador, who attended because the meeting was
sponsored by the Indonesian-Soviet Friendship Institute, demanded the right to reply
and was thereupon jostled by the Indonesians around him. Granted the right to
respond, he criticised Aidit's stand sharply amid catcalls and cries of ' Retool [remove]
the Soviet ambassador! '

Established Forces of imperialism and reaction and the New Emerging Forces of nationalism and socialism, and that non-alignment in the struggle between them was not possible. A vigorous attempt to organise the new emerging forces began with Indonesia's retaliation for the International Olympic Committee's criticisms of the Djakarta-based 1962 Asian Games: the Games of the New Emerging Forces, held in November 1963, were far more successful than anyone but the Indonesians had expected, and they also helped, by the international frictions they generated, to widen the rift between those who favoured the non-aligned bloc and those who promoted an Asian-African one. The games were accompanied by a succession of Asian-African meetings in Djakarta, at which it was apparent that the Indonesians—and not only those from the PKI—favoured neither the Soviet position nor Soviet participation.[7]

The principal gatherings in 1964 were the Asian-African Film Festival, at which China dominated and the Soviet entries were given short shrift, and the Asian-African Ministers' Conference, which was to prepare for the holding of a second A-A Conference, a project which Indonesia had long promoted. The Indonesians hoped that the question of Soviet and Malaysian participation in the meeting would not come up; but it did, being raised by India, which managed to secure the backing of most of the African delegations. As the Chinese were adamant regarding the USSR and the Indonesians regarding Malaysia, no decision was reached, which effectively meant those countries' exclusion. Though the exchange of visits between Mikoyan and Indonesian foreign minister Subandrio in the following nine months awakened speculation that Djakarta might be persuaded somehow to secure Soviet participation, nothing of this nature developed, and soon thereafter the USSR appeared to give up.

Though recent developments in international affairs have brought Indonesia considerably closer to Peking, the PKI has not placed great stress on ties with China. In the first place it wishes to avoid being labelled subservient to any foreign power, a most damaging charge in Indonesia; second, it wishes to escape the special stigma attached to the Chinese by many Indonesians, who demonstrated in May 1963 that

---

[7] One of the major gatherings was a preparatory conference for the Asian-African Labour Conference, scheduled to take place in 1964. A tussle between pro-Soviet and pro-Chinese groups had already developed in the preliminary negotiations before the preparatory meeting; at the meeting itself, which took place in Djakarta at the end of October 1963, the Soviet Union continued its protests, and the Indonesian news agency's account of the text of the resolutions, complete with the appended Soviet reservations, was published in the PKI newspaper (*Harian Rakjat*, 4 November 1963). Two days later it published the version meant for general consumption, with the statement that the previous text should be regarded as non-existent. Presumably its purpose in issuing the first account was to demonstrate Soviet isolation. The Indonesian delegation was headed by Ahem Erningpradja, then Labour Minister and a major enemy of the PKI; in mid-1964 he travelled to Africa in connection with preparations for the conference and declared on his return that the project had foundered on the conflict between the Soviet and Chinese camps.

they had not lost their prejudice against the local minority by holding widespread anti-Chinese riots. It was probably for these reasons that Aidit suddenly announced, on returning from his journey of July–September 1963, that he had decided North Korea formed the model Asian socialist state and the proper example for Indonesian communism. Since then the party has given considerable attention to North Korea, which has reciprocated the Indonesian interest, among other things, by volunteering its entire parliament for service in the struggle against Malaysia. North Vietnam, which is closer and better known to Indonesians, might seem the more obvious choice, but Korea's considerable economic achievements probably impressed the visiting PKI leaders greatly; moreover, Vietnam's proximity is a disadvantage in that Indonesia increasingly considers itself the leading revolutionary force in Southeast Asia, a position the PKI has shown signs of sharing.

IMPORTANT as these international developments have been for the integration of the PKI with the Indonesian regime, it is unlikely that they will determine whether or not the party succeeds in coming to power. Other nations have drawn close to the East, only to drift back again; others have crushed their communist parties while allied with a communist power. What will decide the PKI's fate is its efforts to make itself an indispensable part of the domestic scene, and here its task is considerably more difficult. In the environment of guided democracy, crowded with symbols and slogans, there is little room for political diversity. The factional wills of parties and mass organisations must bow to the general will of the Indonesian peoples as expressed through Sukarno. It is closeness to the ideas set forth by the President, and thus closeness to the spirit of the revolution, that must determine whether or not a political group has a legitimate place on the public scene. The PKI has not attempted to press its claims to leadership of the national revolution, for all that its theoretical statements declare this to be essential. Instead, it has used loyalty to Sukarno and devotion to the principles of his Political Manifesto to demonstrate its legitimacy and to prove that its opponents are at heart disloyal. This approach has so far been most successful, though the communists are still not free from their two principal anxieties: that the party system will be abolished in favour of a monolithic political structure, and that the military may take control in a state of emergency.

Leaders of the nationalist-communist Murba party have been the principal spokesmen for anti-PKI sentiment and for a monolithic political structure; during 1964 they launched a vigorous campaign (some said as a Presidential trial balloon) to promote a one-party system. In mid-1964 sufficient cooperation among anti-PKI political elements was achieved for the establishment of an informal alliance between ten major newspapers under the leadership of the Murba-oriented *Berita Indonesia*; the journals have since coordinated their attacks on the communists, aiming principally at labelling the PKI a servant of China.

Labour organisations have also been exposed to efforts at creating a monolithic system; the non-communist unions have shown more sympathy than the parties for such attempts, probably because the PKI-sponsored federation SOBSI so completely dominates the labour field. The latest effort, launched in 1962, was SOKSI, an organisation that had the backing of the military, management, and various non-communist unions, and that received numerous privileges, among them that of distributing government rice rations to the employees. By mid-1963, however, SOKSI appeared to lose momentum; since then it has declined rapidly, and by mid-1964 seemed to present little challenge to the communist unions.

The state of emergency, which placed Indonesia under military control between 1957 and 1963, gave the PKI a most unpleasant time, for not only did it restrict general party activity but it gave a virtually free hand to the strongly anti-communist commanders of the military districts outside Java, with the result that the development of the movement in the Outer Islands, so important if the PKI is not to retain its label of being a Javanese party, was severely curtailed. The ending of the emergency did not remove the military from the scene, as the army was by then firmly entrenched in governmental, political and economic affairs; but it did give a stronger voice to the civilians in regional government and relaxed control of publications and meetings, of which the PKI has since made good use. Of even greater benefit to the party in its rivalry with the military has been the decline in the power of the army's outspokenly anti-PKI element, which proceeded with particular rapidity during 1964 and has gravely weakened the position of the armed forces chief of staff, General Nasution. This is not so much the product of a rise in pro-communist military sentiment, which appears to remain minimal, as it is of the substitution of officers who are faithful above all to Sukarno for those whose loyalties lie primarily with the army itself. The PKI has tried to mend its fences with the military and police by stressing its willingness to cooperate in preserving law and order and furthering the anti-Malaysia struggle; a whole series of addresses by Aidit on the subject of their common interest has been published in the last two years. Nonetheless, the PKI remains acutely aware of the inherent rivalry between the two groups, and accordingly expressed great concern lest the partial restoration of the state of emergency announced in 1964 as part of the Malaysia campaign be used to take power from civilian hands. It is for the same reason not eager to see the Malaysia quarrel pushed too far, for, as it has publicly stated, this might lead to an embroilment in which 'adventurist elements' might bid for power.

The problems involved in joining the administration illustrate a basic dilemma in the PKI's integration policy: the more the party makes itself acceptable to the regime, the less it differentiates itself from the status quo and the less effectively can it rally popular discontent. The lack of outlets for public opinion makes it difficult to know whether the party's identification with the regime has already caused a decline in its following (it claims a steady increase in membership). This appeared to be a particular danger during the food crisis of late 1963 and early 1964, when the PKI openly acknowledged that 'politics moves to the left but the stomach moves to the right' was a phenomenon that presented it with a serious problem. It is even more likely that the people might continue to see the PKI as representing them, but only within the present system, so that in a future PKI-government confrontation their allegiance would be questionable. Finally, there is the possibility that discontent with things as they are may result in a revolutionary outburst against the regime and with it the PKI; something of this sort appeared to threaten with the May 1963 anti-Chinese riots, which in various places were directed against the regime as well as the Chinese minority and which were notable for being carried out chiefly by students and other young people.

During the past year the PKI has pursued a course which, seen within the Indonesian context, is far from revolutionary. It has been a quite successful year, but within the terms of the PKI's assumptions and not necessarily in terms of ultimate victory. The party denounces the revisionists and the parliamentary road, and argues—when discussing the world communist movement, but seldom when considering its own situation—that the bourgeoisie will never willingly yield power to the workers and peasants. Is its present course the only way or simply the most attractive way? Does not Aidit's denunciation of the revisionists also contain a note of complacency at the positions the PKI leaders themselves have achieved? Many questions can be asked about the actual strength and loyalties of the party's mass following and the ability of its leaders to penetrate the system without being absorbed by it; in the end only the ultimate fate of the integration endeavour can provide an answer, and it is not likely that that strategy will be seriously challenged before Sukarno's death.

(3) JAPAN
Kyosuke Hirotsu

WHEN the Sino-Soviet dispute came out into the open at the 22nd CPSU congress in 1961, the Japanese Communist Party tried to maintain a neutral position. Even when both sides, as the controversy became more marked, published lengthy articles containing reciprocal accusations and attacks, the JCP still kept its formal distance, republishing the articles but strictly forbidding discussion within the party on the rights and wrongs of the substance of the dispute.

However, despite the claim to neutrality, there had already been since 1959 attacks on Shojiro Kasuga's faction, regarded as the pro-Soviet wing, as revisionists. Under the guise of ideological controversy with these revisionists, the central committee defined its position on a whole series of questions, such as its evaluation of American imperialism, war and peace, peace and national independence, peaceful co-existence and total disarmament, peaceful and non-peaceful roads to revolution, structural reform, etc. These problems are all related to the fundamental questions at issue between Moscow and Peking, and the conclusions reached were all at variance with the Soviet position and favourable to the Chinese.

The pretence of neutrality was discarded at the JCP central committee meeting in October 1963, following the breakdown of the Sino-Soviet conference, on which great hopes had been placed, in July, and the conclusion of the three-power test ban treaty. Neither neutralism nor hopes of mediation could any longer be maintained. The JCP therefore decided to adopt the report of its central committee presidium, confirmed by the central committee itself in October, stating that: ' Our party will maintain its autonomous and independent position on the controversy within the international communist movement, based on the principles of Marxism-Leninism and on facts, but it does not intend to adopt a neutral, mediatory, indifferent, or passive attitude towards the truth. So long as controversy exists on questions which have serious political and ideological implications for the future of the revolutionary movements of the whole world, it is only natural for communists to adopt this attitude, to pursue the truth and to assert as right what is right and as wrong what is wrong ' (*Akahata*, 10 November 1963). In the same issue, under the title ' For true solidarity and the advancement of the international communist movement ', the JCP launched an open attack on the Soviet Union, though it named neither that country itself nor Khrushchev. It rejected the argument that Yugoslavia had changed its attitude; the Tito faction had never modified its opposition to the revolutionary principles of the Moscow statements of 1957 and 1960. To treat Tito's party as a fraternal party and to support Yugoslav revisionists was against the interests of the international revolutionary movement. Secondly, responsibility for the open controversy rested on the party [i.e. the CPSU] which had openly criticised a brother party immediately after the 1960 conference, and had engaged in propaganda which distorted the conclusions of the conference. This trend had gone so far as to denounce the other brother party openly at a series of party congresses. Moreover, the party in question had continued its pernicious manoeuvres and had been trying to persuade Japanese party members to take action in opposition to JCP policy. Such interference in the internal affairs of brother parties infringed the principles of the two Moscow statements, and the JCP flatly rejected it.

E ARLIER in the year, the Communist Party of the Soviet Union, which was concerned at the growing support for the Chinese CP line, had sent a letter dated 22 February 1963, requesting the JCP to send a mission to the Soviet Union in order to adjust the differences in the views of the two parties. Two further letters followed towards the end of the year—on 12 October and 26 November—repeating the request.

The JCP finally decided to send four central committee members, Hakamada, Matsushima, Ishizawa, and Yonehara, to the Soviet Union, and a two-party conference was held in Moscow, lasting about two weeks from the end of February 1964. According to a letter dated 18 April 1964, from the central committee of the CPSU to the JCP, during the period from 2 to 11 March 1964, the representatives of the two parties held a series of five conferences, each lasting many hours. The CPSU delegation repeatedly proposed an exchange of views on important matters concerning the international communist movement and the relationship between the two parties, but the Japanese delegation refused to discuss these questions. Instead, they concentrated their efforts on raising ' objections ' to Soviet ' interference in the internal affairs of the Japanese Communist Party '. The true intentions of the JCP delegation in staging such manoeuvres, the Soviet letter added, were clear from the fact that these ' objections ' were raised in the form of an ultimatum, hinting that relations between the two parties might be severed. Furthermore, the Japanese refused to sign any joint communiqué on the conference.

With this visit, the friendly relations between the Japanese and Soviet Communist Parties, which had lasted for several decades, virtually came to an end.

On their way home, Hakamada and the other members stopped off in Peking to confer with the Chinese leaders, and then visited North Korea and North Vietnam, staying one week in each country. The delegation then returned to Peking, staying for nearly two months while they held conferences with Asian communist party leaders before returning home. The substance of these conferences in China, North Korea, and North Vietnam has not been made known, but on their return to Japan, Hakamada and his colleagues reported that their reception had been extremely friendly and enthusiastic. It has been suggested that the delegates probably discussed with the communist parties of these countries such questions as how to deal with the preparatory conference called by the CPSU for December, and how the ' united anti-American front ' could be organised by the Asian peoples in relation to the situation in Vietnam, Laos, South Korea, etc. However that may be, the ' fraternal solidarity ' among the Asian communist parties resolved upon at the JCP's central committee meeting in February 1963 can be considered as in many respects an accomplished fact.

> The communist parties and the peoples of Japan and China have had a common experience in fighting against a common enemy, Japanese imperialism. At present also, the two parties and the two peoples are carrying out joint struggles against American imperialism. The communist parties of China, Korea, Vietnam, Indonesia and other nations and their peoples are bound together with the Japanese Communist Party and the Japanese people in unbreakable brotherly solidarity, and this relationship will never change.

While Hakamada and the other members of the delegation were having their conferences in Moscow with Suslov and other CPSU leaders, *Akahata*, in its issue of 10 March 1964, carried an article entitled ' Kennedy and American imperialism '. The article is significant, for in it the JCP openly attacked the ' peaceful coexistence ' policy of the Soviet Union. At the same time, *Party Bulletin* announced that the JCP was planning to publish a series of theoretical articles criticising the Khrushchev line.

In short, with the failure of the meeting between the Japanese and Soviet representatives, the JCP finally decided on an open demonstration of its anti-Soviet attitude. It was against this background that the Shiga-Suzuki problem developed in May.

YOSHIO SHIGA, one of the foundation members of the JCP, who spent 18 years in prison with Tokuda and Miyamoto, and Ichiro Suzuki, a worker who has had a brilliant career and was a member of the party presidium, supported the ratification of the test ban treaty in the Diet on 15 May, and made public their opposition to the views of party headquarters.

Party Chairman Miyamoto, who had been recuperating in China, returned home at once and convened the central committee, which expelled Shiga and Suzuki from the party. Miyamoto accused the two men of ' engaging in conspiratorial activities, such as secretly contacting the Soviet Union, deceiving and betraying our party ', and of systematically ' dancing to the tune called by the Soviet Communist Party '. An unsigned article entitled ' The Place Where Revisionists Go ', carried in *Akahata* of 28 May, referring to a Moscow broadcast of 15 May which supported Yoshio Shiga's action and openly condemned the four communist members of the Diet who had voted against the test ban treaty, said: ' This open attack on our party is a crude violation of the principles governing relations among fraternal parties as embodied in the Moscow Statement, and we are bound to take a serious view of it. Our party firmly rejects these accusations, and at the same time reserves the right to answer them '.

The two members are not taking their expulsion lying down. Early in October they held a press conference, at which they claimed to be the 'true representatives' of the JCP; they were supported by two leading party intellectuals who protested against the 'bullying' to which they had been subjected.

On 11 July the Soviet Communist Party sent a letter to the Japanese central committee, sharply attacking their attitude:

> In the present situation, when the JCP leaders are, on the one hand, intensifying their attacks on the CPSU, and, on the other, are taking no steps to eliminate the disagreement existing between our two parties, which has now been brought to light, and when they avoid any discussion of our proposals and do not even consider it necessary to reply to our letters, the central committee of the CPSU can no longer conceal this matter from our party or keep the party in ignorance of the present state of affairs. We have decided, therefore, to make public our letter dated 18 April 1964, sent to the central committee of the JCP, together with the present letter, and we hereby inform you of this decision.

The letter of 18 April which the CPSU thereupon published, is an extremely lengthy one, enumerating in concrete terms the anti-Soviet actions which the leaders of the JCP central committee had been taking for several years past, and revealing in detail the speeches and actions of the JCP delegation to the Moscow conference in early March. The letter further refutes item by item the JCP's assertions on the test ban treaty and other questions. Since the JCP leaders had not even informed the central committee of the receipt of this letter, the commotion within the party raised by its publication was expected to have further repercussions. At the time of writing it has not yet been published in the Japanese communist press, although the answer to it (dated 15 July) appeared in *Akahata* of the 20th; this made a sharp attack on the Soviet Communist Party:

> It was your party that started the open controversy at its 22nd congress, thus violating the Moscow Statement. . . . It was also your party that launched an open attack on our party. It was you who published Comrade Zhukov's article in *Pravda* on 25 August last year, and thereby started to attack our party, mentioning our party by name. In addition, you have informed us that you will unilaterally make public your letter, which was sent to us in secret. In view of these facts alone, you bear the greatest responsibility for creating disunity in the international communist movement.

The North Korean party followed up with an article on 27 July condemning the Soviet attack on the JCP, and a day later the Chinese CP severely criticised the CPSU for this further instance of its 'betrayal of proletarian internationalism '.

On 2 September *Akahata* published the full text of the Japanese central committee's lengthy letter (dated 26 August) in reply to the CPSU letter of 18 April, and it was reproduced in the *People's Daily* on 13 September. In the same month Miyamoto visited Indonesia and signed a joint statement with Aidit condemning ' modern revisionism ' (*Akahata*, 10 September). He then went once more to Peking, where he was received by Mao Tse-tung.

SINCE the Chinese communist line is more relevant to underdeveloped than to highly developed countries, the JCP's adherence to it requires some explanation.

To some extent the geographic, racial, cultural, and historical ties between the two countries have engendered a special relationship which is reinforced by the commercial benefits they can gain from reciprocal trade. More important, however, is the fact that a great many of the JCP leaders were trained and educated in China, and have close personal ties with its leaders.

Just as, after the Russian revolution, Lenin and Trotsky placed great hopes on a successful revolution in Germany, so today the Chinese communist leaders are prepared to do much to promote revolution in Japan, which would not only provide strong industrial backing for their own country, but also deprive the United States of its most powerful ally in the Pacific. American imperialism, they assert, is planning to use Japan as a base from which to attack the Chinese mainland.

When a Japanese ' Workers' Educational Association ' delegation (most of its members were communists) visited China in August 1962, Mao Tse-tung is reported to have told them that ' China attaches great importance to the liberation of Japan. The first revolution in the world was the Russian revolution. That changed the world. The second was the Chinese revolution. That, too, has changed history. As we have recently witnessed, colonies have almost ceased to exist, and capitalism has been weakened. The third revolution will be the Japanese. When Japan is liberated, the East will be liberated and that will lead to the liberation of the world. The liberation of Japan will be of the greatest significance to the course of world history '.

Since its own accession to power, the Chinese CP has given strong support to the Japanese communists; it has conducted surveys and studies of the Japanese internal situation, working chiefly through Sanzo Nozaka (one of the JCP's most prominent leaders) and others who had been in exile in Yenan from the time of the outbreak of the Sino-Japanese war in 1937. It also organised the ' Japanese People's Liberation League ' among Japanese prisoners of war, who were given courses in Marxism-Leninism. Some of the prisoners were sent to the ' Yenan School of Industry and Agriculture ', where they were trained in the theory and techniques of revolution, as preparation for their future role in Japan.

At the time of the Korean War, United States headquarters in Japan (the country was still controlled by the American forces) took steps to curb the JCP. Its secretary-general at that time, Kyuichi Tokuda, and many other party leaders, immediately went underground, left Japan secretly, and went to China. There they were said to have been given intensive training in the conduct of illegal activities, based on the Chinese formula for revolutionary movements. It was as a result of this guidance that the JCP adopted and operated the guerrilla tactics which characterised its activities in 1951 and 1952.

In addition to the leaders, a large number of young Japanese communists, many of them being sought by the police, also left Japan for China. They were sent to the ' School of Marxism-Leninism ' and given several years of basic party education and training. Altogether, from 1953 to 1957, China is said to have received about 1,500 Japanese communist ' stowaways '. Many of them returned home in the spring of 1958. They form the nucleus of the pro-China faction within the JCP, and are said to control at party headquarters the organisation department, the personnel division, the trade union department, the financial committee, and the *Akahata* editorial board.

AT the time of the 7th party congress in 1958, the pro-Soviet faction (including Shojiro Kasuga, Tomochika Naito, and Yoshio Shiga) and the neutral faction (including Secretary-General Miyamoto, Harushige Matsushima, and Koreto Kurahara) expelled Shigeo Shida, Etsuro Shiino, and other pro-China elements from the party, but with the return of the young communists from China, and their appointment to important positions at headquarters and in local bodies, the balance gradually swung the other way. The pro-Chinese wing was reinforced by the new members who joined the JCP during the campaign against the Security Treaty in 1960; and, just before the assembly of the 8th party congress in July 1961, the pro-Soviet faction, including Shojiro Kasuga, was defeated in the ' Platform controversy ' and expelled from the party. About 400 party members supporting the pro-Soviet faction were either expelled or resigned.

At the 8th congress itself, the pro-Chinese faction monopolised the important positions at the party centre, and the strengh of Secretary-General Miyamoto's faction, which was said to be neutral, declined. The pro-Chinese leaders are getting abundant Chinese financial aid, and there is no immediate prospect of their losing their hold on the party machine.

Three years ago, when Shojiro Kasuga's faction was expelled from the JCP, the Soviet Communist Party refrained from comment. Its endorsement of the support given by Shiga and Suzuki to the test ban treaty, and its condemnation of the central committee's attitude, was therefore the more worthy of note. It has had its effect on the internal situation of the JCP where, even at headquarters, there were still some who approved the action of Shiga and his faction. In local party organisations, too, there seemed to be a marked tendency to criticise the central committee's devotion to China, though this is probably not a nation-wide tendency.

On 11 June 1964, twelve prominent scholars, men of letters, and artists, all members of the communist party (among them Takashi Ide, Ineko Sata, Hiroshi Noma, Katsujiro Yamada, and Setsu Asakura), submitted a petition on the Shiga question to the central committee:

> Having been deeply perplexed by the dilemma of whether we must blindly follow even such decisions as will obviously lead to an anti-Soviet split, or whether we should observe that international discipline which is a prerequisite for communist parties in all countries, we have come to the conclusion that the latter course would be in the true spirit and responsibility of communism.

Action such as this would normally merit immediate expulsion from the party, but the central committee procrastinated.

Crucial for the future was the fate of Secretary-General Miyamoto's faction which, from an allegedly 'autonomous and independent' standpoint, was striving to maintain a somewhat more neutral position and to promote unity within the Japanese Communist Party. Around 1950, Kenji Miyamoto joined forces with Shiga, Kasuga, Hakamada, and others, to contest the leadership of the Nozaka-Tokuda faction. Most of Miyamoto's comrades in those days are now in the pro-Soviet group.

Miyamoto visited China for about three months, from February 1964; he was accompanied by his wife and children, a doctor, a nurse, and some others, and was said to be recuperating from illness. At that time a rumour was circulating both within and outside the party that he was 'being brain-washed', but an analysis of what he said on his hurried return to Japan to deal with the Shiga problem does not suggest that he has been completely converted to a totally pro-Chinese policy. His visit to Peking, in mid-September, marked, however, another step in the assertion of Chinese control over the Japanese Communist Party, a process which was consolidated indirectly by the removal of Khrushchev and the subsequent Soviet efforts to achieve a détente with Peking. This put the 'Voices of Japan' group led by Shiga, and other pro-Soviet elements, into an impossible position. They were left politically in mid-air, unable to justify their opposition to the party leadership and no longer able to draw ammunition from Sino-Soviet polemics. By the same token, any remaining potentially pro-Soviet elements in the party must have been still more demoralised, and if they had entertained the idea of joining the pro-Soviet communists, they must now have abandoned it. The Chinese position has thus been strengthened and consolidated in the Japanese party and its front organisations. This was perhaps best symbolised by the congratulatory telegram sent to Peking after the explosion of the Chinese atomic bomb, by Kaoru Yasui, the founder and leader of the Japanese Council against Atomic and Hydrogen Bombs (*Gensuikyo*). When, at the 10th conference of this organisation in August 1964 in Tokyo, the Russian and the pro-Russian delegations walked out in protest, *Pravda* expressed its pained surprise that Kaoru Yasui, the Lenin Prize winner (and before the war a leading militarist and pro-Nazi jurist at Tokyo university), should follow the Chinese line, and implied that he had shown some reluctance in conversation with the *Pravda* correspondent. It is unlikely that he was in fact reluctant, considering that at the time *Gensuikyo* was under the complete control of the pro-Chinese leaders of the JCP. But he is certainly even less reluctant now.

The reaction of the JCP to the dismissal of Khrushchev was more immediate and more explicit than the Chinese. On the day following the announcement Miyamoto declared that it made manifest the failure of his policy, but added that 'history teaches us that the errors of a party cannot be corrected merely by changing the central figure of the leadership of the party'. If the new leaders tried to improve their relations with China and stopped 'compromising with the imperialists', the JCP would look towards the restoration of friendly relations with the CPSU, but if they persisted in the wrong policy, they would be firmly opposed by the Japanese communists. Miyamoto expressed the hope that the new leaders would understand that Khrushchev's 'resignation' was 'a clear indication of bankruptcy' and would give up the idea of holding a conference of 26 parties in Moscow (*Akahata*, 17 October 1964).

On 4 November *Akahata* accused Shiga of making a 'conspiratorial trip' to Russia to persuade the new leaders to give their support to the formation of a new pro-Soviet Japanese party. On 12 November the same paper announced the expulsion from the JCP of the ten writers and intellectuals of the so-called 'cultural group' who had protested against the expulsion of Shiga and Suzuki. This is important, for it signifies a break with the intellectuals whose support gave the JCP such a hold on the universities and on intellectual life in general. The decline of Marxist influence among the intellectuals has been visible for some time, and this will accelerate it. The formal proclamation by Shiga of the new pro-Soviet party, 'Voice of Japan Comrades Group' on 2 December can hardly have important repercussions at the moment on Japanese political life, but it may contribute further to the divisions and ferment among the country's Marxist intellectuals.

AUSTRALASIA

T. H. Rigby

OPERATING in economically advanced countries of European population situated on the outskirts of Asia, Australian and New Zealand
communists have been subjected to peculiarly acute pressures by the
Sino-Soviet dispute. Their anomalous geopolitical position accounts for
the roles assumed in the international movement: the Communist Party
of New Zealand (CPNZ) was the only ' white' party apart from the
Albanian which supported Peking, whereas the Communist Party of
Australia (CPA) was the only ' official' party in the South-East Asia area
supporting Moscow, opposed, it is true, by a small but vociferous breakaway party. The CPA is also the only party which has changed sides in
the dispute. All this can be understood only against the specific
historical background of Australasian communism. The dispute
reactivated its particularities and a tactical accommodation between
Moscow and Peking will not make them disappear. A closer examination of the local consequences of the dispute is therefore a necessary
preliminary to any realistic analysis of the prospects of communism
there in the post-Khrushchev era.

A high level of industrialisation along with a working-class movement
which, despite its predominant reformism, contains a strong radical strain,
combined to give Australia relatively the most influential communist
party in the English-speaking world. Nevertheless in neither country
does communism play more than a marginal role. Both parties have
sunk to about a fifth of their membership at the end of World War Two.
Communist candidates regularly lose their deposits in national and state
elections and neither party is represented in parliament. Up to the early
fifties some indirect influence was exerted through front organisations, but
this has been crippled by the disillusionment of most party intellectuals
and fellow-travellers and by the growing sophistication among non-
communists as to the party's methods. Communist strength in the trade
unions has also declined considerably since the early post-war years, but
this remains one field where these parties (especially the CPA) continue
to make an important impact on national life.

Up to 1961, relations between the CPA and CPNZ were extremely
close. The CPNZ originated as an offshoot of the CPA, and the CPA
leadership played a crucial part at decisive points in its history. Although
the Sino-Soviet dispute has allowed the CPNZ leadership to assert their
independence of Sydney (one is again reminded of the Albanian party,
and of the independence which Tirana gained from the Sino-Yugoslav
dispute in 1948), the split in Australasian communism has been deeply
disturbing to the rank and file of both parties.

A certain weakness for ' leftist ', ' dogmatic ', ' adventurist ' policies is
apparent in the history of the CPA. Although no doubt facilitated by

radical working-class traditions, this is usually attributed to the personality and outlook of its General Secretary, Mr L. L. Sharkey. Sharkey was one of the leftists installed by the Comintern in 1929, when Stalin was moving against the ' Right ' both at home and in the international movement, and he has dominated Australasian communism since the mid-thirties. Although the CPA followed the zigs and zags of Stalin's policies with commendable alacrity, observers have detected a ' leftist ' bias in such things as Sharkey's controversy with the British Communist Party in the early post-war period over the proper attitude to Labour governments, the alleged radicalising influence of the CPA on communist policies in South-East Asia at the same time, and the disastrous 1949 coal strike (in which the Federal Labour Government successfully called the bluff of communist-controlled unions in the New South Wales coalfields). Other observers, however, contest this attribution of ' leftism ', and explain such events in terms of Sharkey's single-mindedness as an executant of Moscow's policies.[1] Be this as it may, in the early fifties Sharkey was faced with a challenge to his leadership from the ' Right ', and his victory set the party in a ' dogmatist ' posture which may have influenced its reactions to the divisions in international communism which began to appear in 1956.

In New Zealand CPNZ Secretary Wilcox has been at the helm for a much shorter time, but he is very much a man of the Sharkey mould. The consolidation of his power dates from the 1951 waterfront strike, a party defeat that was comparable in its impact with the 1949 coal strike in Australia. Wilcox and his friends appear to have made deliberate use of the switch to a semi-illegal footing after the strike in order to entrench themselves and to discredit and squeeze out their critics and moderates like ex-secretary Sid Scott.

SOON after the establishment of the Chinese People's Republic, the facts of geography began to modify the Moscow-centrism of Australasian communism. By 1951 a group of CPA cadres was studying in Peking, and by the mid-fifties (reputedly according to a Sino-Soviet agreement on division of training responsibilities), Peking had become the normal training ground for Australian and New Zealand communists. The two parties sponsored a constant flow of delegations, particularly of trade unionists, and party members on their way to Eastern Europe began regularly stopping off in Peking. Works by Mao and Liu Shao-chi became prescribed reading in party study courses. Peking soon became one of the twin Meccas of communism for Australian and New Zealand communists, as it did for their comrades throughout the East and South-East Asian area generally. Young communists in particular, being less set in Stalinist patterns, tended to be attracted by the apparent dynamism, mildness, and absence of bureaucratic rigidity of China.

---

[1] I am obliged to Mr J. Normington-Rawling, author of a forthcoming study on the history of the CPA, for a well-argued statement of this evaluation of Sharkey.

The international communist movement has shown a continuing interest in ' Oceania ', treating it as one of the main areas of the ' national liberation ' struggle.[2] Strategic considerations, highlighted by United States and French nuclear tests, have increased the international importance of the small communities in these scattered islands in recent years. Nevertheless, no autonomous communist organisation is believed to exist in the area. The CPA is responsible for Papua-New Guinea and has a New Guinea Bureau. The CPNZ failed in its attempt in 1947 to establish a communist party in Fiji, but this rapidly developing territory of mixed Indian and Fijian population has been the most important centre of communist attentions. In recent years the CPNZ has concentrated its efforts in the Cook Islands and to a lesser extent Western Samoa and Fiji. The CPA has made energetic use of the communist-controlled Australian Seamen's Union to establish contact with local labour activists throughout the area, and claims to have played an active part in stimulating strike activity and hostility towards the administering authorities.

IF the events of 1956 consolidated the hold of the Stalinoid bureaucracy on the CPA and CPNZ, by removing most of the party intellectuals, they also cast a shadow over the authority of Moscow. According to Mr E. F. Hill, the leader of the present pro-Peking group, the CPA twice tackled the CPSU leadership over their ' capitulationist ' policies during 1956.[3] While doubts about Soviet communism led some Australasian communists into ' revisionism ', others could bolster their faith by focusing on the Chinese alternative. The close contacts of recent years now assumed crucial importance, making Australasian communists immeasurably more aware of the existence of this alternative than were their European comrades. To the leadership, however, the orthodoxy of the CPC remained in doubt in 1956–57, and this inhibited any clear alignment with Peking. It was China's swing to the left in its internal and foreign policies in 1957–59 which dispelled these misgivings. At this stage Peking met the needs of Stalinists and non-Stalinists alike: to the former it offered a halt to destalinisation and uncompromising condemnation of ' revisionism '; to the latter it offered a more dynamic and flexible pattern for building communism untainted by Stalin's ' mistakes '. It thereby provided the focus around which unity and some degree of confidence were restored in the Australian and New Zealand parties after the debâcle of 1956. This explains why these parties emerged as supporters of the Peking line in 1959–60 when Sino-Soviet differences began to disrupt the outward unity of the international movement and to cause parties to stand up and be counted.

2 E.g. the 81-parties statement declared that ' the conference expresses solidarity with all the peoples of Asia, Africa, Latin America and Oceania, struggling against imperialism '.
3 See *Declaration of Australian Marxist Leninists*, Melbourne, 1963, p. 8.

At the 81-parties conference in November 1960, both the CPA (which sat on the 26-party preparatory commission) and the CPNZ apparently supported the Chinese against the Russians on the basic issues under dispute. Together with the Albanians, they were the only parties of European population to do so. Nevertheless it must have been a discon- certing experience for Australasian communists, especially to an old Comintern hand like Sharkey, to find themselves in a minority ranged against Moscow. Sharkey subsequently told of his opposition to the extravagant Albanian attacks on the Soviet leadership and, while making due allowance for the exigencies of intra-party apologetics, it is reason- able to suppose that he was dismayed at the turn the dispute had now taken and began to entertain misgivings at his own party's position.[4]

The CPNZ's refusal to accept Soviet discipline at the 81-parties con- ference was reaffirmed a year later in the Albanian crisis which broke at the 22nd CPSU congress. Although there were some indications in the selection of overseas materials to support the impression that the party continued to favour the Chinese, CPNZ propaganda throughout this period avoided direct mention of the dispute or open identification with either side. This posture was consistent with CPNZ efforts at this time to encourage conciliatory talks between the CPC and the CPSU.[5] Beginning with its national conference in April 1963, however, New Zealand com- munist spokesmen emphatically ranged their party in the Chinese camp. Shortly after the conference Wilcox visited Peking, and a joint statement issued by the CPC and the CPNZ, together with a speech delivered by Wilcox at the Chinese Higher Party School, indicated complete identity of views between the two parties.[6] In August 1963 four CPNZ Political Committee members visited Moscow for ' fraternal talks on ideological difficulties' in response to an invitation issued some five months earlier, but Wilcox's exchanges with Suslov on this occasion served only to emphasise the incompatibility of their positions.[7] Since then the CPNZ has proudly assumed an honoured place in the Chinese camp.

---

[4] Mr Alistair Davidson, who is engaged in research at the Australian National University on the history of the CPA, has suggested that Sharkey's apparent failure to take as unqualified a pro-Chinese position at the 81-parties conference as his mandate from the Political Committee indicated, as well as changes in the tone of party propaganda during 1961, indicate that the CPA began to re-align itself on Moscow in November 1960 and not in November-December 1961 as is usually thought. The present article places this question in a slightly different light, but much remains obscure about this period and subsequent evidence may well lend some weight to Davidson's contention.

[5] See Report of National Committee to CPNZ national conference, *New Zealand Communist Review*, April 1963, p. 3. It has recently been suggested that differences within the CPNZ leadership may have played a part as well, in particular that Party Chairman Jackson, who was replaced in March 1963, may have represented a relatively pro-Soviet tendency and resisted a policy of open identification with the CPC as long as he could.

[6] See *Peking Review*, 31 May 1963.

[7] See V. G. Wilcox, *New Zealand Party's Firm Stand*, Auckland, no date (1963?).

THE history of the CPA since 1960 has been far more complex and eventful. No formal reappraisal of the party's position appears to have occurred till December 1961, and meanwhile the leadership firmly resisted rank-and-file requests for an intra-party discussion of the matters at issue between the CPC and the CPSU. In their rare public references to the international movement, party spokesmen not only refrained from taking sides in the dispute but blandly denied that any serious differences now existed.[8] Beneath the surface, however, the issue was very much alive. Differences of emphasis appeared between the propaganda of the Victorian branch, containing about a quarter of the CPA membership, and the other branches. The Victorian branch was led by E. F. Hill, a member of the CPA's key executive body, the four-man National Secretariat, and throughout 1961 it pursued a strong and uncompromising pro-Peking line. Members who questioned the line and demanded access to Soviet as well as Chinese views were forced out of the party.[9] Two members of the State Executive,[10] who challenged Hill's policies, were eventually forced to capitulate and one was packed off abroad on a study course. In other states, where the propaganda posture could perhaps be characterised as ' neutrality from a Chinese standpoint ', there was less trouble. Nevertheless, there is some evidence of a gradual realignment of ideological positions among party cadres at this period. The failure of the ' Great Leap Forward ' disillusioned many younger members who had formerly taken the lead in the turn to Peking. At the same time, as critics of the Hill machine in Victoria were saying openly, dogmatic, leftist policies were hamstringing the party's work in the trade unions and front organisations. On the other hand there was the agonising dilemma of older Stalinist internationalists, notably Sharkey himself, who, since the 81-parties conference, had realised that their Stalinism might lead to their organisational isolation from Moscow and from the bulk of the international movement. These moods and doubts helped to clear the way for the open desertion of Peking, which occurred at the end of 1961.

The Hill group subsequently alleged that these changing attitudes were in large part induced by personnel changes masterminded in Moscow and carried out by Mr L. Aarons, secretariat member responsible for cadres,

8 See e.g. Sharkey's statement to the Sydney district conference in April 1961 that ' such difference of views as existed ' had been resolved at the 81-parties conference, and that ' the differences no longer existed and are therefore not a subject it would be useful to re-discuss now ' (*Guardian* (Melbourne), 20 April 1961). In an article in the *Communist Review* for April 1961 he said that ' revisionist ranks from our party assist the class enemy by circulating rubbishy gossip about the meeting of the 81 parties about which their knowledge is practically nil '.
9 The most celebrated expulsion of the period was that of Mr G. T. McDonald, a member of the Melbourne District Committee and long-time trade union organiser, who went to unusual lengths to gain publicity for his position. See *Nation* (Sydney), 25 February 1961 and 25 March 1961.
10 Messrs B. Taft and H. K. Stanistreet, who later returned in triumph to the Victorian leadership with the defeat of the Hill group. It has been suggested that these officials were representative of a small section of Victorian cadres and rank-and-filers who had been influenced by the ideas of Italian and Polish communism.

and that Aarons' own increased influence at this period was also connived at by the CPSU leaders. Hill's Moscow-plot myth may contain a few grains of truth. It would be strange indeed if the International Department of the Soviet Central Committee had not made some effort to exploit the malaise in the CPA to shift influential party opinion in favour of the CPSU. Aarons, Hill's most serious competitor for the succession to the ageing Sharkey, was undoubtedly less set in a dogmatic, Stalinist mould than Hill, and of all the national leaders he probably found it easiest to sympathise with the moods of doubt about the party's ' Chinese ' policies, whose existence we have noted. At the same time, Aarons' responsibilities for cadres and the senior party positions held by several members of his family, enabled him to win an organisational predominance in all states except Victoria, and Aarons must have realised that a re-alignment of the CPA with Moscow would destroy Hill's authority and clinch the succession issue in his favour.

Despite these pressures, it seems very doubtful that any decision had yet been agreed when Sharkey left to attend the 22nd CPSU congress on 24 September 1961, whatever point Sharkey's own ideas may have reached by this stage. His speech of greeting at the congress, which failed to condemn the Albanian leadership, suggested that the CPA was still in the Chinese camp, although its tone is probably best characterised as neutral. The CPA delegation's statement on the results of the congress, published a fortnight later, came closer to pro-Soviet positions, but was still very guarded.[11] The CPA was one of the ten communist parties to send greetings on 8 November on the twentieth anniversary of the founding of the Albanian Party of Labour. However, a meeting of the Political Committee convened immediately after the delegation's return to Sydney in December adopted a statement giving unequivocal support to the CPSU and made an explicit attack on the Albanian leadership. This appears to constitute prima facie evidence supporting Hill's claim that Sharkey did not finally make up his mind until some stage during the five weeks he spent in Moscow *after* the 22nd congress closed.[12]

Hill is probably also right in implying that Sharkey's decision was crucial in promoting the party's re-alignment, not only because of the General Secretary's standing amongst Australian communists, but also because of the divisions in the party at large, and, more pertinently, within the leadership. Sharkey could count on Hill's opposition to a re-alignment and on Aarons' support; the fourth Secretariat member, Richard Dixon (who had played Molotov to Sharkey's Stalin since the thirties, and who would probably have been at best luke-warm), was at this time recuperating in Moscow from a heart attack; Sharkey's own weight thrown on one side or the other would therefore be decisive.

[11] See *Tribune*, 8 November 1961.
[12] See *Declaration of Australian Marxist-Leninists*, p. 7.

WHAT were his motives? Of central importance was his fear of isolation from the international movement, which now outweighed his distaste for Khrushchev's ' revisionist ' leanings: it was one thing to push for a change in Moscow's policies, but quite another to range oneself against Moscow with a handful of ' splitters '. At the same time Sharkey must have had an eye for the national as well as the international implications of his decision. Whatever he did, there was a serious danger of splitting the party. But, given the relative strength of Aarons and Hill, and the movements of opinion among the middle cadres, plumping for Moscow afforded him the best chance of carrying the bulk of the party with him and containing any breakaway movement. By this time it is extremely doubtful that a majority could be found for the Chinese line among the CC members, who recognised its tendency to isolate the party within the working-class movement and obstruct its institutional influence on the non-communist left, and Sharkey himself was realist enough to acknowledge the validity of this attitude. In this way the organisational and ideological shifts of the preceding period probably helped to determine his choice.

The spectre of a split was not long in materialising. The Central Committee was convened in February 1962, and Hill vigorously criticised the December statement of the Political Committee and voted against it, along with a small group of supporters. Sharkey and Aarons struck back quickly, and Hill was removed from the Victorian State Secretaryship and from membership of the National Secretariat. The editor of the Victorian communist newspaper, *The Guardian,* was dismissed, and other changes followed. Nevertheless, a substantial proportion of Victorian cadres remained loyal to Hill, including several members of the State Committee and a handful of the Central Committee. By means of a graduated campaign of pressure and threats, the national leadership tried to force their capitulation and so avoid an open split. Hill's supporters, however, continued to attack official policies at all committee levels, and in June 1963, after some eighteen months of internal dissension, Hill was expelled from the central committee. In the following weeks some 200 resignations and expulsions of lesser pro-Peking communists were reported. Hill was formally expelled from the CPA on 22 August. Meanwhile Sharkey and Dixon made a six-weeks visit to Moscow, where they conferred with Brezhnev and Ponomarev, while Hill went to Peking, where he apparently had talks with Indonesian and New Zealand representatives, as well as with the Chinese. On his return, he called a public meeting of his supporters, at which the formation of a ' genuine ' Marxist-Leninist party was predicted, he began to issue a newspaper and a theoretical journal, and to organise support in the Victorian branches of a number of unions. Finally, in March 1964, he convened a meeting of supporters in Melbourne, which agreed ' to reconstitute the Australian communist movement as the Communist Party of Australia (Marxist-Leninist) '.[13]

Meanwhile the battle was also engaged in the ' mass organisations '. After some fierce skirmishes Hill's supporters were eventually silenced in the Union of Australian Women and the Eureka Youth League. In the trade unions, however, they have held their ground, although their influence is still virtually confined to Victoria.[14] In the ' peace movement ', the two parties are working in rival organisations. The CPA participated in the Australian Congress for International Cooperation and Disarmament, held in Sydney at the end of October 1964. (Playing safe, the words ' New Zealand ' were dropped from the original title.) The CPA (M-L) is meanwhile seeking to revive the Peace Liaison Committee for the Asian and Pacific Regions, and an exploratory meeting to this end was held in Melbourne in April 1964. Subsequently the Australian Peace Liaison Committee was formed in Melbourne with the Rev. Victor James as chairman and Mrs Betty Little as secretary. These persons then left for a visit to Peking, and since the Rev. James was a foundation member and vice-chairman of the Peace Liaison Committee for the Asian and Pacific regions when it was founded in 1952, it is reasonable to conclude that his trip to China was connected with a possible link-up between the two organisations.

The attachment of the CPA and the CPNZ to rival camps within the world communist movement shattered the close association which had existed since their inception, and posed the question of their future relations, a question complicated by the existence of the Hill party. In October 1963 the CPA leadership wrote to the CPNZ proposing a meeting of delegations. After three earlier dates had been rejected by the New Zealanders, talks were finally arranged for April 1964.[15] In the meantime, however, Hill had visited Auckland and consulted with the CPNZ leaders, much to the indignation of the CPA. In a speech in Canton, Wilcox justified this meeting with the words ' what were we supposed to do: ignore him and only talk with the revisionists? ' [16]

The CPA-CPNZ talks were held in Sydney on 6–9 April. A joint statement was issued, couched in very general terms and foreshadowing further talks on disputed issues, and separate statements were made by the two parties.[17] The latter contained mutual accusations of betrayal

13 See *Vanguard* (Melbourne), No. 10, March 1964.
14 In the recent Waterside Workers' Federation elections, however, a Hill supporter obtained no fewer than 1,500 votes in the port of Sydney. See *The Bulletin*, 1 August 1964. The existence of two labour parties and two communist parties has given Australian trade union politics a complexity allowing almost infinite possibilities of manoeuvre, of which the Hill group has made able use, not hesitating to support Australian Labour Party candidates to defeat sitting CPA officials. See e.g. Between Moscow and Peking—the CP of Australia (*Current Affairs Bulletin*, University of Sydney, 1964).
15 *Tribune* (Sydney), 1 April 1964, where extracts from the correspondence leading up to the talks are reproduced.
16 *People's Voice*, 18 December 1963; *Peking Review*, 20 March 1964.
17 *Tribune*, 22 April 1964.

of the 81-party statement, but dealt largely with the problem of the Hill group. The CPA claimed that, despite ideological differences, there was considerable room for cooperation ' on the many issues of common concern ', but that the opportunities in this direction were being jeopardised by CPNZ contacts with the Hill group. For their part, the CPNZ leaders stated that ' we will meet and discuss with all Communist Parties matters of common interest; but we will also meet and discuss with anybody matters of Marxist-Leninist theory and principle on the basis of mutual help in the defence of Marxism-Leninism '. In August 1964 Wilcox called for a conference of pro-Chinese parties, as a counter-move to the December conference in Moscow.

Meanwhile the two Australasian pro-Peking parties have been consolidating their links with the Communist Party of Indonesia (PKI). The inaugural conference of the CPA (M-L) authorised Hill to send greetings to the PKI, to which Aidit cabled the following reply. ' Many thanks for your message. In order to increase our knowledge of Australian communist movement we shall be happy to receive you in Djakarta.' [18] Early in June, Wilcox visited Indonesia, where he lectured on CPNZ policies, and held talks with Aidit and other PKI leaders. A long joint statement emphasised that ' the two parties hold similar views on all international questions discussed, including the problems that have arisen recently in the international communist movement '.[19] These moves have further accentuated the geographical isolation of the CPA.

THE CPNZ leaders were now too entrenched in their pro-Peking policies to allow any serious possibility of retreat. Moreover, although the CPA would no doubt have been glad to retaliate for CPNZ collusion with Hill by fostering a breakaway pro-Moscow party in New Zealand, it could not do so. The tiny New Zealand Left could scarcely accommodate a viable organisation in between the ' dogmatist ' CPNZ and the 1956–58 ' revisionists ' grouped around the *New Zealand Monthly Review*.

Observers have detected in the CPA a wide range of opinion from crypto-Hillites, through pro-Soviet dogmatists like Sharkey and Dixon (*plus catholique que le pape*), to younger opportunists looking to Aarons as the future leader, and finally to the small Italian-oriented ' Right '. The last named, already an influential group in the Victorian branch, could become a problem in the future. They are reported to entertain misgivings about the CPA's participation in the preparatory talks called

---

[18] *Vanguard*, June 1964. It is significant that a recent visit to Djakarta by two prominent CPA officials took place with a minimum of ceremony and failed to result in the traditional joint party communiqué (see *Tribune*, 5 August 1964), thus strengthening the impression of PKI preference for the CPA (M-L). Meanwhile it seems likely that Hill, on his visit to China and North Korea in April-May 1964, had discussions with PKI and CPNZ representatives, visiting there at the same time, and there have indeed been suggestions that about this time Peking was the scene of consultations on tactics between a number of parties favouring the CPC.
[19] *Peking Review*, June 19, 1964.

in Moscow to prepare a new world communist meeting. It has been suggested that if this group grows and the Aarons machine fails to absorb it, a further split might ensue in the CPA.[20] Failing such calamities, however, the CPA appears to hold nearly all the cards in its contest with the CPA (M-L). The great majority of party members and cadres outside Victoria have stayed with them. They have retained the established organisation and the established sources of finance, and are able therefore to command the services of well over 100 full-time officials.

The main assets possessed by their rivals are the concentration of adherents in Victoria, the firm and able leadership of Ted Hill, and the support of the Chinese. They have held well-attended meetings, formally established their party, retained a considerable number of trade union jobs, and kept up a constant stream of propaganda (though distribution outside Victoria is meagre), usefully augmented by Chinese material sent out directly by Radio Peking. One of the unknown factors is the extent to which Peking will be willing to help them financially as well as morally. It seems doubtful, however, that the pro-Chinese party will attempt to set up a full-scale organisation with a hierarchy of regular committees and paid officials to match the CPA. The pattern of organisation is more likely to be that of the illegal party, with a minimum of formal organisation and bureaucratic apparatus, and a considerable proportion of undeclared members. One of the main objects of the CPA (M-L) must be to penetrate the CPA with a view to disrupting it and ultimately taking it over. Outside left-wing circles the appeal of its militant and dogmatic propaganda is likely to be very limited, and it will have great difficulty competing with the CPA, except in certain trade union situations. But one should not underestimate its potential appeal for the rank and file and middle cadres of the CPA itself. This is an asset which Ted Hill seems to be quite consciously exploiting. His writings, militant, dogmatic, mythopoeic, at times almost incantational, ring with the authentic note of pre-1956 communism; it was this note that brought a great number of Australian communists into the party, gave them their sense of mission, and sustained them through stress and trouble, and many of them may be tempted to answer the call and take refuge from their doubts.

The Australian and New Zealand parties now find themselves on opposite sides of the fence, but on one question they would be completely agreed: it would have been far better if the fence had never been erected. In the statements issued after their April talks there were some wistful references to the lost Eden when there were ' no such differences between the CPA and the CPNZ '. Both parties attempted to keep the Sino-Soviet dispute from their rank and file and to avoid taking sides publicly for as long as possible, and both have been active in moves to find a

20 According to Mr Fred Wells, the writings of Gramsci have been circulating clandestinely in the Victorian branch. A member of the state executive is reported to have said: ' Why worry about learning Russian—learn Italian.'

formula for agreement. Their reaction to polycentric and fissiparous tendencies differed from that of major communist parties like those of France, Italy, or Indonesia, which have seen these tendencies as far from an unmixed evil. It may well be true that the larger the communist party and the better its chances of achieving power by its own efforts, the less interest its leaders are likely to feel in maintaining the discipline of the international movement and the authority of its top spokesmen, because this discipline and authority militate against the influence they can themselves exert in the movement and the independence they might hope to enjoy in the event of achieving power. Different considerations apply in the case of small parties like the CPA and CPNZ. The only chance their leaders have to play an international role is as agents of the world communist leaders, and their prospects of achieving power are entirely dependent on the fortunes of the international struggle. To quote Sharkey at the 19th CPA congress:

> Our party is still small and maybe sometimes it makes us feel that after all it is too small in relation to other parties in this country and that we are not advancing as rapidly as we would wish. This is true, but the situation is developing in our favour and the contributions at this Congress indicate that we have widespread influence that extends into all spheres of the life of our country. But it must not be overlooked that part of the strength, and a very considerable part, is contributed by the fact that we are not alone in the world but are an integral part of the great communist movement whose vanguard is the Soviet Union.[21]

For this reason their interests are closely involved in the cohesion and discipline of the international movement. What they fear most of all is isolation, and both Australian communist parties made play with this fear in their propaganda. The CPA never tired of stressing that they are lined up with the great majority of parties throughout the world, while the CPA (M-L) emphasised their solidarity with the communists of the Asian and Pacific area. Asserting that their party 'takes its place in South-East Asia alongside the Marxist-Leninist Communist parties of New Zealand, Indonesia, China, Burma, Korea, Malaya, Ceylon, Laos, and Japan ',[22] they wrote of Sharkey, Dixon, and Aarons that in embracing Soviet revisionism, they 'thereby isolate themselves not only from the Australian masses but from the South-East Asian masses, notably from the Marxist-Leninist position of the communist parties of Indonesia and New Zealand.[23]

21 *Communist Review*, August 1961, p. 342.
22 *Vanguard*, No. 10, March 1964.
23 *The Australian Communist*, January 1964, p. 21. This isolation will be further intensified if the present alignments within international communism harden into separate internationals after the projected Moscow meeting in December 1964. A foretaste of this is provided in the CPC's remark in its letter to the CPSU of 7 May 1964: 'The situation is now vastly different from that in 1960. There are two parties in some countries mentioned on your list. In Australia, for instance, there is a party represented by E. F. Hill and another by L. L. Sharkey; the former is Marxist-Leninist and the latter is a revisionist party.'

Although, as suggested above, the rift in the world communist movement and their own mutual estrangement were damaging to both the CPA and the CPNZ, the interest of the two parties in healing the breach is not equal. The CPA suffers more from the present situation because of the existence of the Hill party. The CPA (M-L) makes considerable capital out of the CPNZ's pro-Chinese position in its propaganda attacks on the CPA. Potentially, the CPNZ could also help the Hill group organisationally. It is therefore not surprising that the issue of whether or not the CPNZ has the right to deal with Hill without the agreement of the CPA has caused more bad blood between the two parties than any other issue. Moreover, while the support of the CPA is a serious loss to the CPNZ, they do gain something out of it: greater independence. It is difficult to judge how much weight this is likely to carry with the NZ leadership, but it would be surprising if Wilcox did not derive some satisfaction from telling Sharkey where he gets off, with the confidence that he is backed up by the largest Marxist-Leninist party of the day. The attention which the Chinese pay to their only ' official ' client party of European population must have been flattering to the New Zealand communists, accustomed to being treated as very small fry in Moscow.

This may help to explain why the New Zealanders have been passive rather than active participants in various ' fence-mending ' enterprises. According to the CPNZ, their talks with Suslov and Ponomarev in 1963 took place on the initiative of the Russians, and the CPA have stated that it was at their suggestion that the CPA-CPNZ meeting was held. Originally, it may well have been Ponomarev's idea to hold the CPA-CPNZ talks, and in any case Sharkey would hardly have proposed it to the New Zealanders without first consulting Moscow.

The Russians, for whom the CPA represented the only breach in the Chinese Wall in South-East Asia, were concerned about the bad example the CPNZ was giving to other parties in economically advanced areas and about its help in subverting the CPA. This no doubt is why the CPNZ was attacked more sharply than any other pro-Peking party in Ponomarev's report to the Academy of Social Sciences.[24] The logic of the Sino-Soviet struggle permitted the CPNZ to play a role completely out of proportion to its intrinsic importance.

But the logic of polycentrism does not stop there. The attempts of the new Soviet leaders to achieve some reconciliation with China presented both CPA and CPNZ with a rather tricky problem. First of all, their leaders may have had doubts about its permanence, and turning the tap on and off may affect their standing with their followers. Second, even though they may be particularly concerned about their isolation, they have by now crossed their Rubicons and committed themselves politically and organisationally to opposite courses and loyalties. The CPNZ was the only party which advocated a counter-conference of the pro-Chinese parties without waiting for the signal from Peking. Wilcox

24 *Kommunist*, No. 11, July 1964.

wrote: 'It is to be hoped that the retirement of Mr Khrushchev will create the conditions for the establishment of unity in the socialist world camp and in the world communist movement'; he had been 'the greatest single factor in creating disunity'. The New Zealander added that preparations for a world conference should now be delayed.

For the CPA leaders any political compromise with their rivals in Australia and New Zealand would prejudice their claims to leadership and their position in the party. No doubt communist leaders are only too well accustomed to changes in the party line, but this time the situation is rather different. It is now not a question of adjusting themselves to a new policy, but of accommodating opposite policies within one organisational frame that is now in two pieces. For the leaders of the CPA local reconciliation inevitably spells a degree of triumph for the pro-Chinese Hill, whose Marxist-Leninist party they have excommunicated; it would put a question mark on Aarons' chances of succeeding Sharkey as the leader of the CPA; and it would probably undermine still further the party's chances of extending its influence by 'soft' tactics, unacceptable to the pro-Chinese elements. A militant line makes even less sense in Australia than in Italy, even though Peking is so much nearer and even though, unlike the Italian CP, the CPA does not want to be autonomous. Temporarily left out on a limb by Moscow, like the Indian CP, overtaken by events but reluctant to resume its past conciliatory attitude because of its more militant rivals, the CPA's loyalty to Moscow was again put to the test, whatever its declarations about international communist unity. On the local level, this involves not just 'unprincipled compromises', but decisions painfully affecting the interests of the protagonists who exposed themselves in the conflict and who may have felt like front-line troops deprived of ammunition, or unimportant allies abandoned by the leaders of their coalition. The fading away of prospects of a Sino-Soviet détente, while bringing back all the embarrassments which the conflict caused Australian communists, does at least obviate this feeling.

NORTH AMERICA

Joseph R. Starobin

WHEN the chairman of the American Communist Party died of heart failure during a visit to Moscow in summer 1964, nobody expected that an historic memorandum would soon become public, criticising the way Soviet communists have handled the Chinese and questioning vital aspects of Soviet reality. Nobody expected it, and nothing of the kind happened.

The late Elizabeth Gurley Flynn was not a Palmiro Togliatti. In private, her Irish wit could be caustic, even about holy matters. Her radicalism had roots quite independent of the Comintern which had moulded her *confrères* whom, indeed, she did not join until late in her active life. But neither alive nor dead have the American communists taken any distinctive part in the enormous upheavals of the communist world. That search for identity and autonomous development which appears to be the net, objective consequence of the shattering of the Stalinist monolith has not included the one party which needed polycentrism so badly.

Under any social system, after all, the United States remains a giant, and a movement which lays claim to raising its country from the capitalist slough might have been expected to behave as a great party, even if the role were only potential. It might have stood aside from both Moscow and Peking. Or it could have tried to moderate the schism. Of all the parties in the West, the CP USA was most knowledgeable about China in the Yenan days, and many of its cadres were trained in the Far East; having so often taken advice from Moscow, the Americans might have felt entitled to give some, since they are viewed so sympathetically, as occupying a special, heroically-difficult position in the imperialist heartland.[1] On a more cynical level, the schism might have been viewed as an opportunity. A party which admitted in 1956 its debilitating dependence on foreign influence, and which has such liabilities as the label of 'foreign agent' in a land which takes this charge so seriously, might have used the occasion to dramatise its independence.

Yet there is no sign that the CP USA even dreamed of the comparatively detached stand of Indonesia's communists. Nor did it try, with the British, the Vietnamese and the Italians to ease the Sino-Soviet antagonism, or to exploit the schism, Rumanian style. Miss Flynn and her fellow-delegate, James Jackson, editor of *The Worker*, had rushed to denounce the Albanians, knowing full well that the Chinese were the

---

[1] E. G. Flynn, in *Political Affairs*, November 1963, noted that at the 81-party meeting in 1960 Khrushchev toasted the American party 'immediately after the Chinese party in very glowing terms', and later, again offered a 'special toast to a party bravely fighting for its right to function in the heartland of imperialism'.

true Soviet target, incongruous as such a preoccupation with an exotic Balkan party must have seemed from any vantage-point in the United States. Although the American communists were kept in the dark on the issues of the great dispute,[2] the CP USA's stand was never in doubt. Miss Flynn's final visit to Moscow, her first journey abroad after regaining her passport, was as a member of the 26-party commission which is intended this winter to stake out the Grand Inquest on the Chinese.

THERE is a particular background to the American movement which suggests that the Sino-Soviet conflict causes it great embarrassment. There are ghosts and skeletons haunting its closets. They have been there almost a quarter of a century.

By the middle 1940s, the CP USA had achieved a genuine influence in the newly-emerged labour movement, controlling a third of the CIO's executive, enjoying considerable prestige in the political and intellectual circles of the Roosevelt era. From a membership of 7,000 at the onset of the Great Depression, the communists claimed to have reached 100,000. Their rise was associated with the general secretaryship of Earl Browder who, by 1944, had projected a very distinctive view of the post-war world. He believed that American-Soviet coexistence and even cooperation was bound to follow fascism's defeat; American capitalism, or rather its ' decisive ' or ' intelligent ' circles, would recognise their own interest in such cooperation and the division thus introduced within the bourgeoisie would work in the communists' favour provided they adjusted to it. Browder envisaged a specifically American, constitutional path to social-ism. He thought the two-party system would endure and decided that his party could do better not as an electoral factor but as a sort of *rassemble-ment*, a Marxist lobby, permeating labour and democratic circles with its people, its influence, and its guidance. The CP USA was changed to the Communist Political Association. Himself a veteran Comintern man, Browder believed his projections were consonant with the needs and spirit of the world movement, simply an extension of Marxism-Leninism into post-Comintern conditions.

Quite suddenly, Browder was deposed. His long-time colleague and rival, William Z. Foster (who had gone along with all this, albeit reluctantly) emerged from semi-retirement as the avenger of doctrinal purity when the French communist leader, Jacques Duclos, denounced Browder as a ' revisionist '.[3] The celerity with which all Browder's

---

[2] James Jackson, reporting the 21st congress of the CPSU, considered that Chou En-lai had ' smashed the assortment of lies emanating largely from Belgrade which alleged differences between Soviet and Chinese leaders '. *The Worker*, 8 February 1959. Eugene Dennis, then general secretary, reported to the July 1959 National Committee meeting that ' the solidarity and unity of the socialist camp . . . is stronger and more unshakeable ' than all the ' lies ' suggested. It was not until the November 1963 issue of *Political Affairs*, after the bitter Sino-Soviet exchanges, that Miss Flynn published reminiscences of her 1960 visits to Bucharest and Moscow, making clear how well-informed her party was on the dispute.

[3] *Cahiers du Communisme* (Paris), April 1945.

colleagues abandoned him and hailed Foster's leadership (although the Comintern had chosen the former and repudiated the latter in a desperate effort to revive the CP USA after the faction-ridden 1920s), could be explained only on the assumption that Duclos had spoken for Moscow. Fifteen years' experience in the rough-and-tumble of American life could not cancel out the formative influence of the Lenin School upon the main body of CP USA leaders. Even if the Comintern no longer existed, they behaved as though it did. Characteristically, the Duclos article was immediately dubbed the ' Duclos Letter ', which was typical Comintern language.

The American communists spent the next ten years of their physical and political substance trying to withstand a fierce attack upon them in the changed post-war environment with the armaments of William Z. Foster. To him, United States imperialism was not only the enemy; it had achieved world capitalist mastery and was bent on nuclear war with the Soviet Union and on fascism at home; any divisions within its ruling circles were illusory and of no value to the Left. Coexistence, a concept which began to be heard in the international movement by the end of the decade, was possible. But only if it were imposed by the superior and combined strength of the communist and colonial revolutions. That coexistence might be necessary to capitalism was a Browderist illusion. By the early 1950s, Foster was sure that the over-all strength of the communist camp was superior to capitalism's. This, however, did not promise coexistence, for it would only make capitalism more desperate and determined upon war.

For the purposes of the Smith Act trial of the communist leaders, Foster worked out a theory of transition to socialism via a People's Front. But there was little conviction in it. Any idea of an American road to socialism, implying exceptional tactics or strategy, had an uncomfortable Browderite echo. In February 1951 Foster was narrowly restrained from sending a letter to his British comrades, condemning their newly-published *British Road to Socialism* as revisionist. Only the arrival of private assurances that the Russians had given their advice and consent to this document deterred him.

By this time, the CP USA had expended its hard-won capital in the trade unions and political life by gambling on Henry Wallace's Progressive Party which failed so badly. All the ties of the Left with progressive and centrist forces were severed on the poorly-chosen grounds of foreign policy. With the top leaders facing four-year jail terms, half of them chose to ' go underground '; with a few thousand ' cadres ' trying to maintain a skeletal leadership, Foster declared that his party would some day emerge victorious, as the Italian and Japanese communists had—an unmistakeable indication that both war and fascism were considered imminent.

Foster's chief lieutenant was the chairman of the New York State organisation (with half the total membership), a military hero in both

Spain and the Pacific theatre, Robert Thompson. He had received a lighter sentence and would have been free in 18 months; but so deep was the guerrilla-warfare mentality and so strong the expectation that normal political life would have ceased within those 18 months that Thompson evaded prison and also chose the 'underground'. The late Benjamin J. Davis, the party's most-publicised Negro leader, had by this time evolved the theory that the Negro struggle was replacing the working class as such as the vanguard of the American revolution, and by virtue of its inevitable links with the Asian and African revolution, the American Negro movement must take priority in the CP USA's doctrine and strategy. With Foster, these three were a virtual faction, driving their reluctant colleagues into more desperate adventures by their dynamism and their apparent international prestige. For five years bitter internecine quarrels pervaded the 'underground'. Some leaders tried to halt the 'ultra-leftism' to which they had yielded, but were fearful of being stuck with the label of Browderism which Foster waved against them.

THE CP USA is thus perhaps unique in having had, within a single decade, a precocious and searing experience with a sort of premature Khrushchevism and a premature Maoism. It tried both political lines, and tried to contain both lines within itself. This explains the explosiveness of the upheavals of 1956–57. The main body of members were not only outraged by the monstrosity of Stalinism as revealed by the 20th CPSU congress, but humiliated by the realisation that the Soviet leaders were making a new orthodoxy out of many ideas which the American communists had been forced to abandon on what they were sure were Soviet instructions. For a brief period, at the 16th national convention, Foster was again isolated and was blamed for the debacle. A 'right-wing' under John Gates, joining forces with the late Eugene Dennis as the 'centrist', revised the party's constitution, declared its independence of Moscow, and tried to revive the movement. But too many members and almost the entire body of cadres formed by the 30s and overwhelmed by events had begun to doubt the viability of any kind of communist party, even if they could control it. Many began to re-examine the validity of Marxism-Leninism altogether. With Dennis returning to Foster's fold, and Gates departing, the CP USA was again reduced to a membership of a few thousand, as in the late 1920s. The leaders tried to follow Moscow, but with their followers steeped in Foster's leftism, clinging nostalgically to memories, and unable to digest the entire traumatic experience.

Such a movement was in any case doomed to frustration, which the Sino-Soviet schism was bound to aggravate. In his report to the National Committee in July 1959, the late Eugene Dennis spoke of the 'virulent factionalism' which in his view had hampered the struggle against both revisionism and ultra-leftism. Eighteen months later, Gus Hall, succeeding the dying Dennis as general secretary, noted that 'there are some members of this very national committee who during the whole year since the convention have voted against every major and minor policy presented by the party leadership '.[4]   There is reason to believe that the late Benjamin J. Davis jr. considered himself the logical anchor-man of the new leadership.   Davis had hopes of competing with Hall, who returned to activity in mid-1959, having paid the double indemnity of a long jail sentence after several years of hiding.

At the end of 1961 a majority of the New York State leaders were expelled; their leader, Milton Rosen, was accused of organising fractional meetings ' and speculating on the stand of the Albanian party with which it is in accord '.[5]   Rosen, a quasi-intellectual who had been ' proletarian- ised ' by being sent into industry during the underground days, seems to have had some support in Buffalo, a steel centre.   His group immediately formed the ' Progressive Labor Movement '.   It appears to have thought that the Supreme Court's decision requiring the CP to register as a ' foreign agent ' was a good occasion to wind up the party and make a fresh start.   The main leaders, however, believed that legal means for reversing the Court's ruling were still available.   For them, the franchise of a party, no matter how small, was vital.

The Progressive Labor Movement has few followers but has received a great deal of publicity, having taken part in the Harlem riots, sparked demonstrations against war in Viet Nam, and organised two student pilgrimages to Cuba, much to the State Department's distress.   This group makes up for its small numbers by a feverish energy.   It publishes a weekly, *Challenge*, with a section in Spanish directed to the Puerto Ricans, and a *Marxist-Leninist Quarterly*, its theoretical organ.   The approach of the PLM is fundamentalist; its language has the vigour and arrogance of the most primitive days of Bolshevism, as though nothing had happened to alter an iota of Leninist doctrine.   It has the attraction of the millenarism of the socialist sects of half a century ago.   It is now frankly pro-Chinese; Peking's arrival on the international scene gives the PLM exactly that foreign star which fills the needs of the inferiority complex so characteristic of the CP USA in relation to Russia ever since 1919.   The PLM also lays claim to William Z. Foster, not without some critical observations on his vacillations, as patron saint.[6]

Foster's own attitude towards the Sino-Soviet schism is one of the most enigmatic and fascinating phases of his career.   His ties to the Soviet Union were, of course, historic and profound.   His formative years were those of an anarcho-syndicalist.   His leadership of the CP USA, both before and after the Browder era, had many essentially Maoist features.   In his *History of the Three Internationals* (1952), written as the

[4] *Political Affairs*, February 1961.
[5] *Ibid.*, February 1962.
[6] The claim is made, without proof, that Foster was immensely impressed with the Chinese publication, *Long Live Leninism*, and said ' I've read it carefully—more than just once—and agree with every word in it '.   Foster is also said to have believed that ' the American communists should make a careful study of what the Chinese are saying '.   Fred Carlisle, in *Marxist-Leninist Quarterly*, Vol. II, No. 1.

Stalin era came to a close, he considers Mao Tse-tung the foremost theoretical figure of communism, the inheritor of the Stalin-Lenin mantle. Late in 1958 he sent Mao Tse-tung a long and ambitious document summarising all the themes of his activity since the war; they bear a striking resemblance to what the Chinese communists have since made public as their own position. Foster suggested that he might visit Peking, once he succeeded in getting to Moscow for medical treatment. Mao Tse-tung's reply welcomed the idea of a visit from Foster, but was extremely laconic on the sweeping survey of the world which Foster had hoped could evoke a sympathetic response.[7] The Chinese were evidently not yet ready to make their views public. Much later, in March 1963, after repeated criticisms of the American party, the Chinese declared that ' the leaders of the CP USA can show that they really understand their international obligations and are fulfilling them, if they carry on and enrich the revolutionary tradition of Comrade Foster '.[8]

Foster had in the meantime made his final voyage to the Soviet capital, dying there in September 1961. Death had spared him the excruciating choice between Moscow and Peking. The Soviet leaders, among whom the highest were Foster's pallbearers, could claim William Z. Foster as their own. Yet the irony of this spectacle could not have been lost on his American associates.

Recalling in 1963 the debates at the 1960 conferences, Miss Flynn speculated on the curious personal animosity of the Chinese delegates towards Khrushchev. ' Some felt that on the death of Stalin the Chinese had assumed that Mao Tse-tung would be considered the leading Marxist spokesman in the world and would be so accepted by all parties.'[9] This had, of course, been Foster's view in his *History*, already cited. Miss Flynn noted that as an ' ambiguous concession ' to the Chinese the idea that ' should the imperialist maniacs start war the peoples will sweep capitalism out of existence and bury it ' was incorporated in the 81-party statement. ' I doubt ', she wrote, ' if any such version would be accepted today by the major parties of the world, as it underplays the destructive power of nuclear war.' But American comrades (and ex-comrades) must have remembered that this very expression had been a favourite peroration of William Z. Foster in countless speeches and articles ever since 1947.

HOW to explain the Sino-Soviet schism itself, and how to assess its meaning for communism as such, has troubled the American communist leaders, but one finds little that is systematic in their press. At most, Gus Hall is quoted as saying: ' It seems that after certain Marxist parties become leaders of nations the influences of narrow nationalism tend to weaken proletarian internationalism. These parties

[7] *The Worker*, 17 January 1959.
[8] *People's Daily*, 8 March 1963.
[9] *Political Affairs*, November 1963.

tend to see the rest of the world, including the socialist world, through the eyes of narrow nationalism.' [10] This comment might, of course, have been made to apply retrospectively to the Soviet Union itself in its influence on the American communists. How to function as a party in the wake of the impact of the Soviet Union's ' narrow nationalism ' upon the CP USA has proven a difficult task for Hall and his colleagues since 1959.

Upon his return to activity, Hall judged that ' we remain largely isolated from the main movements and currents of American life ', and added ' that all too often, instead of starting with a thorough investigation of the reality with which we are dealing, we proceed to paint a picture based on fragmentary knowledge and wishful thinking, and thus to work up a situation that has nothing necessarily to do with reality '.[11]

Hall has since tried to steer a new course. It is taken essentially from the CP's earlier days, but he seems to have little to work with. *The Worker's* circulation objectives late in 1963 were to gain 1,500 new subscribers, 500 news-stand sales, and 2,000 bundle orders (the latter having meaning mainly for New York). Judging from similar campaigns in previous years, these objectives were not reached, although *The Worker* now publishes twice weekly. *Political Affairs*, polling its readers in 1960, reported that 65 replies had been received from 13 states, and three from overseas. One third of the replies came from readers over 60 years of age, and two thirds from readers over 40. Meetings to celebrate the party's 40th anniversary brought an audience of 2,000 in New York and 500 in Chicago.

On the other hand, there have been signs of a certain vitality which can be credited more to local peculiarities than to the state of the party's health nationally.[12] In a recent local election in Los Angeles for school board supervisor, a veteran party official, William Taylor, received 34,516 votes, or 13·7 per cent of the total. But it is doubtful whether the American communist leaders would generalise about their situation from any experience in California, where everything and anything can happen.

A major frustration for the CP USA is the attitude of those who have in previous decades been its fellow-travellers and from whom it drew political support, plus financial and moral sustenance. These people do not constitute a movement. They are more of a *milieu*. The *National Guardian*, a weekly which came into being in 1947–48 when the Progressive Party was being organised, was written largely for communist sympathisers; it served as their voice and channel of information at the height of the McCarthy era, when the CP went underground and it might have been dangerous to receive outright CP papers. In recent years, the

10 *Ibid.*, October 1963.
11 *Ibid.*, May 1959.
12 Hall was much encouraged by speaking tours in which he and other associates are said to have reached 100,000 university students over the past three years. *N.Y. Times*, 26 September 1964. Commenting on his own experience, he said: ' You can't speak to this generation in the same way as in the 30s. This generation won't accept agitation as the answer. They want serious discussion '. *Political Affairs*, April 1961.

Guardian has declined. Its influence in left-wing trade union circles has almost vanished, with the virtual disappearance of the unions expelled from the CIO in 1949. Moreover, the *Guardian's* editors have been attracted to what they call independent political action in alliance with the Trotskyist Socialist Workers' Party. This is a major bone of contention with the communists, who are trying to steer into some relationship with the labour movement's endorsement of the Democrats. The *Guardian*, which publishes Anna Louise Strong regularly from her second homeland in China, has become frankly pro-Chinese and contemptuous of the domestic communists. It did not even mention William Taylor's independent candidacy in Los Angeles, as he bitterly complained. It sustains itself on a motley variety of village radicals, picturesque sectarians, and the finances of former CP members who are attracted to the Chinese view in proportion as their own good fortunes have grown in the capitalist prosperity whose imminent end they periodically predict.

With greater intellectual pretensions, there is *Monthly Review*, edited by the economist Paul Sweezy and the labour historian Leo Huberman. It too has disappointed and often irritated the CP USA. This magazine, which has a certain currency among scholars, university professors and students, as well as unattached radicals of all sorts, was founded in 1949 and was bitterly attacked by the CP USA which saw it as a spokesman for the Yugoslav revisionists. Indeed, Sweezy and Huberman were much enamoured of Tito in his defiance of Stalin.

At the turn of this decade, *Monthly Review* was exhilarated by the Cuban revolution, which it welcomed not only for its socialist orientation but its non-communist inspiration; the magazine is much involved now in a Latin American edition. Originally, its editors saw the Sino-Soviet schism in terms that were favourable to Moscow. In the December 1961 issue, they believed that the differences concerned ' what course of action the socialist countries ought to follow to minimise the threat of World War III '. After outlining what both sides were saying at the time, *Monthly Review* declared: ' We have no doubt that the Russians are right and the Chinese wrong. The Chinese position seems to us to be a typical example of the kind of dogmatic leftism that has appeared again and again in the history of the international socialist movement '. Sweezy and Huberman were confident that the ' disease ' would ' abate and eventually disappear ' if China were admitted to the United Nations. They felt the world should be grateful that ' China's foreign policy is subject to the moderating influence of the Soviet Union and the large majority in the Socialist camp which agrees with the Soviet position '.

In May 1963—before the exchange of CPSU and CCP letters— *Monthly Review* reversed its position on the ground that ' our earlier analysis of the dispute did not stand up '. It was based on a ' misconception of what the dispute was all about '. Proceeding from ' new material ', this magazine found the dispute to rest on a difference ' about the nature of the historical period through which the world is passing and what

can and should be done to advance the cause of world socialism . . .
On the main issue in the controversy—whether the struggle for peace or
the struggle against imperialism should have priority—we are convinced
that the Chinese do indeed have the truth on their side. Real peace will
never be achieved, much less guaranteed, as long as imperialism exists.
And we are also convinced that the Chinese are right that imperialism
can and will suffer decisive defeat at the hands of the revolutionary
peoples of the underdeveloped areas.'

The editors were not as ' sure as the Chinese seem to be ' that the
international socialist movement would come around to their position.
They deplored the acrimony of the argument. They wondered why the
Chinese were pushing to a ' showdown ' with the Russians, since history
was surely working for them. *Monthly Review* has since maintained
this position despite the dismay of many readers.

On related matters, such as the Negro battle for civil rights, it has
given much publicity to the ' leftist ' trend that has gained currency among
many young Negroes, to the effect that white allies in the struggle are
quite useless, and non-violent means illusory. The opinions of Robert
Williams, a former NAACP leader of North Carolina, who suggested
taking up arms to defend the Negroes and who lives in Havana when he is
not in Peking, have received wide attention in *Monthly Review*. It is
evidently unaware that the original inspiration for this ' ultra-left ' and
' nationalist' theme was projected by Benjamin Davis jr. before the
communist national committee in the heyday of the late 1940s under
Foster's aegis.

The attitude of both the *National Guardian* and *Monthly Review*
not only confronts the CP USA with serious intellectual competition; it
also disappoints the hope that somehow the CP could resolve its problems
by a unifying move on the Left that would include these journals and
their audience. This was the hope of Gilbert Green, one of the CP
leaders who paid the double indemnity of a four year underground
existence plus a jail sentence that followed on the original Smith Act
conviction of 1951. Green was among those who tried ineffectually to
stem the Foster tide from the underground, without facing the heart of the
problem, which lay in the party's commitment to Soviet policy and indeed
to Marxism-Leninism; he has only recently returned to activity, mainly
with ideological articles. The effort to debate all the old and the new
problems with *Monthly Review* comes a cropper because of the restricted
intellectual arena and the dwindling audience. The Sino-Soviet schism
makes the effort futile.

At most, the Sino-Soviet schism has produced a more detached
attitude towards the Soviet leaders, a recognition of their fallibility which
in an earlier day would have been considered heretical in American
communist circles. But the commitment to the franchise which stems
from Moscow is a firm one. Gus Hall's reaction to Khrushchev's fall

was remarkably debonair, as though the dismissal of the CPSU's general-secretary requires only a few explanations to justify it. In Hall's guess, Khrushchev had become 'brittle and opinionated', and could not take criticism, as is typical of men as they get older. It was so simple, and so sad. Yet the American communist leader considered that Khrushchev had made a 'historic contribution', and even speculated that he might 'continue to make contributions in one capacity or another'. This was rather different from the 'cult of the un-personality' which the Soviet successors of Khrushchev immediately began to develop. Thus, without departing from the basic assumption that everything always works out for the best in Moscow's behaviour, there was a certain independence of judgment in Hall's analysis that would have been unlikely a decade ago. But there was no astonishment or outrage: the American CP is too spent for such passions. The inability to determine where things went wrong in the Foster era (except perhaps in private [13]) paralyses the CP USA, no matter how tenaciously its leaders work for a renewal. The 'perpetual mobility of American institutions' of which Emerson spoke, has brought forth a radically new set of problems. If new radicals arise in American life, they are not going to turn to old bottles, to outworn intellectual or organisational forms. The new problems of American life surely abound. But the Left of the CP's inspiration is far too compromised and exhausted, with the Sino-Soviet schism as a final blow, to contribute to their solution.

---

[13] Hall is known to have remarked at a reception for Elizabeth Gurley Flynn in the fall of 1961, a few days after eulogising Foster, that it was Foster, after all, who 'had wrecked the American Party'.

LATIN AMERICA

Ernst Halperin

IN Latin America, the communist parties do not hold a monopoly of
extreme leftist opinion. In most Latin American countries other groups
also calling themselves Marxist-Leninist are as strong as, or stronger than,
the communist parties. These are not groups of mere fellow-travellers.
They are independent of and frequently antagonistic to the communist
parties. All of them may be described as pro-Chinese, though by
no means uncritically so, whereas the bulk of the Latin American
communists are loyal to Moscow.

The non-communist and dissident communist groups of the Latin
American Left are unanimous in accusing the communist parties of
not being genuinely revolutionary. Remembering the French saying,
On est toujours le réactionnaire de quelqu'un, one is inclined to dismiss
this accusation as stemming from mere envy or blind fanaticism. There
is probably not a single communist party in the world, including the most
successful ones, which has not at times been denounced by rivals and
competitors as having betrayed the revolution, or at least as lacking all
revolutionary fervour. Even Lenin himself was once accused of the foul
heresy of Bernsteinian revisionism by the Mensheviks.

Yet it is an error to apply European standards to Latin American
reality. In other parts of the world it may be merely ridiculous to claim
that the communists are not revolutionaries, but in Latin America it is a
fact that the communist movement has no vigorous revolutionary tradition. There is probably not a single conservative or liberal party in all
of Latin America which has not staged more insurrections, and incited
more civil wars, than the communists. On a continent racked by civil
strife, the communists' record has been one of remarkable quiescence.
Their only major attempt to seize power by force was the Prestes rising
in Brazil, which occurred in 1935, apart from which there have only been
some instances of communist participation in risings organised by non-
communist groups. Of late, the communist party leaders in Latin
America have been under strong pressure from Castroite elements to
switch over to a policy of terrorism and guerrilla warfare, but so far
only the Venezuelan communists have actually succumbed to this pressure
and changed their party line.

Their lack of revolutionary fervour does not mean that the communist
parties of Latin America are democratic. They are totalitarian parties
with a totalitarian system of organisation and a totalitarian mentality,
and whenever they have managed to manoeuvre themselves into a
position where they enjoy a share of real power, as in Chile in 1946–47,
in Guatemala in 1954, and in Cuba from 1960 onwards, their totalitarianism at once becomes manifest in their behaviour towards both their
allies and their opponents.

One vital element of totalitarianism is, however, missing in their
make-up: the drive, the ruthless determination to seize power at all
costs. In general, the communist parties of Latin America do not strive
very hard for power. They are content to play the normal game of Latin
American politics, cooperating both with dictators and with democrats
in return for small benefits. This is understandable in view of the fact
that, until a short time ago, a communist regime in Latin America could
not have expected effective Soviet protection against intervention by
the dominant power of the hemisphere.

COMMUNISM first made its appearance in Latin America in the
early nineteen-twenties, at a time when it was possible to believe that
the revolution in Russia was the immediate prelude to revolution on a
world scale. This assumption proved false. World revolution did not
materialise, and the Soviet Union remained isolated, weak, racked by
internal dissension, and more and more absorbed by the gigantic effort
of industrialisation. It could not have come to the assistance of a revolution that might break out in any Latin American country.

In consequence, the ultra-leftist strategy of immediate revolution—
the so-called 'third period' strategy which was initiated by the Communist
International in 1928, made even less sense in Latin America than in
Europe. The strikes and petty revolts engineered by the Latin American
communists in obedience to the orders of the Comintern all failed
miserably, and the one serious attempt made by a communist party to
seize power by violence—the Prestes revolt in Brazil in 1935—was also a
failure. The Latin American communist parties, which had not been
very strong from the beginning, now lost all influence and dwindled into
insignificance.

But at the very moment of the Brazilian rising another communist
party, that of Chile, was already preparing to implement the popular-front
strategy newly proclaimed by the Comintern. This new strategy, calling
for broad alliances with limited aims, was soon adopted by all the
communist parties of the hemisphere.

From the moment of its adoption, the history of the Latin American
communist parties has been one of the most extraordinary opportunism.
Communist parties have indiscriminately cooperated with dictators and
with democratic parties of the Right as well as of the Left. Sometimes
they have split into two parties with opposite policies, one of them collaborating with a dictator and the other with the democratic opposition,
only to reunite after the political situation had changed.[1]

The communist parties of Latin America were thus allowed almost
complete freedom of manoeuvre by the leadership of the international
movement, while the communist parties of Europe (and that of the United
States) were kept on a much shorter leash, and obliged to respond to any
change in Soviet foreign policy. The reason why the Latin American

[1] Cf. R. J. Alexander, *Communism in Latin America* (1960).

communists were accorded such freedom of movement was undoubtedly that throughout the nineteen-thirties and nineteen-forties, and during most of the nineteen-fifties, Soviet foreign policy had far more pressing concerns than Latin America. The area was beyond the range of Soviet state interest, not only because it was out of reach of the Soviet armed forces, but also because none of the Latin American countries carried enough weight in international affairs for the Soviets to be vitally concerned about their friendship or enmity. Consequently, the activities of the Latin American communists were only rarely considered to be of importance to the Soviet Union. They were not expected to seize power, or to maintain themselves in power if by some fluke they managed to seize it.

Their freedom of manoeuvre enabled them to join in the normal game of political give-and-take to a far greater extent than the communist parties in other parts of the world. Even in those Latin American countries where they are clandestine, the communist parties are a factor taken into account both by the government and by the opposition in their every-day political dealings. It is true that most of them are very small, but that only makes it easier and less dangerous to cooperate with them. The few thousand votes controlled by a communist party may swing an election; its influence among university students may serve to start or quell a riot, its trade-union connections may be of use to a military dictator struggling to improve his image and win a civilian following. And since the Latin American communists' principles are very flexible, their support may be bought, and at a moderate price: perhaps by an amnesty for the imprisoned comrades, and a slight relaxation of police supervision, or by the offer of a few positions in the state-controlled trade-union bureaucracy, or by the permission to publish a daily newspaper, or even a mere periodical.

Visiting Europeans and North Americans are frequently appalled by the average Latin American *politico's* readiness to negotiate and conclude deals with the local communist party. In their experience, that is the road to perdition: those who collaborate with the CP inevitably become its prisoners. But this is not the case in Latin America, where politicians who wish to shake off their communist allies when these have exhausted their usefulness have rarely found it difficult to do so. With the possible exception of Chile, the communist parties of the Latin American countries are simply too weak to constitute a serious danger to their allies.

THIS weakness can be traced to the inapplicability of communist organisational principles and techniques to the specific conditions of Latin America. The organisational formula of the communist movement is ' democratic centralism ', i.e. extreme centralisation and rigid discipline. But loyalty to an organisation representing an abstract principle is poorly developed in Latin America. Perhaps because the traditions of feudalism are still strong throughout the region, the average Latin American prefers to give his loyalty to an individual or to a family. In consequence, 'organisation men' are scarce, and political parties based on ideologies, as well as trade unions, cooperatives, etc., are more difficult to build up and tend to be far less efficient than in Europe.

Furthermore, Latin American communists have been led by their Marxist credo to concentrate their organisational efforts on the industrial workers, and especially on those groups already organised in trade unions. Unfortunately for the communists, these groups usually constitute a privileged stratum of the Latin American proletariat, a 'labour aristocracy', as Lenin called it, and are not really a revolutionary element.

To put it briefly: the Marxist-Leninist concept of revolution by the organised working class is not applicable to Latin America, first because the Latin American working class as a whole can hardly be organised, and second because those sectors that can be organised are not revolutionary.[2]

That is why, in the communists' view, conditions in Latin America are never quite ripe for revolution, because revolution has to be made 'by the masses', and 'the masses' have to be prepared for revolution by a long and patient labour of organisation and propaganda which is never quite completed. Typical of this argument is the Peruvian communist Jorge del Prado's statement in an article characteristically titled: 'Mass Struggle—the Key to Victory', in the *World Marxist Review* (May 1964):

> International experience—including the experience of the Cuban Revolution, and also the experience of our own revolutionaries, reinforces our conviction that *revolutions are made by the masses*, that there can be no revolution without the support of the masses. ... Although the events show that the majority of our people feel the need for radical changes, although a powerful movement is under way in this direction, still the masses have not yet come to see the need to fight for political power.

The Latin American communist parties have often repeated this argument against immediate action right up to the moment when some other group has actually started the revolution, usually in some highly unorthodox, typically Latin American manner.

The need for a long and patient labour of organisation and propaganda is also used by Latin American communists—and probably in perfectly good faith—to justify their many unprincipled pacts with dictators. Organisation and propaganda are rendered extremely difficult if the party is obliged to operate in complete clandestinity, with its newspapers suppressed, and its leaders imprisoned. It thus becomes the duty

---

[2] There are, of course, some exceptions to this rule. Thus, the well-organised tin-miners took a decisive part in the Bolivian revolution. It is, however, significant that these miners were not organised and led by communists, but by a typical Latin American Caudillo, Juan Lechin.

of the party leaders to obtain and safeguard the privileges of legality, even at the cost of some morally dubious compromise with a dictator. In this manner, the very dictum that the masses must be organised for revolution has served as an excuse for the most shady deals with such dictators as Trujillo, Somoza, and Batista. Thus, most of the Latin American communist parties have degenerated into small machines run by professional politicians who hire out their services to dictators and democrats alike in return for petty concessions.

THE second strong current of leftist extremism in Latin America is composed of groups that are motivated by sentiments of violent nationalism, or ' strategic hatred ', as Eduardo Frei called it. This hatred is of course directed against the power that exercises political and economic hegemony over Latin America—the United States.

The protagonists of ' strategic hatred ' or total rebellion against the United States hegemony do not want to settle specific grievances or negotiate better terms with the United States, as do the moderate nationalists like Romulo Betancourt of Venezuela, Belaunde Terry of Peru, or Eduardo Frei of Chile. They will not be satisfied by anything less than the complete withdrawal of the United States from Latin America. They are not against any specific United States policy, but against all United States policies. Their obsessive anti-Yankeeism is not caused by mere mistakes of American policy; it reflects the wound to their pride inflicted by the very existence of United States superiority, the mere presence of the United States in Latin America, regardless of the forms in which this presence manifests itself. They are proud men who cannot bear to live in wealthy Uncle Sam's backyard, and have come to the conclusion that the only way to free themselves from their backyard status is to burn down the big house in front.

Since the combined might of the Latin American states would not suffice to destroy the United States, the extreme nationalists seek the aid of an outside power capable of fulfilling this task.

To seek the support of one big power against the other has been a policy followed by the weak throughout the course of history. But in our times, power politics take on the form of ideological strife. The real issues, which in this case are the relationship between Latin America and the United States, and the attempts of a foreign power to set foot in the Western Hemisphere, are thereby obscured to the onlooker, and to some extent even to the participants themselves.

In the nineteen-thirties and during the Second World War, Latin American extreme nationalism sought the aid of Germany and Italy against both the United States and Britain, which at that time still held strong positions in a number of Latin American countries. In the process, the extreme nationalists adopted the language and organisational forms of European fascism. After the defeat of fascism in the Second World War, they sought and found a new ally against the United States—the

Soviet Union, and they now began to talk the language of Marxism-Leninism.

The Soviet Union, besides being the only power capable of defying the United States, also stands for a programme of complete social and economic transformation which makes it even more attractive to many Latin Americans. The desire for social change is widespread in Latin America. Such change would, of course, also affect the American-owned enterprises which play a preponderant role in the economy of many Latin American countries. And since Washington has frequently declared its determination to protect the interests of American investors abroad, the United States itself appears to Latin Americans as one of the major obstacles to the social change which they desire.[3] Nationalist resentment of United States hegemony, and the desire for social change, to which the United States appears to constitute an obstacle, have thus blended in the post-war period to produce a powerful upsurge of pro-Soviet and anti-American sentiment.

For the first decade of the post-war era Soviet opportunities in Latin America were, however, still severely limited by the fact that the Western Hemisphere was out of reach of Soviet military power. This was drastically changed when in 1957–58 the USSR put the Intercontinental Ballistic Missile into service—a technical innovation which has brought about what may well be termed the greatest revolution of military strategy in the history of mankind. The ICBM made it possible for a power situated literally on the other side of the globe directly to threaten the Western Hemisphere with destruction. The Soviet Union was now able to resort to nuclear threats in order to protect a base established in Latin America; it could threaten massive nuclear retaliation against the United States itself if such a base were attacked.

No more than three years after this hypothetical possibility had emerged, the Soviet Union did in fact establish a base for political and military operations in the Western Hemisphere. It is significant that it did not obtain the base through the offices of a Latin American communist party, none of which was in a position to seize power, but through alliance with a Latin American nationalist.

It is questionable whether Fidel Castro contemplated a complete break with the United States, and the inclusion of Cuba in the ' socialist camp ', when he first took up the Soviet offer to back him in 1959. At that time he may well have been thinking only in terms of a balancing act between the two powers. The United States did not intend to tolerate

3 It is true that the Alliance for Progress advocates social reforms. But it also advocates an increase in private investment. Many Latin Americans regard these two postulates as contradictory, since those governments which really implement social reforms are not the ones likely to inspire confidence in the domestic and foreign private investor. Actually, the contradiction is more apparent than real. The example of Venezuela shows that reform governments easily win the investor's confidence once they have demonstrated a certain stability.

the existence of a pocket Nasser in the Caribbean, but its counter-measures were worse than self-defeating. Instead of warning the Russians that it would on no account permit their expansion into the region, it applied pressure on the small states seeking Soviet aid. In doing so, it gave the impression of being afraid to face the Soviets directly, and encouraged Castro to draw closer to his new protector.

THE failure of the United States to prevent Soviet economic and military assistance to Cuba, and its apparent unwillingness to face up to the real threat to its interests in Latin America—which was the Soviet Union and not little Cuba—had a galvanising effect on Latin American nationalism. Here was what the extreme nationalists had been waiting for: the chance to free their countries from United States domination with the assistance of a great foreign power. They were all too ready to interpret the apparent weakness of the United States as confirmation of the Soviet claim that the world balance of power had shifted decisively in favour of the ' socialist camp '. Marxism-Leninism now became the ideological cloak of Latin American extreme nationalism, as fascism had been earlier.

The Latin American communists, these one-time revolutionaries degenerated into machine-politicians, were unable to take full advantage of the wave of pro-Soviet feeling that now swept the Latin American Left. The bulk of the nationalists who had become admirers of the Soviet Union stayed outside the communist parties, forming Castroite groups of their own.

The ideology of these Castroite groups, for whom Professor Alexander has coined the name ' the Jacobin Left ', is Marxism-Leninism; they all stand for revolution and the installation of a regime on the Cuban pattern in their own country. They are completely independent of the communist parties, with whom they are often engaged in bitter controversy.

The issue at stake in this controversy between the communists and the Castroite groups is a highly practical one: the timing and strategy of the revolution. The Castroite groups want their revolution now; the communists say that conditions are not yet ripe for revolution, because ' the masses ' have not yet become convinced of its necessity. The Castroites want a violent revolution, to be sparked off by guerrilla warfare in the countryside, and a campaign of terrorism, sabotage, and strikes in the cities. They point out that there is no instance of a socialist system having been established without violence, by the ' peaceful road '. In some countries, the communists openly state that they prefer the ' peaceful road ', in others they evade the issue by asserting that the choice between the peaceful and non-peaceful roads depends primarily on the attitude adopted by the ruling classes when faced with the revolutionary advance of the masses. In any case, the communists reject the Castroite thesis that the revolutionaries need not wait until the conditions for revolution are mature, but can create these conditions by starting a guerrilla war.[4]

In this debate, the Latin American communist parties enjoy the tacit support of the Soviet Union. Even before the Caribbean crisis of October 1962, when Soviet policy was still in a highly aggressive phase, the Soviet leaders were reluctant to allow the tempo of their advance into Latin America to be dictated by outsiders, firebrands like Fidel Castro, who often proved unamenable to both reasoning and pressure. The Caribbean crisis has made Moscow aware of the need for a period of retrenchment and consolidation, i.e. 'peaceful coexistence' in the sense of a slackening of tension with the United States. Those Latin American communist parties that remain loyal to Moscow follow suit by moderating their policies, and this naturally increases friction with the Castroite extreme nationalists.

We thus see that the position of the Castroite groups coincides with that of the Chinese communists on three vitally important issues: first, in their rejection of the Soviet interpretation of 'peaceful coexistence' as a lessening of tension with the United States; second, in their insistence on an aggressive policy of promoting revolution everywhere, and, third, in their rejection of the Soviet thesis of 'the peaceful road to socialism', which they consider to be a mere excuse to avoid revolutionary action.

THIS triple coincidence does not mean that the Castroite groups are Maoists, or in any way inspired by Peking. The coincidence arises from a community of interests: both are interested in pressing forward with revolution now regardless of any embarrassment this might cause the Soviet Union, and both are interested in preventing any rapprochement between the Soviet Union and the United States. Although taking place in the general context of the Sino-Soviet dispute, the conflict between the Castroite groups and those Latin American communist parties that remain loyal to Moscow was not sparked off by that dispute. The issue at stake is a genuinely Latin American one, which would have arisen even if the conflict between Moscow and Peking had not broken out at this precise moment.

The once pro-Soviet Castroite groups are now sympathetic to China, but they do not display as fervent an enthusiasm for China as they once did for the Soviet Union. As long as the Soviet Union appeared to be

---

4 In the article already quoted Jorge del Prado wrote: '. . . we cannot accept the thesis that all that is needed to "kindle the flame" of revolution in any place and in all circumstances is to "ignite the spark" of guerrilla warfare. Considering the demands of the present stage of the revolutionary process and contrary to the adventurist policy of the "ultra-lefts" who are causing confusion and who follow the Chinese splitters, we uphold the tactic of actively gathering strength'. The 'thesis' is obviously the Castroite one formulated by Che Guevara: 'It is not necessary to wait until all conditions for making revolution exist; the insurrection can create them' (*Guerrilla Warfare*, New York, 1961, p. 15).

engaged in an all-out struggle against the United States, it had their unreserved and completely uncritical admiration. Their attitude towards China, though sympathetic, is far more reserved. They do not wholeheartedly support the entire Chinese platform, but agree only with some of its points. Other points, such as the Chinese defence of Albania and glorification of Stalin, the denigration of Trotsky, and even some of the harsher criticisms of the Soviet Union, are shrugged off as irrelevant to Latin America, or even as slightly ridiculous. They show little interest in China's efforts to wrest control of the communist world movement from the Soviet Union, and tend to deplore the split in that movement.

The reason for this rather reserved attitude is no doubt that China, in the eyes of the Latin American nationalists, has one great defect: it is not a military power capable of defying the United States in the Western Hemisphere. What they would really like is not that China should take over the leadership of the communist movement, but that the Soviet Union should change its foreign policy in accordance with Chinese criticism, i.e. that it should revert to a policy of all-out hostility to the United States. As long as there is the slightest chance of that happening, and, specifically, as long as the Soviet Union has not made it absolutely clear that it has completely lost interest in Latin America, few, if any, Latin American nationalists are likely to come out unequivocally in support of China.

China therefore only has a very uncertain and lukewarm ally in the Latin American extreme nationalists. That is why, besides encouraging the Castroite groups in their policy of subversion and open rebellion against the governments of Latin America, it is also attempting to split the communist parties in the region in order to win to its side cadres accustomed to strict discipline and motivated by Marxist-Leninist doctrinal considerations, and not by mere nationalism.

*   *   *

Three distinct tedencies have thus emerged in the Latin American extreme Left: Party-line communists loyal to Moscow, Castroite nationalists (the 'Jacobin Left') disappointed in Moscow and harbouring pro-Chinese sympathies, but unwilling to commit themselves wholeheartedly to the Chinese cause, and nuclei of Maoist communists ideologically—and financially—dependent on Peking.

Cuba is the main stronghold of the extreme nationalists; the only country in which they have managed to seize power, and thus actually to implement the policy of 'strategic hatred' against the United States. Since this policy was based on a serious underestimation of American and overestimation of Soviet strength, the Castro regime now finds itself in an extremely difficult position.

Castro had assumed that Soviet protection would enable him to carry out his scheme to 'convert the Andes mountain range into the Sierra

Maestra of all Latin America ', i.e. to spread revolution throughout the continent, and thus to deal a mortal blow to ' Yankee imperialism '.[5]

The Caribbean crisis of October 1962 proved this assumption, and indeed Castro's entire estimate of the ratio of strength between the Soviet Union and the United States, to have been completely wrong. Since then it has become increasingly clear that the Soviet Union does not want another show-down in Latin America, and is therefore anything but eager for the establishment of a second Castroite regime in the area. Indeed by now Castro has reason to doubt the Soviet Union's willingness to support Cuba itself against United States pressure. The Soviet government is constantly urging him to ' settle his differences ' with the United States, and since it does so in spite of the United States government's refusal to take up negotiations with him, Castro must be beginning to feel that Moscow wishes to have the Cuban issue settled at any price, even that of capitulation and the dismantling of ' the socialist regime '.

Castro's predicament is heightened by the latest developments in the Sino-Soviet conflict. His attitude towards this conflict has hitherto been one of neutrality with a definite pro-Chinese bias. Neither of his two visits to the Soviet Union resulted in a change of attitude; press agency reports that he had been won over to the Soviet side were based on a completely inadequate analysis of the speeches and documents produced by these visits. In his television interview on his return from his first visit in May 1963, Castro actually defended the Chinese against the Soviet charge of war-mongering. Subsequently he refused to sign the test ban treaty, siding with China, North Korea, and North Vietnam in this matter. His second visit in December 1963 did not cause him to relent; he continued to withhold his signature, and the communiqué issued on the termination of the visit did not include a condemnation of China or even of Albania—the very minimum that Khrushchev could have expected of him at this stage of the conflict.

President Dorticos' visit to Moscow coincided with the fall of Khrushchev. The new Soviet leaders assured him of continuing support, but Cuban press reactions to the change were non-committal; the official communiqués were reproduced, but not the *Pravda* editorial giving the explanation, nor were Khrushchev's portraits and writings immediately withdrawn, as they were in Moscow. Since the new men will have to proceed cautiously at first, pressure on Castro will be relieved, at least for the immediate future.

Meanwhile, events have also shown that Castro had vastly over-estimated the prospects for revolutionary development in Latin America. In less than a year his Latin American policy has suffered three major setbacks: the Venezuelan elections of December 1963, the ignominious collapse of the leftist Goulart regime in Brazil in March 1964, and the Chilean presidential election of September 1964.

---

[5] Sierra Maestra: the Cuban mountain range which was Castro's stronghold during his two-year guerrilla war against Batista. Castro first launched this slogan in his speech on 26 July 1960.

Venezuela is the country in which the Castroites have made their most determined revolutionary effort.   As early as 1960, the left wing of Romulo Betancourt's democratic government party, *Accion Democratica*, broke away to form an ardently Castroite opposition movement, MIR (*Movimiento de Izquierda Revolucionaria*).   MIR, together with leftist elements of the main opposition party URD, and the Venezuelan Communist Party, one of the strongest and most radical of the Latin American communist parties, combined in a National Liberation Front (FLN). Late in 1962, the FLN initiated a campaign of terrorism and guerrilla warfare on the same pattern as that which in Cuba had led Fidel Castro to victory against the Batista dictatorship.   Early in 1963, the FLN officially constituted its military branch, the FALN (*Fuerzas Armadas de Liberacion Nacional*), comprising both urban guerrillas, i.e. groups of terrorists, and rural guerrillas operating mainly in the desolate Falcon mountain range in Western Venezuela.   The decision of the Communist Party of Venezuela to participate in this campaign coincided with a change of its position in the Sino-Soviet conflict: at the congress of the East German communists in January 1963 the Venezuelan party was no longer among those Latin American parties which condemned ' the provocations of the Albanian leaders ' and deplored ' the activities of those who appear to be seeking the division of the communist movement ',[6] i.e. the Chinese.

The attempt to overthrow the democratic Betancourt regime by force culminated in the FLN's decision to sabotage the 1963 presidential and parliamentary elections.   Terrorism in the cities was stepped up, and the population was called upon to boycott the ' electoral farce '.   But on election day, long queues formed in front of the polling-stations, and abstention was hardly higher than in the previous election, in which the extreme Left had participated.   The results brought heavy losses to the left-of-centre opposition parties, and gains for the right-of-centre Christian Democrats and Independents, proof that the overwhelming majority of the population rejected the terrorist methods of the extreme Left.

The FLN has not recovered from this blow.   Today there are still some guerrilla bands operating in the Sierra Falcon, and occasional acts of terrorism in the cities, and the extreme Left still commands a majority in the student body of Caracas University.   But the movement is now deeply split.   The leader of the MIR has issued a statement calling for an end to violence.   The Communist Party is still dominated by an extremist group led by the guerrilla chieftain Douglas Bravo, but there is a strong faction of moderates which is struggling to regain control, and, incidentally, to lead the party back into the Soviet fold.

Brazil was the first country to have two communist parties, one pro-Soviet, the other pro-Chinese.   The Brazilian communist leader, Carlos Prestes, had been a nationalist guerrilla leader in the nineteen-twenties,

---

6 The Chilean guest delegate, Orlando Millas, speaking in the name of the communist parties of seventeen Latin American countries; the list included neither the Cubans nor the Venezuelans.

and after his conversion to communism, had led the one serious attempt to seize power by force in the history of Latin American communism— the 1935 revolt. Since the failure of that attempt, he has been a firm believer in the peaceful policies of alliance, collaboration, and infiltration. Under his leadership Brazilian communists supported the Goulart regime.

Needless to say, Prestes supports Moscow in the Sino-Soviet conflict; but in 1962, a number of his most able and experienced lieutenants rebelled against his line, and split off to form the ' Communist Party of Brazil '. This new pro-Chinese party had disciplined, well-indoctrinated cadres, but since it follows the highly sectarian line imposed by the Chinese, it has failed to develop any mass appeal.

A third, specifically Castroite, movement were the Peasant Leagues founded in 1960–61 by a young socialist lawyer, Francesco Juliao. Since he advocated violent revolution, Juliao was denounced as an ' ultra-leftist adventurist ' by the Prestes communists.

In March 1964 the Brazilian army moved against Goulart. The general strike called by the communist trade union leaders failed to materialise, and Goulart was deposed without being able to offer any resistance. The new regime immediately suppressed all leftist organisations and arrested their leaders. The rapid success of the coup demonstrated the extreme weakness of the Left in South America's most populous and most important country—a crushing blow to Cuban hopes of a continental revolution. Since Goulart's fall the pro-Chinese elements everywhere claim that it demonstrates the failure of the ' collaborationist ' (i.e. pro-Soviet) line of the Prestes party. The official, but now really illegal Brazilian CP has not remained unaffected by these events, and Prestes, it is said, has been removed from his post as party secretary by his more radical colleagues.

Chile has by far the strongest and best organised communist party in South America (12·4 per cent of the vote in the 1963 municipal elections), as well as a socialist party which is almost as strong (11·1 per cent in 1963). The Chilean communists are staunchly loyal to Moscow, their leader, Luis Corvalan, being the main Latin American spokesman for the Soviet Union in the conflict with China, and also the most voluble advocate of the ' peaceful road to socialism '.

Since 1956, the communists have been linked in an uneasy alliance with the Chilean socialists, who are not social-democrats, but nationalists with a typically Latin American history of participation in military conspiracies and coups. They also have a most remarkable record of ideological instability. In the brief space of thirty years, the Chilean socialists have been militant anti-communists, members of a communist-sponsored Popular Front, admirers of the Argentinian fascist regime of Juan Peron, Titoists, and finally enthusiastic pro-Cubans; of late, their left wing has developed pro-Chinese tendencies. But two factors have remained constant throughout these changes: their violent nationalism and their dislike and distrust of the communists. For them, their alliance with the communists is a mere matter of expediency: its purpose was to obtain communist support for the socialist presidential candidate Salvador Allende. In the 1958 presidential election, Allende had polled 28 per cent of the vote, running a close second behind the victorious candidate of the right-wing parties, Jorge Alessandri. In the 1964 election, held on 4 September, Allende was heavily beaten by the Christian-Democrat Eduardo Frei, although he managed to increase his share of the vote to 38·9 per cent. Since the combined forces of the socialists and communists had never before polled more than 30 per cent in any Chilean election, this would appear to be a substantial success. Nevertheless, the election result plunged the entire extreme Left into a state of demoralisation and despair. For this was no ordinary election. It was held at a time when one 'socialist regime', Cuba, was already in existence in the Western Hemisphere. The Cuban regime is in severe straits and is in urgent need of support from another Latin American country. Chile's failure to supply that support may thus well mean that Marxist socialism has lost its last chance of victory in Latin America.

There is also a small pro-Chinese communist group in Chile, composed of perhaps two dozen rank-and-file members who were expelled for pro-Chinese activities in 1963. The group has no leader of stature, and its publications testify to a well-nigh unbelievably low level of intelligence and knowledge. Nevertheless it is barely possible that it will reap some benefit from the crisis into which the loss of the election has plunged both the Socialist and the Communist Party.

Peru has a small Communist Party which is seriously affected by the Sino-Soviet conflict. The party leaders supported the victorious left-of-centre candidate Belaunde Terry in the 1963 presidential election, and have since been acting as a pressure-group among the President's followers. But a sector of the party's central committee opposed this moderate policy and in January 1964 staged a coup by announcing the expulsion of the old leaders and the formation of a new leadership. Since then there have been two Communist Parties in Peru, each claiming to be the authentic one. The rebels appear to have rallied a large part of the party cadres and the overwhelming majority of the young members to their cause. They have proclaimed allegiance to Peking, while the old-guard leadership is loyal to Moscow. The Peruvian Castroites are represented by the MIR, formerly APRA Rebelde, which is active among the peasants of the mountain regions.

Ecuador and **Bolivia** also have nuclei of pro-Chinese communists. In **Argentina**, the small and singularly ineffective Communist Party, led by the ancient Comintern veteran Vittorio Codovilla, formerly cooperated with the semi-fascist Peronista movement in opposing the military regime, but after the moderate democrat Illia's surprise victory in the 1963 presidential election, deserted its allies in order to give qualified support to the new government. It has now reaped its reward in being restored to full legality after many years of semi-clandestinity. Meanwhile, the extreme left wing of the Peronistas, which is under Castroite influence, has constituted itself as a separate *Movimiento Revolucionario Peronista.* Castroite guerrillas are operating in an outlying tropical province, but neither they nor the scattered bands operating in **Colombia** and **Guatemala** appear to constitute more than a local nuisance.

*   *   *

Thus, after an impressive upsurge in the years 1959–62, leftist extremism in Latin America is now deeply divided and obviously in a period of decline. The turning point was the Caribbean crisis of October 1962, although it took more than a year for the full effect of the Soviet Union's climb-down on that occasion to become apparent.

The pro-Chinese tendencies which have since manifested themselves in the Latin American Left are symptoms of disappointment over the Soviet Union's failure to live up to expectations. They are not likely to develop into a revolutionary movement of any importance. For there is a strong streak of realism in the Latin American character, even in that of the utopian dreamers and romantic guerrillas of the extreme Left. Latin American interest in and enthusiasm for the Soviet Union developed in direct proportion to the growth of that power's military strength and willingness to interfere in Latin America. China has not the means, i.e. the military strength, to inspire anything like the same enthusiasm, and even if it had, the Latin Americans would fail to react to it positively. The explosion of the Chinese atomic bomb elicited no admiration in South America; approval was not forthcoming even from the communists.

The fall of Khrushchev has caused no great excitement either. Only the Chilean CP (in an article by Luis Corvalan in *El Siglo* of 20 October 1964) expressed concern about the manner of his removal. Other parties endorsed the official Soviet explanation.

It is highly significant that of all the issues at stake in the Sino-Soviet conflict, the only ones that really inspire interest and debate in the Latin American Left are those concerned with revolutionary strategy and with Soviet foreign policy. Such issues as political and cultural destalini-sation and economic revisionism are regarded as quite irrelevant to Latin American reality. As a matter of fact, the pro-Soviet parties have never properly informed their followers about the problems of destalinisation, and the Latin American left still has the same naive pic-ture of the Soviet Union which European leftists harboured in the nine-teen-thirties; the heart-searchings of East and West European communists and fellow-travellers are completely unknown to them.

One Chilean leftist to whom the present writer gave a copy of *One day in the life of Ivan Denisovich* said indignantly that it presented an unfair picture of the Soviet Union. This only demonstrates that the Latin American Left is not genuinely interested in the Soviet Union itself; it is interested only in what the Soviet Union represents in terms of power, as an ally against the United States, and it is in the light of this attitude that the post-Khrushchev leadership will be judged.

AFRICA

William E. Griffith *

COMMUNISM came to Africa from Europe, along with and as part of European culture and politics.[1] Africa's communist parties and groups were originally established by Europeans; they have long remained multi-racial; and like other European political movements they have never obtained any serious African mass support. The Marxist-Leninist emphasis on the proletariat, on multi-racial internationalism, and on atheism, have always run contrary to African traditions and culture; and the few Western-educated intellectuals who have become communists have been largely submerged in, when not suppressed by, the rising wave of anti-colonialism and radical pan-African nationalism which characterises the new, modernising African intelligentsia. To most black Africans the Russians are as European as any other whites; moreover, manipulation of European and African communist parties and groups by the Russians for purely Soviet purposes soon disillusioned most of their early African sympathisers. Furthermore, the rationalist ideology of Marxism-Leninism, or indeed any political ideology at all, has little if any appeal to any but the most Westernised Africans, who are fully prepared to give lip-service to communist ideological and policy formulas when it serves their purpose, only to abandon them when that seems more in accord with their interests. Africans tend to be undogmatic and pragmatic and to prefer the achievement of consensus to prolonged ideological struggle. South of the Sahara and even in North Africa, therefore, political theories and ideologies mean much less than north of the Mediterranean. Those African intellectuals and radicals who have been much influenced by Marxism-Leninism have been so first by its organisational aspects and then by such general Marxist-Leninist concepts as state ownership and control of the economy and economic determinism, which they see as simultaneously allowing both the recovery of pre-industrial communal virtues and modernisation via industrialisation. Most of them have not taken over Marxism's hostility to religion, its stress on the 'leading role of the working class', or the belief in the necessity of an elite, rather than a mass party, oriented towards an urban proletariat rather than the peasantry. (This last omission makes particularly clear the preference of many radical Africans for Chinese, as opposed to Soviet, policy

* I have profited much from two trips to Africa, to West and East Africa in 1962 and to southern Africa in 1963, in connection with which I should like to record my gratitude to the Center of International Studies at MIT and to the Carnegie Corporation for making the trips possible.

[1] For discussion of communism in Africa see Z. Brzezinski, ed., *Africa and the Communist World* (Stanford, 1963); George Padmore, *Pan-Africanism or Communism?* (New York, 1956); David L. Morison, *The USSR and Africa* (Oxford U.P., 1964), Fritz Schatten, *Afrika—Schwarz oder Rot?* (Munich, 1961).

positions.) Finally, some radical African nationalist leaders influenced by Marxist-Leninist concepts (e.g. in Guinea and Mali) probably by now think of themselves (as Castro in all likelihood does) as Marxist-Leninists who have successfully adapted the best of that doctrine to their national circumstances.

Indeed, they are probably convinced that the Russians and the Chinese have also adapted ideological Marxism to their specific conditions, thereby both contributing to and influencing for the better a much looser, more permissive current in the international communist movement than that which previously existed. That the Sino-Soviet split itself is moving all communist parties towards differentiation further encourages such thinking.

It is true that some African students who were fed strong doses of leftist, including communist, ideology while being educated in London and Paris in the 1940s and 1950s retained a liking for both communist terminology and its organisational aspects. However, for these young African intellectuals communism was primarily a method of rapid modernisation; of the establishment, organisation, and discipline of a new, modernising intellectual African elite; and of obtaining aid from communist states. Thus state ownership and central planning, the Leninist model of one-party organisation, and economic and sometimes political ties with the Soviet Union have remained characteristic of some new African states, notably Guinea, Ghana, and Mali.

The primary focus of the African elites—pan-African nationalism—did not come from communism. Being modernisers and thus determined to depose the traditional African tribal elites, the new elites could not base their power upon the tribes, while the colonial boundaries were creations of the colonisers and could thus only with difficulty serve as their rallying symbol for modernisation and independence. Their goal of a united black Africa was the result. In turn, pan-Africanism plus modernisation has led to such general concepts as 'African socialism', a varying mixture of Marxism and utopian socialism combined with such African attitudes as consensus, the charismatic concept of the tribal chieftain, common ownership of land and property, and extended family.

In fact, pan-Africanism has made little political progress, and the resulting disillusionment and the consequent need of the new modernising elites for a substitute focus have made them turn to nation-building within their own states, artificial and colonial as their boundaries may be, as the prime symbols of the nations that do not yet exist in Africa but which they hope to create. Only radical African leaders such as Nkrumah and Sekou Touré, who have the most effectively established their supremacy over traditionalist tribal elements, can afford to spend much energy on pan-Africanist political activity.

However, although on the whole it remains a frustrated if still powerful dream, pan-Africanism and the present African rulers stand as the major obstacles to Soviet and Chinese ambitions in Africa. For the desire to form a group strong enough to keep Africa out of the cold war is an integral part of the drive for pan-African unity. This near unanimous African objective not to become the pawn of either Western or communist interests has been largely formed by the African states' experiences in the United Nations. Undeniably, the radical African elites greatly fear what they consider the dangers of continued if indirect (i.e. economic) domination by the ex-colonial powers. 'Neo-colonialism' is still a persistent cry, particularly among the young radical modernisers to whom those African rulers who came to power by the will of, rather than in struggle against, the colonial powers (Senghor, the Sardauna of Sokoto, and Houphouet-Boigny, as contrasted with Nkrumah, Sekou Touré, and Kenyatta) seem merely disguised perpetuators of European hegemony. Yet the Soviets have several times overplayed their hand, most notably in Guinea and the Congo, and the Chinese have done the same in Malawi. Most African leaders have learned not only the danger of letting communist as well as European powers go too far in Africa but also, and more importantly, how relatively easy it is to outplay the communists at their own game. On the other hand, there does remain one area of potentially serious communist penetration within the modernising sectors of African society. For the successes of some African states in secondary and higher education, contrasted with their slowness in economic development, are producing rising numbers of 'academic proletarians', whose desire for the power and privileges of the post-independence elite, and whose attraction to the communist model of rapid modernisation in the hands of new, disciplined intelligentsias, furnish an increasing base for Soviet and Chinese influence.

Before starting on a survey of communist parties and groups in Africa, and of Soviet, Chinese, and other communist activities there, several important but often neglected preliminary points must be made.

First, the number, size, and significance of communist parties and groups in Africa is very limited; the influence and activities of communist states is much more significant. Furthermore, communist influence is increasingly exercised not upon or through disciplined communist individuals or groups, but rather upon and through radical African nationalist movements.

Second, in the context of the radical nationalist movements, African politics is carried on by blacks and whites, but it cannot be accurately portrayed by any such dichotomy. The appeal of communism to radical African nationalists is organisational rather than ideological. The extent to which these individuals may come under communist influence hinges in large part upon how long their goals are frustrated, the depth of their impatience with the lack of victory, and their inability to find support elsewhere.

Yet, third, the temptation of the radical African nationalists to turn to the communist powers for aid may have been blunted by the Sino-Soviet rift. This dispute has given the Africans a free show in communist polemics that has made Marxist-Leninist ideological quarrels seem not only irrelevant but often ridiculous, and indeed a threat to the concentration of all anti-colonial forces.

Finally, because of the political and economic exigencies facing the Soviets and the Chinese alike, Western and particularly American, British, and French policies and actions will probably continue to have significant influence in Africa, most notably in moments of crisis, during which they also influence African attitudes towards the Soviets and the Chinese.

North Africa: Of its independent countries, the three ex-French ones, Algeria, Morocco, and Tunisia, are a part of the Mediterranean as well as of the Middle Eastern and African worlds; and French influence, even in Algeria, remains great. Libya is only now reluctantly entering the active Middle Eastern as well as the African political worlds; and Egypt, despite Nasser's pan-African ambitions and his support for radical African movements, remains primarily a Middle Eastern power.

Not only has communism in all of North Africa been almost entirely a phenomenon of European origin, but its adherents have been largely Europeans as well. It has never gained substantial support, and all communist parties in North Africa are now illegal, small in number, harassed, and negligible in their significance. Their failure and impotence have been made even greater by the increasing tendency of both Moscow and Peking to deal directly with Nasser, Ben Bella, and other rulers, without paying any attention to the local communists.

Algeria and Egypt have been special objectives of Soviet and Chinese economic and military aid, political influence, hopes, and conflicts. Both Ben Bella and Nasser have been influenced by Marxist and Leninist ideas, particularly (as has Sekou Touré) by their organisational aspects; both have been impressed by Tito personally and by some of the deviant Yugoslav communist ideology (but more by its guerrilla and peasant background). In sum, although both have ambitions which far exceed the bounds of their countries, they are both primarily radical modernising nationalists who have so far known how to take aid from East and West and to give no firm allegiance to either in return.

Tropical Africa: Communism in tropical Africa is also by origin a European phenomenon. It may therefore conveniently be treated according to the areas colonised by the four European powers: France, Great Britain, Italy, and Belgium.

1. *The ex-French colonies*: French intellectual, cultural, and social influence upon Africans has probably been greater (with the exception of British influence in South Africa) than that of any other European colonial power. Furthermore, the French Communist Party (PCF) has long been large, powerful, and very active in the French African

territories both as a party and through the trade union federation (CGT) which it dominates. As in France, its most significant influence in Africa has been among intellectuals and trade union leaders. And when, after World War II, anti-colonialism began to be significant in the French African territories, of all French parties the PCF was the most vocal about it. The first African party in the Fourth Republic, the RDA, therefore quite naturally allied itself with the PCF in the French Chamber of Deputies, and the CGT (and the World Federation of Trade Unions [WFTU] of which the CGT was a member) became active in French African trade unionism. Yet the PCF's subordination to Soviet policy, its far from complete anti-colonialism, notably with respect to the Algerian rebellion, and above all the fact that it was European, drove the overwhelming majority of the French African leaders of the RDA to break with it in the early 1950s, while retaining much of the Marxist-Leninist organisational model. The only faction of an RDA section which remained allied with the communists, the *Union des populations du Cameroun* (UPC), waged guerrilla warfare for a time, in the process became dependent on Chinese support (the Soviets having previously refused aid), and is by now of no significance. The influence of Marxism-Leninism, as strained through the PCF and the CGT, remains of considerable importance in such radical populist nationalist governments as those of Sekou Touré in Guinea and Modiba Keita in Mali, but, as with Ben Bella, anti-colonialism, anti-Europeanism, Islam, and radical agrarian populism, plus the desire to remain independent and the confidence that this is possible by taking Soviet, Chinese, French, or American aid (or indeed all four), and balancing the assisting countries against each other, are more important than disciplined Marxist-Leninist contributions to their thought.

Guinea represents perhaps the most clear failure of Soviet short-term objectives in Africa. Sekou Touré was able to defy General de Gaulle in 1958 because of his tightly-organised *Parti Démocratique de Guinée* (PDG) and because he had cemented an alliance between his own tribe, the Malinke, and the more numerous Foulahs. Since de Gaulle thereafter refused to aid him, and the other Western powers followed this example, he turned to the Soviet Union, East Europe, and China. Although the occasion for his break with Moscow in late 1961 was the unrest in the teachers' union, followed by a short-lived strike in the *lycées,* its main cause was the ineffectiveness of communist economic aid. Some of the teachers' union leaders probably were communists, but the unrest was primarily that of young, frustrated, radical intellectuals against an established and privileged, albeit radical, state bureaucracy.

After 1961 communist aid was rapidly replaced, first by West German, then by American and some French aid, and Touré publicly resumed the non-aligned posture which he had always expressed in private. His appeal in radical African circles is still strong, and he remains willing to ally with Moscow and Peking in the UN and elsewhere to further his own, and African, interests. But, like Keita in Mali, he no longer has any illusions—and he probably never had many—about the incompatibility of Soviet and Chinese ultimate objectives and his own. By now the Soviet Union and China deal with Touré and Keita primarily on a state-to-state, not party-to-party, basis.

The only Marxist-Leninist party now active in black ex-French Africa, the small illegal *Parti africain d'indépendance* (PAI) of Senegal (whose leadership is mostly in exile in Mali), is composed mainly of a few French-educated intellectuals. It has no base in either the peasantry or the urbanised proletariat. Furthermore, it is rent with factionalism as a result of the Sino-Soviet rift. Not surprisingly, therefore, it is of little significance.

2. *The ex-Belgian Congo.* There is no evidence that the small Belgian Communist Party had any significant influence among Africans in the Congo. Lumumba was not a disciplined communist, nor are either his present successors in exile in Brazzaville or the rebel leaders in Stanleyville, Kivu, or Kwilu. Yet sufficient evidence is available to demonstrate that the Chinese (and perhaps the Soviets) have been aiding the neo-Lumumbaists both in Brazzaville and from the small border state of Burundi. This aid has consisted of money, guerrilla training, and advice. Even more than in Zanzibar, recent developments in the Congo show how much, and until the present with what profit, the Chinese concentrate on radical ' national liberation movements '. Developments in both areas also demonstrate more clearly than any others in Africa the basis of Chinese and (to a much lesser extent) of Soviet calculations there—a reliance on often radical, tribally hostile, and locally anarchic forces. It is not surprising that the anarchic tide has run so high in the Congo. Belgium's political and cultural heritage was too thin, the number and quality of educated Africans too small, ethnic diversity too great, the clashing moves of African and non-African powers there too destabilising, and its area and diversity so great that it would have been surprising had anything less chaotic happened.

3. *British West Africa.* The Gold Coast, the first British colony on the west coast of Africa, was the first to become independent; not surprisingly, therefore, its intellectuals, educated in London and in Accra, were the most Westernised and Europeanised of any in British West Africa. Some of them were attracted to communism. Nkrumah himself, educated in England and America, where he was influenced by Marxism, was primarily a pan-Africanist, an orientation in which he was strengthened by his close associate, the West Indian ex-communist, George Padmore. Nkrumah's drift to the extreme left at home and abroad, like Castro's, has been influenced more by his determination to maintain and consolidate his personal dictatorship than by any disciplined ideological Marxist-Leninist allegiance or Soviet or Chinese influence. There is, however, a small group of young African intellectuals in Accra, centred on the regime-sponsored paper *The*

Spark, who do seem to be something close to disciplined communists, under the inspiration if not the control of Moscow via the British Communist Party; and their influence with Nkrumah is said to be growing. Furthermore, like Touré's PDG and Keita's *Union Soudanaise,* Nkrumah's CPP has sent 'fraternal observers' to Soviet and other communist party gatherings. Yet, like the state parties of Guinea and Mali, Nkrumah's CPP is essentially anti-intellectual, staffed largely with the 'verandah boys' who did not make the academic grade, while the opposition to it is found largely among the frustrated and harassed intellectuals.

In Nigeria, potentially the most powerful country in tropical Africa, the North remains Moslem and feudal, while the South, which is booming economically, retains strong elements of the British democratic tradition. However, Nigeria's rapid increase in population, and notably in half-educated semi-intellectuals, bids fair, even at the present rate of economic growth, to create increasing discontent and native radicalism. Only very small Marxist-Leninist 'study groups' and more recently a 'Marxist-Leninist' party, the Socialist Workers and Farmers Party (SWAFP),[2] headed by Dr. Otegbeye, have appeared publicly in Nigeria. It has influence within the Nigerian TUC, the left-wing trade union federation, which, together with the United Labour Congress (ICFTU-affiliated) and the Nigerian Workers Council (IFCTU-affiliated), formed the Joint Action Committee which won the June 1964 Lagos strike. It seems doubtful, however, that communists in Nigeria will exercise any significant political influence, unless and until the present relative stability there deteriorates markedly. Yet inter-tribal and inter-regional rivalries and the successful Lagos strike have shown that Nigeria's time of troubles may only now be beginning. The result cannot be predicted.

4. *Former British East Central Africa.* The relatively small number of educated Africans in East Africa (as compared with West and South Africa) has until recently precluded the growth of any significant number of disciplined communists, and there are no communist parties in the region with the exception of the Sudan. Recently, however, many East African students have gone first to London and then to communist countries, and Marxism-Leninism has had considerable influence on them. Jomo Kenyatta himself was strongly influenced in London in the 1930s by Marxism, and he even made a trip to Moscow. As his experience indicates, any significant influence of Marxist-Leninist ideology has usually required a considerable exposure to European cultural influence. It is not surprising, therefore, that such influence first became apparent in Zanzibar.[3] There, a small group of Arab and

---

[2] The inaugural conference of SWAFP is said to have been held in August 1963; by November it had enrolled 2,000 members in twenty branches. *The African Communist,* January-March 1964, p. 67.

[3] See Mohamed Babu's interview in *Révolution,* May 1964, and another in *L'Unita,* 27 July 1964.

part-Arab young nationalist intellectuals began plotting against the traditionalist Arab minority elite which dominated the majority of Africans. Gathering around the young Sheik Abdul Rahman Mohamed Babu, who had been influenced by Marxism-Leninism while studying at the London School of Economics, these young radicals came under the influence of Chinese and Cuban communism in the late 1950s and early 1960s. Even so, the willingness of the Chinese to finance them probably played at least as great a role in their actions as did ideological commitment to anything much more specific than romantic revolutionary passion.

Babu's group began as the extreme left-wing of the ruling Zanzibari Nationalist Party (ZNP) of which Babu was secretary-general. However, when he was expelled from the ZNP, Babu formed his own Umma Party, which after the coup joined the majority Afro-Shirazi Party— headed by Sheik Abeid Karume—in setting up the new government. This particular combination of forces within the new regime, combined with the rapidity with which communist powers (notably the Soviets and the East Germans) came to the aid of the new Zanzibar government, and the slowness of Western powers in establishing contacts with that government, helped Moscow and Pankow, and to a lesser extent Peking, to acquire major influence on the island. Karume was hampered by his own lack of experience, the influence and skill of Babu, and the pro-Soviet tendencies of the other main Afro-Shirazi leader, Hanga. He thus turned for support to Tanganyika. In order to forestall a communist-controlled Zanzibar, Nyerere joined with Karume to unite the two states. However, Babu and Hanga, and even Karume, who did not relish giving up his power to Nyerere much more than to Babu and Hanga, strongly resisted Dar's attempts to implement the union. The issue polarised around the East German embassy in Zanzibar, which provided the main external resource needed to maintain Zanzibar's autonomy vis-à-vis Dar. The result remains in doubt. In the meantime, the Zanzibar radicals, his own indecision, and the after-effects of the abortive coup in Dar moved Nyerere towards a less pro-Western position, while in both Dar and Zanzibar the Soviets and Chinese fought bitterly for influence.

The Chinese drive to gain influence in Africa also figured in the governmental crisis in Malawi. The question whether to accept a £18 million Chinese loan (which Dr Banda refused) was certainly one issue, although clearly not the crux of the matter, in that cabinet upheaval. As so often in Africa, the whole affair reflected a conflict of generations, and the tension between a more traditional-style leader of an independence movement and younger, more intellectual, and more radical elements. Nevertheless, in spite of Chinese denials, it was confirmed by one of Dr Banda's ministers that the Chinese Embassy had indeed offered Malawi a £18 million loan, the very size of which, apart from the appeal it may have had for some of the dissident ministers, certainly indicates the extent to which Peking is prepared to invest in Central Africa.

In Kenya, Oginga Odinga, the Vice-President and a well-to-do Luo merchant, frankly stated that he takes Soviet and Chinese money (in large sums) primarily because he needs it to build up his party machine and because he could get it nowhere else. Corruption is rife in black African states, and Moscow and Peking have been clever enough to use it for their purpose, although it is unlikely that all the Africans who have been bribed will stay bought. Indeed, one may suspect that there will be few if any changes in their behaviour as a result of the bribes, which aid them in attaining their own objectives more than the further long-term—as opposed to immediate—Soviet or Chinese purposes.

5. *The ex-Italian colonies.* Communism remains illegal and persecuted in Libya and Ethiopia, nor is there an organised communist party in Somaliland. As to the influence of the Italian Communist Party in these countries, its efforts were short-lived and (despite increasing participation in African trade union activities) it is not a significant force. In Libya suspected Italian communist organisers were expelled in 1951 and 1952.

In Somaliland, although communism itself is insignificant, the territorial disputes with Ethiopa and Kenya have made Mogadishu ready to accept first Chinese and later Soviet arms aid.[4] So far this does not seem to have brought major political gains to either Moscow or Peking, but Somali irredentism is one of the most explosive issues in East Africa, and (as the recent Soviet-Cyprus arms agreement showed) irredentism makes strange bedfellows.

The White Redoubt. It can reasonably be argued that the problems and condition of southern Africa, and their implications for independent black Africa, offer the Russians and Chinese perhaps their best opportunity to increase their influence on the continent.

1. *Portuguese Africa.* Most colonial powers have dreamed of assimilation; not so many years ago France boasted of *l'Algérie française*. Portugal has held the longest to this policy, and, it must be said, with the best justification. As modern Brazil demonstrates, Portuguese tradition is particularly tolerant towards miscegenation and the resulting multiracial society. Yet the gap between Portuguese theory and practice in Africa remains great. The existence of a few *assimilados* in Luanda and Lourenco Marques could not long cloud the fundamental point: Portuguese colonial practice in Africa, as distinguished from its theory, was and remains largely one of economic exploitation and political repression.

---

4 John Drysdale, *The Somali Dispute* (London, 1963); Mesfin Wolde Mariam, ' Background to the Ethio-Somalian Boundary Dispute ', *Journal of Modern African Studies*, July 1964.

The few, mostly mulatto *assimilados* in Angola's and Mozambique's capitals therefore quite naturally have provided the most likely targets for pro-communist activity.

Angola has been the main centre of educated mulatto activity in the Portuguese African territories. Northern Angola includes the southern part of the Bakongo tribal area, the greater part of which is north of the border in the (ex-Belgian) Congo. Once the Congo became independent and the Bakongo became influential in Congo politics in 1961, a largely tribally-based revolt led by Holden Roberto and his *Uniao dos Populacoes de Angola* (UPA) broke out in northern Angola. The revolt was and still is planned, supplied, and directed from across the border in the Congo.

The other, more intellectual, much more left-wing group, the *Movimento Popular de Libertacao de Angola* (MPLA), was led by a group of almost entirely European-educated mulatto *assimilado* intellectuals from Luanda. Their first major move, a short-lived and rapidly crushed rising there, also occurred in 1961. The extent of communist influence and of Marxist-Leninist inspiration in the MPLA is controversial; and as with all such organisations of a largely clandestine nature, such matters are difficult to determine. Some of the MPLA leaders, in particular the mulatto *assimilados* Mario de Andrade and Viriato da Cruz, have long had close ties with Portuguese and Soviet communists, and more recently da Cruz has been in close relations with the Chinese.[5] However, like most African extreme leftists, they are probably neither disciplined communists nor unquestionably loyal either to Moscow or to Peking. Yet, like Babu in Zanzibar, they are not entirely African, and this very disadvantage makes them naturally inclined to rely on outside support for compensation—which in the present political constellation can only be communist (since the Western powers are allied with Portugal in Nato).

Thus, the MPLA remains small, intellectual, and mulatto-dominated and, for pan-African tastes, too closely allied with the communists. Most important, it has never succeeded in launching any significant guerrilla activity, while the UPA, which was consistently supported by Holden Roberto's friend, ex-Prime Minister Adoula in Léopoldville—until Tshombe replaced him—kept guerrilla warfare going (although with no decisive success) from 1961 until most of its guerrilla activity in northern Angola was crushed by the Portuguese in early 1964. That the UPA was fighting and the MPLA was not, was the decisive reason why in July 1963 the OAU's Liberation Committee recognised Roberto's group as the Angolan Government-in-exile (GRAE) and as the sole Angolan organisation worthy of support.

[5] Lowenthal (in Brzezinski, *Africa and the Communist World*, pp. 258–259, ftn. 20) cites a statement by Andrade in *Pravda*, 6 February 1961, that the MPLA originated from a 'small Marxist underground group' (identified in 1962 by *Afrika Segodnya* (Moscow, 1962) as the Angolan CP, founded in 1955) and a larger African one with a near-Marxist programme. See also Viriato da Cruz, 'Angola: Quelle indépendance?' *Révolution*, February 1964.

The Angolan rebels have not been able to make decisive advances against the Portuguese. Portuguese victories over Roberto's forces, the mid-1964 replacement of Adoula by Tshombe, who has long had good relations with the Portuguese, plus the activities in the Congo of extremist rebels with Chinese contacts, have further weakened Roberto's position. Furthermore, Dr Banda and Dr Kaunda have decided to maintain peaceful relations with the two Portuguese territories, lest they be denied access to Angolan and Mozambique ports, and the Angolan and Mozambique rebels cannot therefore count on Malawi or Zambia for support. The consequent frustration in UPA ranks has been increasingly disruptive. Angolan guerrillas in training in the Congo have at least once almost mutinied against their leaders, who themselves have become increasingly divided into conflicting military and political groups. Holden Roberto's position has been further undermined by the resignation of his chief aide, Jonas Sawimbi, in the summer of 1964. No Western aid being available, and OAU aid being slow and increasingly limited by the domestic problems of its members, Roberto has naturally been tempted to turn to the communists, and, among them, to the power which seems the most willing to give aid: China.

Meanwhile, the MPLA itself, having lost out to Roberto in July 1963, split into a majority wing headed by the African physician, Dr Agostino Neto, but actually probably still largely influenced by the pro-Soviet mulatto, Mario de Andrade, and a minority wing headed by the mulatto Viriato da Cruz. Da Cruz soon made it clear that he was receiving Chinese support. Not surprisingly, given the very pragmatic, not to say cynical, Chinese use of radical African nationalist movements, communist or not, da Cruz soon tried to join with Roberto's GRAE, a move in which he succeeded in early 1964. (Conversely, Sawimbi, after his split with Roberto, is said to have made overtures to the Andrade-Neto MPLA faction.) Only Roberto's menaced position and perhaps his hope of getting Chinese arms could explain the reversal of his previous hostility to MPLA mulattoes, who, he rightly feared, would use their much greater education to gain control over his African associates, and his willingness to welcome them into his movement. However, da Cruz and his supporters must have been impressed by Chinese willingness to help the previously anti-communist Roberto; it seems unlikely that they will be more firmly committed to China or any other communist power as a result.

Mozambique is a different and much shorter story. In the first place, it has few mulattoes, not such close intellectual ties with Portugal, and therefore practically no significant communist or *communisant* movement. Second, since serious guerrilla warfare has not begun there, the tensions of the Angolan liberation movement are not yet a dominant feature of the Mozambique emigré scene. Third, since most of its African nationalist intellectuals were educated in Protestant mission schools, they have less inclination to embrace Marxist views. Having no ethnic or minority problems, the natural tendency of Mozambique African intellectuals was towards pan-Africanism, and, as in East Africa, such influence as the communists have has been won by their money rather than their ideological appeal. The main emigré group, FRELIMO, in Dar-es-Salaam, headed by the American-educated anthropologist Eduardo Mondlane, is not under serious communist control or influence, nor is his main rival, Gumane. Yet, as in Angola, FRELIMO's frustration at not even being able to start guerrilla operations in Mozambique (due in part to Tanganyika's fear of Portuguese retaliation), made communist support more attractive. In December 1963 Mondlane went to Peking where he was ceremonially received by Mao. Communist influence in the Angolan and Mozambique African nationalist movements thus seems likely to increase the longer and more successfully the Portuguese hold out. Since at present Salazar is winning and Roberto and Mondlane are losing, Moscow and Peking appear likely to gain, and the West to lose influence.

2. *Southern Rhodesia.* With Malawi and Zambia now independent, less than a quarter-million whites of Southern Rhodesia remain between black African nationalism and South Africa itself. The educated African elite of Southern Rhodesia is small in number; there is no communist party and apparently few communist sympathisers among the Africans there. Nevertheless, as in Angola and Mozambique, the extent of future communist influence may well vary directly with the length and intensity of the white settlers' resistance to African majority rule. Should African nationalist frustration in Southern Rhodesia continue for some years, there, as in the Portuguese colonies, Moscow and Peking will find increasingly fertile fields for their efforts.

3. *South Africa.* The three million whites in the Republic of South Africa, by far the wealthiest, most industrialised, and most powerful state on the continent, and particularly their inner core of 1·8 million Afrikaners, represent the single remaining ruling racial autocracy and also the strongest and most defiant barrier to the complete conquest of the continent by black African nationalism. The thousands-strong African elite (to say nothing of the Coloureds and the Indians) have backgrounds and training that could make an African-ruled South Africa the predominant power on the continent, yet Verwoerd's policies condemn them to oppression and frustration.

Until a few years ago Africans could still attend South African universities, and the many who did were thoroughly exposed to European culture—including its radical Marxist-Leninist variety. Further, communism in South Africa has had something to work with available nowhere else on the continent: an industrialised country with a substantial proletariat, white and African. The main inspiration of South African communism came at first from Britain. Later many if not most of its white members were drawn from the same minority which so largely staffed East European communist parties: Jews from Poland,

Lithuania, and Russia, who came to South Africa after the beginning of the century. Many of these people prospered, and all suffered varying degrees of racial and religious discrimination. From its beginning after World War I the South African Communist Party (SACP) [6] was multiracial; it included whites (who have always been predominant in it), Indians, Coloureds, and Africans. Like its East European equivalents, it was racked by factional feuds and by the rapid shifts in Moscow's line during the 1930s. Declared illegal after the Nationalist government came to power in 1948, it has since remained underground. However, it has continued to operate within and thus in part to control other organisations, primarily racial by nature. The SACP leadership remains pro-Soviet in the Sino-Soviet dispute,[7] despite visits by some of its African leaders to Peking.

Until recently, when it was driven underground, there also existed, primarily among Cape Coloured intellectuals, a radical pro-violence movement, the 'Yu Chi Chan Club' (taken from the title of Mao's work on guerrilla warfare), of which the two leading figures were K. G. Abrahams, who was originally from Southwest Africa, and Dr Neville Alexander. This group, whose members came from the youth wing of the Trotskyite and largely Coloured Non-European Unity Movement, were strongly influenced by Maoist doctrine. Alexander (who received a Ph.D. in German literature at Tübingen), is now in jail. Abrahams, after being kidnapped from Bechuanaland, where he had been active in the Southwest African Peoples Organisation (SWAPO) which is affiliated with the African National Congress (ANC), was allowed to return there by Pretoria after British protests.

Until the 1950s the South African Communist Party made relatively little impression upon the traditionally-oriented leaders of the ANC, the main African nationalist movement in South Africa. However, as the Nationalist government steadily increased its pressure, the SACP began to influence the younger, more westernised, and radical African nationalist leaders. For until the foundation of the Liberal Party in 1953, the South African Communist Party was the only political party in the country which offered membership to Africans on an equal basis with whites; and many of its white members fought heroically against apartheid. From the beginning, therefore, the ANC did not exclude communists from its ranks. By the late 1950s the communists succeeded in capturing significant influence within the ANC and this

[6] There is no satisfactory history of the SACP; Mr. Sheridan Johns' forthcoming Harvard Ph.D. dissertation on the subject will fill this gap until 1949. I am grateful to Mr. Johns for allowing me to read some of his manuscript and for discussions on the subject. The SACP's monthly, *The African Communist* (London), which now also has a French edition, is a valuable source for the line not only of the SACP but of communist parties and groups throughout Africa. See also the SACP programme, *The Road to South African Freedom*, and C. and M. Legum, *South Africa: Crisis for the West* (London, 1964), pp. 182–86.

[7] See Terence Africanus (pseud.), ' 100 Years of the International Marxist Movement ' *The African Communist*, July-September 1964.

influence has more recently been on the rise as so many of its non-communist leaders, notably Luthuli, have been banned or imprisoned, and as the frustrations of the ANC's exile leadership and the lack of effective Western and OAU support for it make Soviet and Chinese aid more attractive. The extent of SACP influence in the ANC is naturally highly controversial. During the Pretoria treason trial no proof was adduced for the charge that the ANC was infiltrated or controlled by the SACP. It has also been said that Mandela has admitted his secret communist affiliations; but his speech at the Rivonia trial leaves this in doubt; and even if he were or is a communist, he would hardly be totally responsive to SACP directives in all circumstances.

However, Govan Mbeki, J. B. Marks, and Moses Katane, all ANC leaders, are declared by the SACP to be among its members.[8] Finally, the *Umkanto We Sizwe* (Spear of the Nation), the covert ANC para-military arm, was particularly infiltrated by the SACP.

Even in the 1950s African frustration arising out of Nationalist oppression had produced a trend towards pan-Africanism and the endorsement of violence as the only hope of defeating the Nationalists. Because the communists were multi-racialist, both before and after they were outlawed in 1950, and because until 1961 they rejected violence, a group of younger pan-Africanist intellectuals under the leadership of the university teacher Robert Sobukwe broke away from the ANC in 1959 to form the Pan-Africanist Congress (PAC). Since then the ANC and the PAC have been bitter enemies.

The 1960 Sharpeville shootings led to a police crack-down on African nationalist as well as communist activities so severe, and within a few years so successful, that by 1963 both seemed to have been organisationally broken within South Africa. Communist and African nationalist leaders were either in exile in London, Dar-es-Salaam, or Leopoldville, or in prison in South Africa. In this situation, as always in exile, the ANC-PAC competition grew more intense since there was no effective public opinion at home to decide it; and all African nationalist exile leaders increasingly turned to the search for foreign help. Because of the relatively passive policy towards South Africa of the United States, the United Kingdom, and the West European powers, the Soviets and the Chinese were both quick to give aid to the ANC and particularly to the communists in its leadership. After the OAU Liberation Committee was established in 1963 it gave some (but little) aid to both ANC and PAC. Nevertheless the apparent communist influence within the ANC caused increasing concern to some African nationalists in black Africa. This apprehension seemed likely, however, to be over-come by their need, due largely to the lack of external support, for arms, sabotage and guerrilla training, and financial support. Meanwhile, in 1963–64 the PAC split into several warring factions, one of which was subsequently in contact with Peking.

---

8 *African Communist*, July-September 1964, p. 11.

The post-Sharpeville police repression, the increasing support for Verwoerd by the English-speaking whites, the effective—if perhaps only temporary—collapse of organised African nationalist activity in South Africa, and, at least as important, the instability in West and East Africa and the resultant concern of their leaders with their own affairs rather than with the struggle for South African liberation—all showed the African nationalists from the White Redoubt that only massive force from outside the African continent could subdue the Afrikaners. Angola, Mozambique, and Southern Rhodesia may still be viewed as areas where internal weakness and foreign pressure will ultimately bring African majority rule. South Africa is something very different. True, some of the more liberal members of the predominantly English-speaking United Party had split away in 1959 to form the Progressive Party, which has called for a transitional, qualified, but multi-racial franchise. However, popular support for the Progressive Party has rapidly declined. The Liberal Party, committed to ' one-man one-vote ', is now a persecuted sect, while the ' liberal Afrikaners ', who in the late fifties grouped around The South African Bureau of Relations (SABRA) have been condemned by Dr Verwoerd to political impotence.

However, the increasing crisis, and the enormous potential forces facing the South African whites, have led to some proposals for compromise. The United Party now favours a very gradual increase in African rights, and the Nationalists have expanded Verwoerd's new policy not of apartheid but of ' separate development ' into the ' Bantustan ' plan—the setting up of entirely African republics in predominantly African areas, with South African economic aid and, Pretoria anticipates, political hegemony.

Yet none of these compromise proposals, whatever may be their other faults, faces up to the real South African problem: the urbanised African intellectuals, the source of leadership for the African nationalist movement. Furthermore, all of them have come almost certainly too late, since by 1961 all of the African nationalist leaders had accepted violence and one-man one-vote as basic policies. This did not mean that they had all become racists. On the contrary, most of them are so westernised that they find it difficult to conceive of a purely black South Africa. But two facts have become apparent which bode ill for an even partially peaceful transition and for the opponents of communism. First, the only dialogue and cooperation still existing between Africans and whites of any political significance is within the South African Communist Party, at home and in exile. Second, and more important, barring the unlikely event of Western intervention, only the Soviets and the Chinese can and may furnish the arms, supplies, technicians, and training which alone might eventually bring the Afrikaners to their knees.

Nor does it seem likely that the three present British High Commission Territories—Basutoland, Swaziland, and Bechuanaland—will play any major role in South African problems in the near future. True, they are on their way to independence. Even so, the facts of their economic dependence on the Republic and of their geographical propinquity (in the case of Basutoland amounting to actual encirclement by South Africa), the overwhelming South African military superiority, and above all, the unlikelihood that any government in London would feel it could commit substantial military forces in their defence, all make any defiance of South Africa on their part unlikely. Rather, like Dr Banda vis-à-vis Mozambique, they are likely to tread carefully in dealing with their powerful and ruthless neighbour.

The Communist Party of Lesotho (Basutoland), the only legal communist party on the continent of Africa, is perhaps more of a *rara avis* than a serious political movement. Indeed, it has been suggested that it is primarily a cover for SACP activities in Basutoland, especially for infiltration of the Maramatlou Freedom Party, whose rival, the more radical Basutoland Congress Party, has sent a delegation to Peking. In any case, the Lesotho Communist Party's activities, and its attitudes towards the Sino-Soviet rift,[9] are perhaps made easier by the low ideological level of its cadres (to whom the dispute must appear to be in a very far country) and the ideological assistance it gets from the SACP.

The SACP has not been untouched by the Sino-Soviet split, and although its leaders have attempted to minimise the dispute, to continue their over-all support of the Soviet line, and to use Sino-Soviet differences to some extent for their own purposes, they have been faced with the fact that the Chinese racist and violent line, and the previous unwillingness of their white leader to adopt a policy of violence, are bound eventually to split the party, with its African members siding with the Chinese.

Soviet Policy in Africa

THE COMPETITION FOR THE FAVOUR of non-communist African states which resulted from the Sino-Soviet rift intensified a Soviet policy shift formally initiated by Moscow in 1955 when Shepilov first visited Cairo. A pragmatist, activist policy such as Khrushchev envisaged for Africa and other underdeveloped areas required a more flexible approach, even though, or, more accurately, in part because the African 'national bourgeois' regimes stifled rather than encouraged the development of native African communist parties. Since Khrushchev abandoned Stalin's rigid two-camp, anti-neutralist line, Soviet policy towards Africa has had as its immediate minimum objective the denial of the continent to the West and in particular to the United States. The tactics were to encourage the rise of 'positively neutral' albeit non-communist African states which would be pro-Soviet and anti-American, which would push

9 See the Lesotho CP CC's statement of 15 May 1964 in *World Marxist Review* Information Bulletin No. 16 (Toronto, 18 August 1964).

towards the 'second revolution', and thus eventually would move towards 'scientific socialism'. That such a policy worked against the immediate interest of communist parties in Africa was thought unfortunate but necessary, both for Soviet state interests and the interests of world communism.

The new approach made for an increasingly friendly attitude towards African nationalism, pan-Africanism, and the radical African nationalist movements. Nor did Soviet policy change after the UAR, Guinea, and Congo developments of the early sixties. On the contrary, the leading Soviet African expert, the late Professor Potekhin, took a largely positive view of pan-Africanism [10]; at the end of 1963 a new phrase, 'revolutionary democracy', was introduced by Moscow [11] (thus further identifying radical 'national bourgeois' regimes with revolution); increased emphasis was given to various methods of non-capitalist development; and one Soviet writer even suggested that the world socialist system might provide an international proletariat while the ex-colonial countries provide the masses, i.e., that socialism can eventually be constructed in Africa without a working class (communist) party. Soviet enthusiasm for radical African nationalists became even stronger during Ben Bella's visit to Moscow, when—in spite of the FLN Congress's slight shift away from Marxist-Leninist influence—the final communiqué spoke of the establishment of 'fraternal relations between the CPSU and the FLN' (Pravda, 7 May 1964).

Shortly thereafter a 'prominent Algerian Marxist' (i.e. communist), Bashir Hajj Ali, declared, in a clearly Soviet-endorsed statement, that the FLN, 'a vanguard party', was built 'in the course of the revolution launched by the proletariat of town and country' rather than having 'preceded the revolution' (as did the Algerian CP). Furthermore, he went on, although the FLN's 'socialist road' did not involve 'the adoption of Marxist philosophical principles as a whole', it was advancing towards socialism by creating the objective conditions for socialist construction. Finally, the statement was remarkably favourable to Islam (which the recent FLN congress had endorsed more strongly than before) and concluded with the rather un-Leninist statement that 'the Algerian masses are marching to socialism with the Koran in one hand and Capital in the other'.[12]

Indeed, although before Khrushchev's visit to Cairo Nasser released some of the imprisoned communists,[13] and although while there

---

[10] I. I. Potekhin, 'Africanism and the Struggle of Two Ideologies', Kommunist, No. 1, 1964.

[11] Pravda, 6 December 1963; Khrushchev's interview with African newspapers, Pravda, 21 December 1963.

[12] L'Unità, 30 June 1964, quoted from Information Bulletin No. 18, Supplement to World Marxist Review (Toronto, 18 August 1964).

[13] See the reference to the release of the 'imprisoned Marxist patriots' in the article by Desmond Buckle, 'The United Arab Republic: A Bastion of Anti-Colonialism', The African Communist, July-September 1964.

Khrushchev publicly took exception to pan-Arabism,[14] Soviet policy (as was shown in Zanzibar) has become almost completely pragmatic. The Soviets have built up extensive aid, as well as cultural and education exchange programmes in Africa. Their relations with radical African governments, however, have been only moderately successful. For in general the Russians know too little about Africa. They are heavy-handed in their dealings with Africans; they are inescapably European, and—as elsewhere since the Cuban crisis—they prefer not to take excessive risks in supporting the national liberation struggle.

Chinese Policy in Africa

FOR THE FIRST TIME in centuries, a powerful, expansionist, and revolutionary Asian power exists. Japan was militarily strong, but not revolutionary. Rather, as a traditionalist imperialist power with stress on naval and land power, Japanese eyes turned to China and Southeast Asia, not Europe or Africa. China, on the other hand, is a revolutionary, imperialist force within both the international political sphere and the international communist movement. Unable to compete at the military level, the Chinese concentrate on their Maoist strategy—revolutionary, peasant-based violence and guerrilla warfare.

China, as did Imperial Japan, considers the great *status quo* power, the United States, its principal enemy; the Soviet Union it regards as an expansionist and hostile power, which seems to Mao to have allied itself with the United States against him. Not surprisingly therefore, Peking talks of a ' second intermediate zone of peace ' composed of the coloured, radical revolutionary elements in Asia, Africa, and Latin America, which will eventually surround and foil white Americans and Soviets alike and thus engage the forces of both. As Lowenthal writes:

> Step by step Peking has come to count on the colonial revolutions first for weakening the imperialist enemy by a ubiquitous war of attrition, then for disturbing any attempt at a Russo-American dialogue by a succession of crises, and finally for proving its superior revolutionary zeal in the factional struggle for the world communist movement. The further the conflict with Moscow has developed, the larger the importance of the colonial struggles for liberation has loomed in the consciousness of the Chinese communists, until they have finally come to see these struggles as ' the *focus* of world contradictions ' and as *decisive* for the victory of world communism—a view that is closely bound up with their vision of themselves as the champions of a world-wide front of the coloured masses that is to achieve that victory.[15]

A separate Chinese strategy in Africa first became apparent in late 1959, within the context of China's determination to replace the Soviet Union as the predominate party within the world communist movement.

[14] *Le Monde*, 19 May 1964. For pro-UAR declarations thereafter, see especially Khaled Bagdash, ' Some Problems of the National Liberation Movement ', *World Marxist Review*, August 1964.

[15] R. Lowenthal, ' China ', in Brzezinski (ed.), *Africa and the Communist World*, p. 202.

China was the more inclined to emphasise armed struggle in Africa, since Soviet reluctance to risk preemptive American intervention as a result of such struggle, combined with the power and obduracy of the South African White Redoubt, made radical African nationalists tend in that direction in any case. Chinese operations in Africa have included massive radio and printed-word propaganda, visits by radical African nationalists to Peking, some scholarships, and support of such radical nationalists as the FLN (before it came to power), Moumié's UPC in the Cameroons, Babu in Zanzibar, and various rebel groups in the Congo.

Thus, contrary to much of their ideology, the Chinese have not concentrated only, or even primarily, on support of communists in Africa. True, they have criticised the Soviet Union for its too excessive support of non-revolutionary regimes. Yet even in the 1940s the Chinese took a remarkably conciliatory line towards the Chinese 'national bourgeoisie', within the context of Mao's theory of the 'people's democratic dictatorship'.

Internationally this conciliatory line was first strongly stressed by Chou En-lai at the 1955 Bandung Conference. The Chinese shift to the left in 1957 made them more antagonistic to 'national bourgeois' regimes and more favourable to such extremists as Moumié and Babu. The mutinies in East Africa, the increasing instability in West Africa, the rise in leftist influence in Zanzibar, and the near-anarchy in much of the Congo, have certainly further encouraged them in their optimistic estimate of prospects for radical or communist movements in Africa.

Nevertheless, in competing with the Russians, the Chinese have shown an increased willingness to cooperate with and support radical African nationalist movements whether or not they are Marxist-Leninist in inclination, or even whether or not they have suppressed existing communist parties. This is all the more true in Africa, since the few communist parties there, particularly in North Africa, have been pro-Soviet in the dispute. Rather than attempt to split them, therefore, the Chinese have adopted the more pragmatic policy of establishing the best possible relations with the non-communist radical nationalist groups (such as the FLN and the ruling parties of Guinea, Ghana, and Mali), both to advance their own aims and to counteract simultaneous Soviet operations with the same objective. Paradoxically enough, as Professor Benjamin Schwartz has pointed out,[16] and perhaps largely because of the example of Castro, the Chinese have even gone so far as to assert that Marxism-Leninism is not and need not be the monopoly of communist parties, that (by implication) a socialist revolution can be carried out by Marxist-Leninists 'without the Communist Party', and that the process of their publicly declaring themselves to be Marxist-Leninists and establishing or taking over control of an already existing communist party is essentially a matter of public self-definition.

[16] 'The Polemics seen by a Non-Polemicist', *Problems of Communism*, March-April 1964.

All these themes were stressed by Chou En-lai during his five-week visit to Africa in December 1963 and January 1964. The duration of the visit, by far the longest ever made to the continent by the Prime Minister of a major world power, plus Chou's diplomatic talents, combined to give him some success in what was perhaps his main objective, good will for China, and he scored some gains by arranging to establish diplomatic relations with African states (notably with Tunisia and Ethiopia) and by pushing China's claim to UN membership.

Finally, even if Chou did not visit East Africa, it seems in retrospect that his African trip signalled a major shift in Chinese activities there. (Emphasis has moved away from the ' Casablanca ' powers.) They are now concentrating their efforts on the militarily weaker and less stable East and Central African states; in particular, Kenya, Tanganyika and Zanzibar, Malawi, Burundi, and the two Congos. They are cultivating alternative radical leaders both within and outside the present governments, and are especially interested in influencing the exiled leaders of ' national liberation ' movements; as their support of one PAC faction after having failed with the ANC shows, they are almost completely pragmatic in their aid for any and all radical elements attempting to overthrow the *status quo*.

In north and west Africa this policy has had significant success only in Mali. Peking has been overshadowed by Moscow in Somaliland and in large part—via the East Germans—in Zanzibar. The Chinese have certainly made enemies of Kenyatta and most of his government, and they have antagonised Dr Obote in Uganda. Dr Nyerere must be highly suspicious of them, but is still, after the coup, too weak to move decisively against them, while Dr Banda has certainly become their enemy. In the near future their chances do seem considerably better in the split, demoralised, and frustrated ' liberation movements ' from the White Redoubt, and it would not be surprising to see the Chinese expand their activities in this area still further.

Although Chou did not succeed (as he must have anticipated he would not) in forestalling another Belgrade (non-aligned) conference (an objective pushed hard by two of his major opponents, Tito and Nehru, as well as by one of his hosts, Nasser), he did gain increased support for a new (Afro-Asian) Bandung conference, which is scheduled for March 1965 in Algiers. He also stressed that Chinese aid came without strings and without its personnel having any special privileges.

Chou's most delicate problem was to project an image of peace and cooperation with ' national bourgeois ' regimes while at the same time encouraging armed revolutionary movements, a dilemma made more difficult by the January coup in Zanzibar (after which Chou discreetly cancelled his scheduled visit to East Africa). Even so, his emphasis on liberation of southern Africa could not be gainsaid by any African power. And, as the events in Angola and the revolts in the Congo provinces of Kwilu and Kivu demonstrated, it was quite in accord with the temper of African times.

Sino-Soviet Competition

THE AFRO-ASIAN PEOPLE'S SOLIDARITY ORGANISATION (AAPSO) and its related specialised affiliates (with its secretariat in Cairo) remained for some time largely under Soviet and UAR control. As Chinese activities developed, however, Peking apparently decided by 1962 at the latest and probably much earlier to attempt to gain control of the AAPSO and in any case to set up new specialised Afro-Asian organisations as one of their prime international instruments against the Soviets, and also as an organisational framework within which to cooperate with and influence radical nationalist movements. At the Afro-Asian solidarity meeting at Moshi (Tanganyika) in February 1963, Chinese influence over the central AAPSO organisation, particularly on the issue of the relative priority of general and complete disarmament as opposed to the national liberation struggle, showed a marked increase. This was followed in April by the establishment in Djakarta of the Afro-Asian Journalists Organisation, from which for the first time the Soviets were excluded as full members. At a subsequent AAPSO meeting in Cyprus in September 1963 the Soviets recouped some of their losses by exploiting the test-ban treaty issue. Chinese and Indonesian attempts to set up an Afro-Asian Workers Organisation scored only a partial success, but Peking succeeded in excluding the Soviet Union from the second Bandung conference.

More significantly for Africa, an AAPSO meeting at Algiers in March 1964 made clear what Nyerere's reference at Moshi the year before to ' the second scramble for Africa ' had foreshadowed: African nationalists were becoming increasingly concerned by the rising intensity of Sino-Soviet polemics, which more and more came to occupy the AAPSO to the exclusion of effective activity for the national liberation struggle. As one Kenyan delegate at the Algiers meeting said:

> We are not Marxist-Leninists, and most of us have never read a single line of *Das Kapital*. So what interest do you have in our participating in your doctrinal quarrels? I have had enough, when I am eating a sandwich, of being accosted by someone who asks me what I think of the Soviet positions and, when I am drinking coffee, by someone who questions me about the Chinese arguments. I would like to be able to eat in peace.[17]

*   *   *   *

The black African liberation movements and states want the White Redoubt to fall quickly. This is not necessarily true of Moscow or Peking; on the contrary, they want primarily to use that struggle to radicalise and influence African leaders. For these purposes a long, costly war would be better than a quick one, and, as Stalin showed during the Spanish Civil War, major communist powers can effectively pursue deliberately dilatory policies.

[17] Quoted in *Le Monde*, 28 March 1964.

Thus Moscow or even Peking may well not send aid rapidly. Both know that a quick victory would leave the African nationalists free to prove themselves ungrateful. But if only enough communist arms go in to prevent a long albeit uneasy African truce with the White Redoubt, they may help replace the post-independence black African leaderships by more radical and more pro-communist ones. Finally, Soviet hesitation may be outweighed by fear of successful Chinese competition— the more so since Chinese activity will probably continue to rise, particularly if it is not contained by the West. There is, however, the other possibility that Moscow and even Peking (although the Chinese have not yet been frustrated by American preemptive action) may be so busy with their own problems and so fearful of such counter-action that they will not try or at least will not succeed in the gamble outlined above.

What, then, will the black Africans do? First, they know that they dare not falter too obviously in their struggle against the White Redoubt. True, leaders like Dr Kaunda, whose geographical propinquity and economic need require caution, may get away with moderation. Mr Tshombe also has enough troubles and may well need European and White Redoubt support as well as that of his white mercenaries. But what of the rest of black Africa? The Soviets because of the Chinese, and the Chinese in any case, seem likely to continue training ' students ' in sabotage and guerrilla warfare and offering arms and technical aid to ' liberation movements '. Therefore, will not such movements be forced to accept Soviet and Chinese aid because (a) unless they do their leaders will be overthrown by more radical (or venal) competitors, and (b) they can get such aid nowhere else? The same questions face the leaders of most of the black African states. Furthermore, in such a situation would Soviet influence replace the West's, or, as in the case of Somaliland, only that of the Chinese? It is also true that the black African states may render only lip service to the struggle against the White Redoubt and, fearing Soviet and Chinese influence, shy away from communist aid. This second possible black African response—one which during the next few years is perhaps more likely—would encourage communist withdrawal.

The extent of Soviet and Chinese influence in Africa remains a function not of the appeal of Marxism-Leninism or the size and effectiveness of communist parties, but of the success of Soviet and Chinese state power in infiltrating, buying, and supplying military aid to the radical racist nationalism of black Africa, as opposed to Western reluctance to take action. But, above all, it remains in the end a function of African affairs themselves: their confusion, instability, and intractability to all foreign attempts at control.

SINO-SOVIET RIVALRY AND THE NATIONAL LIBERATION MOVEMENT

Elizabeth Kridl Valkenier

OPPOSED interpretations of the importance and course of the national liberation movement occupy a prominent place in the Sino-Soviet conflict. More important, however, these views far transcend the realm of theory, now that the Moscow-Peking rivalry for leadership of the world revolution has come out into the open. Despite frequent lapses from proclaimed theory in the actions of both countries, the rival interpretations of the revolutionary situation in the third world are worth examining, for they serve as the basis of a wide range of policies that cover diplomatic and economic relations with governments in power, the control of local communist parties, and the guidance of front organisations.

From the very start of open polemics, the CPC made the issue of national liberation movements a pivotal one in the bid for revolutionary leadership. Its proposals of 14 June 1963 ' Concerning the General Line of the International Communist Movement ' advanced a new thesis that ' the whole cause of the international proletarian revolution hinges on the outcome of revolutionary struggles ' in the ' vast areas of Asia, Africa, and Latin America ' that are today the ' storm-centres of world revolutions dealing direct blows at imperialism '. Marx's opinion, expressed in 1870, that ' only in Ireland can a decisive blow be dealt to the British ruling class ', is held in Peking to justify its contention that the revolts of the oppressed peoples actively promote the proletarian revolution, a view shared by Lenin when he said that a ' great new source of world storms has emerged in Asia '.[1] For Chinese theoreticians today, however, the unrest of the oppressed peoples has become the *principal* source.

Accepting the challenge, the Soviet leaders in their reply of 14 July 1963, vigorously denounced this ' " new theory " according to which the decisive force in the struggle against imperialism . . . is not the world system of socialism, not the struggle of the international working class, but . . . the national liberation movement '. This new thesis, they argued, would ' isolate the national liberation movement from the international working class and its offspring, the world system of socialism ' —and they condemned it as un-Marxian, since it would transfer the leadership of the anti-imperialist struggle from the working class to the bourgeoisie, or, even worse, to ' certain patriotically minded kings,

---

[1] Kuo Fang, ' The Revolution of Oppressed Nations is a New Source of World Storms ', *People's Daily*, 15 October 1963.

princes, and aristocrats ', at the head of nationalist movements.[2] To substantiate the Soviet claim to leadership in Marxist terms, both this letter and numerous subsequent Russian commentaries asserted that the vanguard role of the proletariat in the anti-imperialist revolution could be provided for the developing countries (in most of which there is either no proletariat or a very weak one) through cooperation with the communist bloc. ' Only under the leadership of the world proletariat and in close alliance with it can the objective, anti-capitalist potential of the national liberation movement be revealed.' [3]

The Chinese have not dealt adequately with this over-all class analysis of the liberation movement today.[4] Instead, they have concentrated on discrediting their rival by pointing out that Russian theories about proper leadership embody a ' scornful ' attitude that assigns a passive, secondary role to the liberation struggles. In their fourth reply (21 October 1963) to the open CPSU letter, which was wholly devoted to the colonial question, the Soviets were attacked for ' belittling and ignoring the role of the national liberation movement ', and for ' asserting that [it] should be " led " by the socialist countries and the working-class movement in the metropolitan countries '. The ' proper relationship ', according to Peking, should be that of ' mutual support '.

THE Russians trace the origins of the new Chinese theory to the abandonment of the class approach in favour of a racial one. Peking for its part has been asserting all along that Soviet indifference to the cause of the colonial and ex-colonial peoples is due as much to the Russians being white and indistinguishable from the other imperialists, as to their being bad Marxists.[5] Moscow continues to emphasise the correctness of its

2 Later the CPSU dropped this charge in favour of one that accused Peking of making the peasantry the moving force of the revolution (Cf. *Pravda*, 11 May 1964; Kuusinen's speech at the February 1964 Plenum, *ibid*. 19 May 1964.) This might be in part due to Soviet recognition that ' revolutionary-minded ' members of the middle class could initiate the transition to socialism.

3 *Izvestiya*, 16 July 1963.

4 Some pro-Peking Marxists outside China seem, however, to have been disturbed by the charge that the CPC was giving the non-proletarian forces in the developing countries control over the world revolution. Writing in the pro-Peking Paris-centred *Revolution*, Pierre Jalée answered it by a textual analysis of official Chinese statements. Their terminology convinced him that emancipation movements of a non-revolutionary character were definitely not designated by the CPC as ' storm centres ' (November 1963, pp. 8–9). But there is little doubt that among the less exacting Marxists of the third world the Chinese theory will find a different response. The January 1964 resolution of the Indonesian Party's CC plenum called the antagonism between the oppressed nations and imperialism the major contradiction, repudiated ' the idea that Europe is the centre ', and held that ' in order to win the victory of world revolution, the world proletariat must assign an important place to revolutions in Asia, Africa, and Latin America ' (*Peking Review*, 27 March 1964, pp. 16–18).

5 The Russians seem fully alive to the explosive character of this issue. Within the past years Soviet commentators have studiously sought to dispel the notion that such outbreaks as the Mau Mau movement and the revolt in Zanzibar had any racial overtones. (V. Kudriavtsev wrote in the February 1964 issue of *International Affairs* that the Mau Mau did not engage in any exclusively anti-White terrorism but in a particular form of peasant war against land-grabbing.) In Angola the attitude towards the racist

' class ' approach, arguing that the international workers' movement is a higher type of revolutionary movement and that the liberation struggles can play only an auxiliary role in the transition from capitalism to socialism. Although such arguments are likely to offend local sensibilities, they provide the only basis on which the USSR can claim leadership in the revolutionary movements of the colonial and semi-colonial countries.

It is interesting to consider certain political and diplomatic moves in the light of the conflicting theories about the colonial revolution and its relationship to the Soviet Union. The most obvious examples are the Chinese efforts to have the USSR excluded from the Afro-Asian Conference (the ' second Bandung '), and to set up exclusive Afro-Asian front organisations. Less obvious but equally telling was the tone of the speeches delivered by Chou En-lai, Khrushchev, and, after his fall, by Shelepin on their respective trips to Africa.

Reasserting his country's leadership, Khrushchev reminded his hosts that the October revolution had opened new prospects for colonial peoples, that the postwar power of the USSR enabled them to gain independence, that Soviet aid and the Soviet example were now guiding their development towards a better future. Any slackening of ties with the USSR would weaken the UAR and other newly independent states vis-à-vis the imperialists. By contrast, Chou in all his speeches carefully made the point that every forward step taken by the Africans in opposing imperialism and building up their own countries was of tremendous help to China. As though to encourage the spirit of self-confidence, the ' will to dare ' on which Chinese revolutionary theories are based, he extolled what the Africans had done for themselves by their own efforts.

The visit to Cairo in December 1964 of the Soviet delegation headed by Shelepin was designed to reassure Nasser about the continuity of Soviet policy in the area. Shelepin stressed that it ' remained unchanged ' and he was even more emphatic than Khrushchev in promising that the Soviet Union ' will give all the necessary assistance ' to peoples fighting against ' imperialism and neo-colonialism ' in Africa, Asia, and Latin America. Obviously, the dismissal of Khrushchev has not changed Soviet diplomatic objectives in the third world though it may have affected Soviet tactics there. It rendered it imperative to show greater ' anti-imperialist ' resolution in order to strengthen Soviet positions and possibly to regain some of the influence lost in the competition with the Chinese.

JUST as the Chinese in open rivalry have advanced a new thesis on the locus of the revolutionary centre, so the Soviets have formulated an equally novel concept about the possibility of ' revolutionary democrats ' leading their countries towards socialism.

excesses of the peasants has been one of the issues in dispute between the pro-Moscow and pro-Peking groups (*Revolution*, January 1964, pp. 17–18).
6 *Peking Review*, 27 December 1963, p. 7.

Despite generally positive appraisal of nationalist leaders, Soviet writings on the national bourgeoisie were until 1960 very equivocal in acknowledging its role in the liberation process. This sector of the middle class, it was conceded, could contribute to the elimination of imperialist influence, but its divided loyalties, its proneness to compromise with the colonialists in its own selfish interests, were also stressed as a reminder that the party of the proletariat should use the middle class but never rely on it. This approach was well summed up by the 1960 Statement of the 81 parties:

> In the present conditions the national bourgeoisie of colonial and independent states, which is not tied up with the imperialist circles . . . maintains its ability to participate in the revolutionary struggle against imperialism and feudalism. In this sense it has a progressive character, but it is not stable. Along with its progressiveness, it is inclined to compromise with imperialism and feudalism . . . With the growing aggravation of social conditions, the national bourgeoisie increasingly shows an inclination towards compromises . . .

In the following year or two, Soviet pronouncements began to stress the first part of the statement while underplaying its qualifications, putting less emphasis on manipulating the middle strata and more on the broad cooperation of all the national and democratic forces, less on class interests and more on vital national interests. At the same time attacks were made on ' the dogmatic notion that in our time the dominating tendency in the evolution of the national bourgeoisie is permanent conservatism and rapprochement with international reaction '.[7]

In their opening salvo of June 1963, the Chinese made the political role and character of the national bourgeoisie one of the issues. Thesis number nine discussed this class in the same terms as the 1960 Statement, stressing its limited potential rather than its usefulness. It gave a warning against the lure of such class concepts as ' interests of the entire nation ', and enjoined communists never to become the ' tail of the landlord and the bourgeoisie '. The fourth Chinese article (21 October 1963) accused the CPSU more specifically of believing that ' a country can build socialism no matter under what leadership, including that of a reactionary nationalist like Nehru '.

7 *Narody Azii i Afriki*, January 1963, p. 36. A good illustration of this change, which is not always easy to pin down since the Soviet position shifts in the effort to accommodate both the Chinese challenge and the ambitions of the nationalist statesmen, is offered by two editions of *Osnovy marksizma-leninizma*, a basic political handbook designed to provide an authoritative interpretation of communist ideology as refurbished at the 20th CPSU congress and after. Apart from describing how the national bourgeoisie joined the anti-imperialist movement because of a clash of interests with the colonialists, the first edition (1959) had nothing specific to say about any contribution this class could make to the liberation movement. Instead it reiterated the warning that the middle class was unreliable. The 1962 edition stressed that a ' considerable segment ' of the national bourgeoisie was interested in carrying on the revolution after independence. To support this interpretation, it used the above-cited quotation from the 1960 Statement but omitted, without any indication, the qualifying clauses, merely adding in a less emphatic manner that both the Statement and the new CPSU Programme took notice of the national bourgeoisie's instability.

This called attention to the fact that the Russians now thought ' national revolutionary leaders ' capable of initiating the transition to socialism. The delegates of the ' revolutionary democratic parties ' of Ghana, Guinea, and Mali attended the 22nd congress of the CPSU in 1961. The list has since been extended to include the Algerian FLN and the Burmese Socialist Programme Party, with all of which the CPSU maintains official relations; and Nasser's Arab Socialist Union seems likely to be the next candidate for membership. Until very recently Soviet politicians and scholars criticised the variants of the socialism which these parties claimed to be building, but as the debate with Peking went on, less and less has been said about the petty-bourgeois and unscientific nature of the Asian, Arab, and African versions of socialism, and more and more about their being a step in the right direction. Some eyebrows must have been raised, and not only in Peking, when the *New Times* editorial of 10 June 1964 explained what the attitude of communists should be towards the socialism proclaimed by more and more Asian and African governments: ' There are two approaches. One, the dogmatic . . . is to disregard such proclamations since their authors are not Marxist-Leninists. The other, constructive . . . is to treat them with the greatest attention and sympathy. That is the approach of the Soviet communists '.

So far, the Chinese have not accepted the claims of the nationalist leaders to be building socialism.[8] In its reply of 9 September 1963 to the open letter of the CPSU, the CPC insisted on the correctness of the thesis about ' the thoroughgoing completion by the newly independent countries of their national democratic revolutions '. The Chinese view that national revolutions cannot as yet break out of the framework of bourgeois-democratic revolutions and begin the transition towards socialism has not been the major issue in the dispute, but it does set the tone of Chinese diplomatic dealings with the new states.

During his African tour Chou made no attempt to interpret local reforms in Marxist terms. When referring to domestic developments he invariably resorted to bland praise of the ' success achieved in building up the country, developing the national economy and culture '. Africans were courted as fellow Afro-Asians, fellow fighters against imperialism, and not as political comrades.[9] Even in his most militant pronouncements (made in Somalia at the end of the African tour) about the excellent revolutionary prospects throughout Africa, Chou was careful to point out that the various forms of struggle waged in Africa ' all fell within the scope of nationalist revolution '.[10]

---

8 Algeria seems to be a special case, due to its winning independence through armed struggle as well as to the long and close association between China and the FLN.
9 In at least one case this approach did not succeed. According to Tanyug, 22 January 1964, Ghana was dissatisfied with Chou's visit because he completely ignored the role of the People's Convention Party and Ghana's determination to build a socialist state.
10 *Peking Review*, 14 February 1964, p. 11. In this respect Chinese theory seems not to have changed in recent years. A captured Chinese army document, dated April 1961, stated: ' What matters now in Africa is anti-imperialism and anti-colonialism; anti-feudalism is not yet important. It is time not for social revolution, but national revolution '. *China News Analysis*, No. 501, p. 1.

In striking contrast was the repeated Soviet praise of the socialist direction of such Algerian and Egyptian measures as nationalisation, industrialisation, and cooperative farming—praise coupled moreover with meddlesome prescriptions of how to carry on the domestic revolution. This line is based on the current Soviet theory that no matter how far removed from ' scientific ' socialism the local variants may be, closer relations with the communist bloc will enable the emerging nations to find the ' correct ' road. Clearly, the Russians hope that their own efforts at ideological assimilation will have the desired effect on the ' revolutionary democrats '.

SOVIET ideas about the role of the communists in the national demo-cratic stage of the revolution have also undergone considerable revision since 1960. Whereas the 1960 Statement described communists as ' the leading part of the liberation movement ' and spelled out how they should act in a broad national front—when to support the national government, when to ' unmask ' reaction, how to unite ' progressive forces '—the 1961 CPSU Programme did not assign them such an active role. Instead of prescribing specific policies, it laid down in bold type the maxim that ' Communist aims are in keeping with the supreme interests of the nation ', and made the general statement that the communists struggle actively to consummate the anti-imperialist, anti-feudal, democratic revolution.[11]

A secondary role for communists, even if only temporary, is emphatically rejected by the CPC. Its June 1963 Proposal, like the 1960 Statement, was explicit about the duty of communists to guide the liberation process. It held that the party must lead the broad national front; it must maintain its ' ideological, political, and organisational independence . . . put forward a programme of its own . . . work independently among the masses '. The statement of 21 October 1963 said more succinctly that ' in the national liberation movement it is necessary both to insist on proletarian leadership and to establish a broad anti-imperialist front ', and accused the CPSU of wanting the proletariat to ' roll up [its] patriotic banner of opposing imperialism and struggling for national independence and surrender it to others '.

To meet this particular charge, the CPSU, in its letter of 14 July 1963, took the line that Chinese extremism regarding the role of the communists serves ' to alienate the popular masses from the communist parties that have won the sympathies of the people '. For it has been Moscow's policy in recent years to create an image of the communist different from that of the hot-headed revolutionary; in order to gain the acceptance of nationalists, he is pictured as the irreproachable democrat,

---

11 The shift was again well illustrated by the two editions of *Osnovy marksizma-leninizma*. The 1959 version held that communists should use united-front tactics to exert pressure on the national bourgeoisie in favour of consistent revolutionary policies. The 1962 edition stressed instead the theme of collaboration, of outright support for the progressive sector of the bourgeoisie.

the ardent fighter for national independence and its staunchest defender. Indicative of this trend was the January 1963 conference on ' Communists and Democracy ', organised in Prague by the editorial board of the *World Marxist Review* (reported in its April 1963 issue). Its participants argued that terms like ' dictatorship ' alienate potential allies, while ' democracy ' is understandable and appeals to many peasants, artisans, and tradesmen. Underlying this policy is an awareness of the impossibility of creating and maintaining a broad anti-imperialist front while insisting on proletarian hegemony. The intention is not to permit an extended and essentially unchallenged middle-class leadership but to achieve effective infiltration through broad coalitions that blur the dividing line between communist and non-communist.

Unconvinced by this argument, the CPC answered that whenever a party did not insist on actively leading the masses in revolutionary struggle it forfeited the confidence of the masses and ended up as a tool of the bourgeoisie.[12] To combat such erroneous views the CPC has started to encourage the formation of truly revolutionary parties that base their programmes and actions on the Chinese version of Marxism-Leninism.

In each case the pro-Peking group has denounced the established leadership for collaboration with non-Marxist parties. In India the dissidents have accused the CPI of preparing a united front with the Congress Party (*Pravda*, 23 June 1964). In Ceylon they have objected to the formation of a United Left Front, asserting that ' unity was useless until such time as all the parties accepted Marxism-Leninism ' (*World Marxist Review*, December 1963, p. 13). In Burma, it was the pro-Moscow United Workers Party which agreed to join the Burmese Socialist Programme Party and to cooperate with the Revolutionary Council (for the Russians supported Ne Win's efforts to establish unity behind his programme), whereas the pro-Peking Communist Party of Burma has not done so because its demand to retain freedom to organise has not been met. In Chile, the dissidents described as ' tagging along at the tail of events ' the party's participation in the Popular Action Front and its endorsement of a non-communist candidate in the presidential elections (*Revolution*, December 1963, p. 115).

While many of the pro-Soviet parties have abandoned their revolutionary opposition to their governments, Moscow is trying to exert diplomatic pressure on some countries to let the communists participate in political life. It is clear that during Ben Bella's visit to the USSR the Soviet leaders tried either to peruade or to pressure him into giving the communists greater scope. In the joint communiqué, the CPSU pointedly wished the FLN ' success in the further unification ' of all the leading patriotic and democratic forces.

12 The eighth in the series of Chinese answers to the CPSU letter. *People's Daily*, 31 March 1964.

THE 1960 meeting of the 81 parties introduced the new concept of the national democratic state to justify the tactical desirability of communist support for nationalism during the transitional stage. Proposed by the CPSU, the new formulation received formal Chinese endorsement.[13] Since then Moscow has continued to advocate the concept, and several parties have accepted it in their programmes; but Peking, by choosing to ignore it, in effect has opposed it.

Given the premises of the 1960 Statement about the bourgeoisie's limited potential and the proletariat's duty to promote liberation movements, this transitional state structure with its democratic rights and privileges was primarily seen as affording the communists freedom of action to work and organise for the eventual take-over. But the Soviets have modified the original concept. The 1961 CPSU Programme omitted any reference to conditions facilitating communist activities, placing its emphasis on participation in government. It held that the political basis of the national democratic state was a bloc of all the progressive, patriotic forces fighting to win complete independence and broad democracy and to consummate the anti-imperialist, anti-feudal democratic revolution. This was clearly a liberalised interpretation of the original formula. The 1960 Statement said nothing either for or against communist participation in the government, but the concept of the national democratic state was not originally adopted to encourage this particular policy.

Without any mention at all of the national democratic state, the Chinese Proposal of June 1963 prescribed that each party 'must put forward a programme of its own which is thoroughly for national independence and people's democracy'. The Soviets have taken the latter term to mean 'one of the forms of the dictatorship of the proletariat'.[14] In one of their most candid statements they argued that, unlike the dictatorship of the proletariat, the state of national democracy 'eases the carrying out of the future socialist changes in a peaceful, bloodless way and makes it possible to avoid armed struggle and civil war'.[15]

This explains why the CPC has not accepted the formula of the national democratic state. Peking, unlike Moscow, is not interested in changing the existing state of affairs through piecemeal structural reforms. Nor does it deem this possible. Hence its insistence on the non-peaceful means of the transition to socialism—the dictatorship of the proletariat.[16]

---

13 W. T. Shinn, Jr., ' " The National Democratic State ": a Communist Program for the Less Developed Areas ', *World Politics*, April 1963.

14 *Kommunist*, No. 11, July 1963, p. 25.

15 *International Affairs* (Moscow), October 1963, p. 5.

16 The Chinese have not excluded peaceful means altogether. The June 1963 Proposal stated that ' communists preferred peaceful transition ' and objected only to having this method made into the ' strategic principle for the international communist movement '. (They also foresee the possibility of a peaceful transition, provided state power is in the hands of the working class during the democratic stage of the revolution.) Practically, however, the Chinese leaders have argued that there have been no

The only way of changing the existing situation, the Chinese insist, is to seize power, smash the old state apparatus, and establish the dictatorship of the proletariat. The eighth in the series of Peking's replies to the open CPSU letter, dated 31 March 1964, was given over wholly to refuting the possibility of a parliamentary road to socialism. It argued that ' even if . . . a communist party should win a majority of seats in parliament or participate in the government as a result of an electoral victory, it would not change the bourgeois nature of parliament and government; still less would it mean the smashing of the old and the establishment of a new state machine. It is absolutely impossible to bring about a fundamental social change by relying on bourgeois parliaments or governments '. In consequence, ' violent revolution is the universal law of proletarian revolution '.[17]

The Russians counter this intransigent position in two ways. On the one hand, they continue to pay formal homage to the concept of the dictatorship of the proletariat: ' No matter how the transition from capitalism to socialism takes place, it is possible only by way of a socialist revolution and the establishment of the dictatorship of the proletariat ' (*Kommunist*, No. 14, September 1963, p. 27). On the other hand, and with far greater eloquence, they stress its changed nature as well as its limitations. Soviet theoreticians argue that it is wrong to identify the rule of the proletariat with violence and they have been stressing the constructive, not the destructive, tasks of the communists. Accordingly, the dictatorship of the proletariat has been called ' a truly democratic power of the majority ', and it has been stated that ' leadership of the proletariat in the revolution . . . implies not only and not so much coercion as education of the masses in the spirit of social discipline '.[18]

In a more down-to-earth vein, the Russians have been pointing out the complexities of the liberation revolution, not the least of which is the complete absence or the great weakness of the working class. This leads to the obvious questions, ' Who . . . will lead the struggle for the dictatorship of the proletariat in those countries where there is no proletariat and its party? And what sort of dictatorship of the proletariat is it without

examples in history of peaceful communist take-over (the Soviet citing of the Czechoslovak example notwithstanding) in support of their contention that the communist parties have to master and rely on extra-legal methods.

[17] This approach is reflected in the programmes and proclamations of the pro-Peking groups and parties. The dissident Communist Party of Brazil advocates the overthrow of the existing state power and the establishment of a ' true people's government '. It castigates the pro-Moscow Brazilian Communist Party for seeking to establish a national democratic government that would only realise partial structural reforms within the existing set-up (*Peking Review*, 13 September 1963, pp. 39–43). The splinter group in India insists that it is absolutely essential to replace the present bourgeois-landlord state headed by the big bourgeoisie by a state of people's democracy led by the working class (*The Hindu Weekly Review*, 6 April 1964, p. 3). The dissidents in Chile challenge the pro-Moscow leadership to abandon its policy of ' parliamentary cretinism [that] accepts the rules of the game of the bourgeoisie ' in favour of a ' proletarian revolution and the dictatorship of the proletariat ' (*Peking Review*, 1 May 1964, pp. 26–28).

[18] *World Marxist Review*, July 1963, p. 64; August 1963, p. 56.

the proletariat?'[19] To supply the missing prerequisites, it has been argued that with its power and preponderance the socialist camp can serve the developing countries as a substitute for the dictatorship of the proletariat.

SOVIET allegations to the contrary, the Chinese do not count on world war to promote the national liberation movement. But they do hold that revolution is best advanced locally by armed struggle and that the communist states can exert their chief influence on world revolution by supporting this struggle. And Peking's charges to the contrary, the Russians do not abjure the use of force altogether, for they believe it has a certain effectiveness on the local level, as does cautious support from the communist camp.[20]

In his December 1963 interview Khrushchev stressed that 'taking up arms' was only one of the forms of the 'liberation struggle'. He clearly indicated the Soviet attitude towards violence by noting that at present the main emphasis of the national liberation movement was not on fighting for independence or overthrowing reactionary pro-imperialist regimes, but on achieving economic and social progress. At the February 1964 plenum of the CC of the CPSU, Suslov criticised the CPC for its 'stereo-typed tactics' of armed struggle, asking what the workers of such countries as Ghana, Mali, or Algeria would accomplish through armed uprisings.

But even for those liberation struggles which the Russians admit do call for the use of force, they prefer to stress the effectiveness of peaceful methods though never ruling out recourse to violence. They argue that peaceful coexistence favours the emergence of new states, that the United Nations can be utilised to liquidate colonialism, that independence gained through negotiation need not be spurious. The Chinese, on the other hand, insist that independence is achieved only through the anti-imperialist struggles of the people, and, to be genuine and complete, liberation requires the forcible expulsion of the colonialists and displacement of the bourgeoisie.

While both parties sanction armed revolts to overthrow oppressive regimes, the CPC is the more vocal about the advisability of such a course. To pin down the attitude of China and Russia towards reactionary governments is difficult, for each measures the oppressiveness of a given regime by its foreign policies; but China lists many more countries than

---

[19] *Kommunist*, No. 11, July 1963, p. 25. This is not the place to go into the fascinating field of communist 'Eastern studies'. But there is an obvious parallel between the increased sophistication and detailed factual research work of Soviet scholars and the growing awareness of the actual conditions in the developing countries that Soviet leaders show in trying to adapt their theories to reality. By contrast, the rigidity of the Chinese position is undoubtedly related to the absence of serious studies and of discussion of the social and economic trends in the third world.

[20] However, the Russians like to point out that according to Lenin, 'the countries of victorious socialism will show their chief influence on the development of world revolution by their economic success' (*Kommunist*, No. 8, May 1964, pp. 3–4).

does Russia as suffering under unpopular rule. The difference in reactions toward the coup in Zanzibar is instructive. Jacques Vergès, chief spokesman for Peking in the West, hailed this revolt as an illustration of the fact that ' in no former colony is any lasting solution conceivable without completely overturning the social and economic structure ' ; nor did its lesson, he suggested, apply only to the existing colonies.[21] The Russian commentator was careful to approve this and other armed revolts, provided they were against colonial rule, conditions were ripe, and the colonialists resorted to arms first.[22] To counter Chinese accusations that the USSR fails to support liberation struggles, the Soviets point to their military aid, proclaim that liberation wars are inevitable and ' holy ', and try to make Soviet policies seem more militant by resorting to the argument that the UN Declaration on Granting Independence, sponsored by the USSR, sanctions anti-colonial wars of liberation.[23] More revealing, however, than any of these ritualistic assertions of unflagging support was the clarification offered in *Pravda* (22 September 1963) of the Soviet attitude towards different types of war. It explained that the USSR was decidedly opposed to a world war and also in general to wars between states. Then the article drew a significant distinction between local and national liberation wars, explaining that the Soviet Union adopted ' a most watchful attitude ' towards the former because they might lead to a world war. In turn it accused the CPC of viewing local wars ' as an acceptable and expedient method of the policy of socialist countries . . . for the export of revolution '. As for national liberation wars, civil wars, popular rebellions—wars waged ' within a single country ' and where there was no question of ' using nuclear weapons '—the USSR had always supported them.

An example of this distinction is Soviet caution in Vietnam, where the fear of escalation has led the Russians, reinforcing their case with offers of generous aid and trade terms, to urge the North Vietnamese to be less provocative. The Chinese express no anxiety on this score; in their theory any conflict with the imperialists is a ' just ' war entitled to the unqualified backing of all communist states (the assumption being that the imperialists will not resort to nuclear weapons when faced with resolute action). Moreover, to Peking such support does not in any way involve the export of revolution, since revolutions are generated internally and the communist countries encourage and aid revolutions only after they have broken out.[24]

[21] *Revolution*, January 1964, pp. 7–10.
[22] T. Kolesnichenko, in *Pravda*, 11 March 1964. Caution about recourse to arms is also shared by the pro-Moscow parties. The ' revisionist ' Peruvian leader, del Prado, has argued that the situation must be fully ripe before armed action can bring the desired results. ' We cannot accept the thesis that all that is needed to " kindle the flame " of the revolution in any place and in all circumstances is to " ignite the spark " of guerrilla warfare ' (*World Marxist Review*, May 1964, p. 12). Some Central American parties that advocate armed action at home nevertheless denounce the Chinese position that denies the practical and theoretical validity of any other way.
[23] Y. Konovalov in *International Affairs* (Moscow), April 1964, p. 40.
[24] ' Questions of War and Peace ', *People's Daily*, 19 November 1963.

Despite the distinction the Soviets draw, their policies towards a 'popular rebellion within a single state', such as is now taking place in the Congo, are not clear-cut. Reports that both communist camps supply arms and advisers indicate that each country will fish in troubled waters to gain influence, to weaken the West and to keep its rival from pre-empting the field. But, to judge from comments in their press, it is obvious that the Russians are much slower to publicise their endorsement of local revolts, and are significantly cautious about the conclusions they draw. By March 1964, the Chinese were hailing the Congo insurgents as patriotic armed forces whose actions proved that it was men, not weapons, that counted, while *Pravda* was still giving factual reports. Only in November 1964, after Stanleyville, did the Russians decide to expel the Congolese governmental legation from Moscow and to come out with greater public support for the rebels against 'the traitor Tshombe'. They also stiffened their position on Vietnam after Khrushchev's fall.

THE *People's Daily* article of 21 October 1963 denounced the CPSU for making economic development the 'central task' of liberation. Moscow contends that with the almost complete elimination of colonial rule, the national liberation movement has entered a new stage wherein the chief problem is to overcome backwardness. The Chinese admit the need to build up an independent economy, but this, the article emphasised, must be subordinated to the political struggle for complete independence and 'must never be separated from the struggle against the forces of imperialism, old and new colonialism, and their lackeys'. Peking is incensed at Soviet preoccupation with the economics of underdevelopment, which 'obliterates the conflict of class opposition, drugs the people's revolutionary determination, halts their flourishing national and democratic revolutionary struggles' (*Peking Review*, 1 November 1963, pp. 16–18).

To take the edge off some of this criticism, Soviet leaders have been stressing that the newly independent states face the problem not just of economic independence but of social progress as well. However, they still tend to rate the economic tasks uppermost, expecting political and social changes to follow. As Khrushchev put it in his December 1963 interview: 'In my opinion, the chief problems confronting the young national states are deliverance from backwardness and poverty, creation of an independent economy that can ensure progress, strengthening of political independence, and development of democracy'. The Russians have also been placing more emphasis on the choice of a non-capitalist path (consisting of such measures as nationalisation, planning, land reform, economic cooperation with the communist bloc) than on setting up national democratic states as the path of transition toward socialism.[25]

[25] During the 'reconciliation talks' in July 1963, the Chinese called the concept of non-capitalist development 'pure nonsense'. There is indeed considerable confusion among Soviet communists about the relationship of the national democratic state to non-capitalist development, and of both to socialism. G. Kim wrote that the

Moscow's readiness to accept the validity of some economic policies of the new states—specifically, state capitalism—is also under attack from Peking. While the CPSU has recommended the expansion of the public sector as a progressive measure, inasmuch as it is aimed against Western interests, the CPC denies that state capitalism will enable the new countries to rid themselves of imperialist exploitation and feudalist oppression. What the Soviets accept and advocate, it claims, amounts to no more than ' bourgeois nationalisation ' which leaves intact the political power of the bourgeoisie, prolongs the exploitation of the working people, and in no way promotes the revolution. It accuses the revisionists of peddling the idea that this type of nationalisation is not an ordinary reform but a measure containing a ' socialist element ', ' a step toward socialism' (*Peking Review,* 26 April 1963, pp. 13–19).

Reacting to Chinese criticism, the Russians have somewhat modified their endorsement of state capitalism. One writer admitted that ' it would be wrong to think that the existence of state capitalism . . . can by itself lead to socialism ', while another stated it was not enough for the public sector to have an anti-imperialist direction; it should have an anti-capitalist character as well and aim at restricting private capital.[26] As a convenient way of providing anti-capitalist content without abandoning state capitalism altogether, the Russians have added workers' management to the list of reforms marking the non-capitalist path of development.

Another bone of contention, of far greater practical import, is the issue of economic aid. The Chinese article of 21 October 1963 objected to Khrushchev's statement that Soviet aid stimulates progress and accelerates those internal processes which help newly independent countries along the ' highway leading to socialism ', on the ground that ' in no case can it be said that . . . national independence and social progress are due solely to the economic aid . . . received from the socialist countries and not mainly to the revolutionary struggles of the . . . people '.

While Chinese theory denies the revolutionary effectiveness of economic aid, Chinese practice of denigrating Soviet aid shows that Peking is well aware of its diplomatic value. To the participants of various extremist Afro-Asian gatherings Peking's delegates have been explaining that Soviet aid weakens the people's struggle against imperialism. During his tour of Africa and Asia Chou sought to undermine Soviet claims

state of national democracy completes the liberation revolution and starts a country on the non-capitalist course, the course of building socialism (*Aziya i Afrika Segodnia,* October 1962). A. Sobolev disagreed, contending that the national democratic state is virtually synonymous with non-capitalist development and that it only prepares the ground for socialist construction (*World Marxist Review,* February 1963). The first post-Khrushchev contribution on the subject to the *World Marxist Review* (November 1964), by G. Adhikari, pointed out that Mao's formula of the ' new democracy' is inapplicable in India, and that national democracy is the most suitable state form to ensure ' the non-capitalist path of development '.

26 *International Affairs* (Moscow), February 1963, p. 37; *Aziya i Afrika Segodnia,* October 1963, p. 13.

about the exceptional features of their aid by propounding the radically different eight principles underlying Chinese aid policy.

He asserted that China never rendered aid as a 'kind of unilateral alms' but strove to make the recipient self-reliant. This was a pointed reference to the Soviet penchant for lecturing the recipients of Russian aid on its far-reaching benefits and for insisting that closer relations with the communist bloc will provide a panacea for all their economic problems. He noted that Chinese loans are free of interest and that Chinese technicians live in the same conditions as the local experts, drawing attention to the fact that Moscow does charge interest (no matter how low) and that its specialists insist on privileges. In the light of recent Chinese revelations and charges of Soviet interference in their internal affairs by means of aid, and of the low quality and high cost of Soviet equipment, Chou's claim that his country granted aid unconditionally and supplied best quality equipment at world prices could have only one purpose. He also managed a dig at such key projects in the Soviet programme as Bhilai and Aswan, and at Russian claims about inaugurating industrialisation by stressing that China undertook projects which required less investment while yielding quicker results (*Peking Review*, 1 May 1964, pp. 9–10).

Interestingly enough, Chinese charges have had some effect on the Russians. During his visit to Indonesia in the summer of 1964, Mikoyan was obviously reacting to charges of Soviet condescension when he first acknowledged that Indonesia, being a great nation, could very well shoulder the burden of economic development by itself, and only then argued that cooperation with friendly countries would help it to reach this goal more quickly. Moreover, as though to outdo the Chinese in selfless generosity, Moscow has been giving large gifts on top of sizable credits, which certainly was not its practice in earlier years. As for the Chinese charge of interference in internal affairs, the Russians are hard put to it to square their theory that Soviet aid contributes to 'progressive developments' with their desire not to offend the sensitivities of the newly independent states. In the UAR, Khrushchev attempted this by saying, on 16 May 1964: 'We came to help the UAR so that the workers, peasants, working intelligentsia, all the progressive forces of the nation could proceed faster in building the new life. Here it was correctly stated that the USSR renders aid without any political conditions. But I will say openly that we give aid with great pleasure to countries which have taken the path of building socialism.' Shelepin went further in his wooing of Nasser: in his speech in Cairo he simply endorsed the Egyptian policy and dropped the Khrushchevian qualifications.

*   *   *

In assessing the Sino-Soviet rivalry one has to consider its impact on the underdeveloped world, as well as on the policies of the two powers themselves. There is little doubt that the crude accusations of hegemony-seeking levelled at each other by Moscow and Peking before the very people whose support they seek have demonstrated that the communist powers are as eager to create their own spheres of influence as are the proverbial imperialists. Already there are signs of resistance to Soviet and Chinese intrusiveness, whether it is Nyerere's warning to Africans not to become involved in the quarrels of others, or the efforts of the Organisation of African Unity to control the aid rendered in anti-colonial struggles. This suggests that the rival theories themselves are equally suspect.

Soviet and Chinese theories are, however, being taken at face value by local communists and other radicals. It remains to be seen how much further the pro-Moscow parties will modify their policies to win political acceptance, and how many adherents Chinese theories will gain among extremist individuals who may succeed in crystallising around themselves the ever-present discontents.

Moscow's policies, it seems probable at this point, will continue to evolve in the direction of flexibility, making it more likely that the Soviets will assimilate local developments in their theory than that the newly independent states will pattern themselves on the USSR. In a review of the 1964 political situation in Africa, *Izvestiya* (29 December 1964) pointed out that the ' last bastions of imperialism in Africa ': Angola, Mozambique, Southern Rhodesia, and South Africa, cannot be liberated without the active help of other African states. Therefore the Organisation for African Unity, and more particularly such states as Algeria, Egypt, Ghana, Guinea, and Mali, will ' play a decisive role in the strengthening of the anti-imperialist, anti-colonialist unity of the African countries, a unity which in the present conditions is the most effective instrument in the struggle for the full liberation of the continent '. This, according to the Belgian communist journal, *Le Drapeau Rouge* (30 December 1964), is ' an implicit warning against a tendency to deepen the division between the African states which may lead to a split in the OAU and which may be followed by the setting up of a revolutionary organisation opposed to the " bourgeois " African states. Such a tendency has recently been manifested on many occasions by certain revolutionary leaders of the extreme left '.

Chinese policies do not show any signs of change. Militant theories to differentiate genuine revolutionaries from revisionists will continue to be proclaimed; diplomatic efforts to win Afro-Asians and to isolate the USSR will be undertaken. The discrepancy between the two approaches has not gained many more friends for China, but it will serve the good purpose of demonstrating to the uncommitted nations the need to be wary and to find their own independent road to a more promising future.

INTERNATIONAL CONSEQUENCES OF THE SINO-SOVIET DISPUTE

Helmut Sonnenfeldt

THE unfolding of the Sino-Soviet dispute has been one of the most fascinating spectacles in recent history. It has already had considerable impact on the complexion of international affairs and there is much speculation about its longer-term implications. But any effort to describe and analyse the international consequences of the dispute confronts numerous handicaps.

In the first place, the Sino-Soviet relationship is not static. Conceivably at some point there may be an improvement, though this is hard to visualise at present. The calculations of those who act in world affairs will depend on the state of the dispute, or at least on how they perceive the state of the dispute, and on their expectations about its future course. Clearly, different inferences about one's own options and interests would be drawn, for example, if one thought Moscow and Peking were on the verge of open warfare or if it appeared that they had found some formula to contain their disagreements.

It seems apparent that Peking and Moscow are still uncertain about how to conduct themselves in the light of their dispute. For example, while each of them has all but accused the other of violating their 1950 alliance, they both still consider it expedient to proclaim its continued validity. Again, while the Soviets have taxed the Chinese with conduct and attitudes that conflict with the obligation of the UN Charter, they have not yet brought themselves to oppose Chinese membership in the world organisation. There are numerous other instances where their statements show a far greater divergence than their actions. In any event, there is likely to be for quite some time considerable uncertainty and experimentation as Moscow, Peking, and other communist countries attempt to draw practical implications from the Sino-Soviet antagonism, while outside countries attempt to decide how best to protect and advance their own interests in the light of what is happening in the international movement. In this situation, the policies of outside powers may themselves influence more than heretofore the evolution of Sino-Soviet relations. This fluid process of adjustment to changing facts and perceptions, and the complex interactions of the calculations and policies of various countries, greatly complicate the effort to project the impact of the Sino-Soviet split on international politics.

Of course, this is not the only important phenomenon in international politics, and to attempt to project some of its longer-term implications without also considering other factors with which it interacts may be quite misleading. However, at the risk of some distortion, this article will concentrate rather narrowly on the consequences and implications of the split.

THE most obvious consequence of the split is that the USSR and China are increasingly being viewed as separate and even competing states, and are being treated as such by the world at large. It is true that even when both countries proclaimed their monolithic unity, they were treated as formally separate entities. Several countries established diplomatic relations with Peiping after 1949. Few, however, of the countries which established relations with the new regime expected to be dealing with a state whose policies would differ significantly from those of its great northern ally.

Peking's emergence in the last few years as an antagonist of Moscow has served to establish its credentials as an independent state, and this in turn has led an increasing number of other states to recognise it. Of the countries which have done so, France is of course the most important, not only because it is a European power and member of NATO, but because its example weighs heavily in the former French colonial regions of Africa. These acts of recognition have not reflected any hostile intent towards the USSR; rather they give evidence of a desire, in the first instance, to get into communication with an important actor on the international stage. Beyond that, however, there has also been a tendency to think in terms of advantages that might be derived from the changes in the Sino-Soviet relationship.

One clearly visible outgrowth of the Moscow-Peking estrangement is the interest among developing countries to use and even to stimulate Sino-Soviet competition for their own profit. The Soviets and the Chinese have each made clear that they do not intend to permit the other to obtain or maintain a position of monopoly influence in the developing countries, and many of the latter have been willing enough to become recipients of the munificence of both competitors. Thus, the African states have been the scene of a series of simultaneous or alternating visits by Soviet and Chinese dignitaries, offers of military, economic, technical, educational, and cultural cooperation, and other competing attentions. The Chinese, less affluent than the Soviets, have nevertheless sought to match Soviet economic and military aid in virtually all sectors of the continent, the more significant cases being Algeria, Tanzania, Kenya, and Somalia. Both have also made efforts to establish a presence in the former French territories. The Chinese have no doubt been aided in their overtures by French recognition. In the special case of the Congolese rebels, Moscow found it expedient for a time to leave the field substantially to the Chinese—partly because of its own unfortunate experiences in the Congo, partly because it seemed uncertain about the prospects of the rebels, partly because of its apparent desire to avoid a new, open cold war confrontation. But later, it gave more open support to the rebels. The general pattern in Africa is likely to continue to be one of broadly matching Chinese and Soviet efforts. In Asia, Pakistan may provide an example of Soviet concern lest Chinese policy preclude a more influential Soviet role. Japan is another example of the fact that Russia and China do not necessarily confine their competing overtures to non-aligned countries.

This is not to suggest that Moscow and Peking would not be active in the developing countries if there were no dispute between them. The colonial regions of the world have preoccupied the Soviets since the revolution and, in the postwar period, Moscow gave increasing attention to the developing countries well before the dispute with China erupted. The Chinese likewise were active in the field from the earliest days of their assumption of power, but it is clear that the dispute, which in part turns on how to conduct the 'national liberation struggle', has given each side a powerful additional incentive to press its quest for influence in the developing world. In the case of the Soviets, in particular, it is probable that their programmes of economic and military assistance have recently been reinvigorated because of the Chinese challenge. And Moscow's open boasts during the past years of the military assistance it has actually or allegedly given to sundry 'liberation movements' were undoubtedly provoked by Chinese charges that the Soviet Union had made common cause with imperialism and betrayed the national liberation struggle.

THE spectacle of the Sino-Soviet conflict and the strife it has engendered within the international communist movement, and within individual parties, has probably tended to reduce the ideological appeal of communism and the effectiveness of communist parties in much of the developing world. At the same time, the fact that neither Moscow nor Peking has been squeamish about bestowing its favours on what their doctrinal discussions describe as reactionary or anti-revolutionary ruling groups, has probably reinforced the complacency of many politicians, especially in Africa, about the dangers of inviting the two communist competitors into their countries. Although some leaders have become disenchanted with the Soviets, and others have been slow to warm to the Chinese, their fears and resentments continue to be largely directed against the West. They may be aware that the attention coming their way from Moscow and Peking is not entirely altruistic, but for the moment they seem largely confident that the dangers are manageable. Moreover, they seem to believe that the time-tested devices of non-alignment by which they have in past years sought to obtain help from both the Soviet Union and the West without letting either side achieve predominant influence, can also be utilised as between Moscow and Peking. So far, events probably tend to confirm them in such optimistic calculations.

At the same time, the developing countries have given some indication that they intend to resist the more overt forms of solicitation by one of the protagonists for support against the other. By and large they have managed to steer a middle course. It is true that an overwhelming number of the developing countries adhered to the test ban treaty even though they were aware of Peking's opposition and of Moscow's attempts to use the treaty as a club against the Chinese. But (apart from India with its special problem with China), this did not reflect a general inclination towards Moscow and away from Peking.

The Soviets evidently intended Khrushchev's proposal of 31 December 1963 on the peaceful settlement of territorial disputes to serve anti-Chinese purposes. The Chinese, at any rate, indicated that in their view Moscow was attempting to draw them into a deal which would preclude them from pressing territorial claims against the USSR. Moscow sought to drum up enthusiasm for its initiative among the developing countries by exempting national liberation wars from the proposed ban on the use of force in territorial issues. But while most developing countries answered Khrushchev's letter politely, and Moscow apparently judged that it had received sufficient general support to place the proposal on the agenda of the UN General Assembly, the move did not spark any stampede to the Soviet side of the Sino-Soviet dispute.

Many of the developing countries have found themselves under pressure from Moscow to back its participation in the Second Afro-Asian (Bandung II) conference against Chinese objections. But despite large new aid commitments to Indonesia, Moscow failed to get even Sukarno to put himself on record in favour of Soviet participation; and Khrushchev evidently could not get Nasser's support during his Egyptian trip in May 1964. Moscow subsequently suspended its open lobbying, having apparently realised that further pressure would not only fail to get it admitted to the conference but would also annoy governments who want to avoid taking positions clearly opposed to Peking.

So far, however, Chinese appeals to the developing countries on the basis of racial affinity, their efforts to establish Peking as the leader and spokesman of these countries and to arouse resentment and suspicion against the USSR as well as against the West, have had inconclusive results. Many leaders, especially in Africa, have thought it expedient and desirable to establish good relations with China, to visit there and to be visited in return, and to receive various kinds of assistance, but few if any of them seem disposed to rely exclusively or predominantly on Peking for the protection of their interests. Among the leftists and dissidents in Africa, China has managed to broaden its contacts and has to some extent come to be regarded as the fountainhead of revolution. But it operates under the handicap of being physically remote from much of the developing world, of having by its own admission limited resources available for assistance, and of running up against the desire of governing groups to keep Soviet, Chinese (and Western) influence in some balance.

THE success of several of the developing countries in establishing profitable relations with both communist powers, while avoiding being engulfed by either, is stimulating others to follow the same path. They feel that the emerging pattern of many-sided competition for influence in developing countries has its own built-in safeguards. The idea seems to be that somehow no one competitor will be able to establish such an influence within a country or over its policies as would endanger its freedom of movement or imperil the power position of the current ruling group. Indeed, there may even be something of an expectation that the competitors themselves will see to it that no one of them achieves over-riding influence in any one place.

It is of course a question whether such calculations will turn out to be accurate over the long run. There is no assurance that bilateral, trilateral, or multilateral competition is going to be self-limiting, or that a nice balance of the various competitors will always be maintained. At any rate, neither the Soviets nor the Chinese (nor other communist states) regard themselves as precluded from seeking to maximise their influence in a particular country; nor does their present support of ' national bourgeois ' regimes preclude them from attempting to nudge these regimes toward the left, or from building communist cadres and supporting ' progressive ' elements with the eventual goal of displacing existing regimes; nor, of course, are they prevented from other forms of subversion. And it is clear that both communist protagonists are trying to narrow the US and Western positions throughout the developing regions of the world and to promote the alienation of these countries from the West.

The West should be under no illusion that in the developing countries one of the issues over which the Chinese and Soviets are at loggerheads is precisely the issue of which of them can best give backing to and promote anti-Western sentiment. And it is not by any means clear that local leaders will always have the skill or the inclination, or the Western powers the leverage, to arrest trends inimical to Western interests. If one looks at East Africa, for example, it is apparent that the lively competition between Moscow (and some of its friends) and Peking has been accompanied by serious problems for the West and has resulted in a decline in Western influence.

The fact that Moscow is on the whole viewed as the less militant and more responsible of the two communist contestants (not altogether deservedly, it should be added) invites the thought that in some cases the West and the Soviet Union might develop a common interest in containing Chinese inroads among the developing countries. If such a parallelism in Western and Soviet interests were to emerge, and if Western and Soviet policies were adjusted to it in practice, it would represent a significant change.

But this prospect must be viewed with the greatest caution, since an interest in excluding or reducing the Chinese presence in one or another place is not the same as agreement on constructive social, economic, and political objectives or on methods of achieving them. So far, while perhaps willing enough to join the West in some tacit, unspoken way in halting Chinese inroads, or to participate with the West in a few international bodies concerned with assistance to developing countries, Moscow has not renounced its basic prescription for the developing countries.   Indeed, it is propounded now even more vigorously than when Khrushchev was in power.   Nor has Moscow abandoned its conviction that this prescription must ultimately exclude or at least reduce to a minimum any constructive association between the developing countries and the West.   Moreover, when thinking about the possibility of enlisting Soviet help in containing the Chinese, it is worth remembering that whatever else the Chinese may be doing in the developing countries, they may by their attacks on the Soviets alert local leaders to the dangers of accepting Russian assistance.

In general, then, the dispute has drawn both Russia and China more actively into the affairs of the developing world, and will probably continue to do so.   Although the two are rivals, their goals and activities will remain largely inimical to Western interests, and the leaders of developing countries will usually be able to count on support from both in disputes with the West.   And while Moscow may tend to exercise greater caution where its support of a developing country may embroil it with a Western country, especially with the US, it will nevertheless be driven by the fear of being outbid by Peking to refrain from applying the restraints it might otherwise consider wise.   The Chinese on the whole make the more inflammatory pronouncements and have proved somewhat more willing to assist dissident elements— although even they hesitated to recognise the Stanleyville ' People's Republic of the Congo '.

But the Soviets are the more powerful and affluent of the two competitors and, through their UN membership, are able to hamstring efforts at mediation and the promotion of orderly change.   Moscow is therefore likely to remain at least as disruptive an influence as Peking.   This will probably continue to be the case unless and until Moscow views, or Western diplomacy forces it to view, the normalisation and improvement of its relations with the West as having a clear priority over promotion of the ' liberation ' of the developing countries, and becomes convinced that the latter jeopardises the former.   Such a reshaping of priorities, in itself a profoundly difficult task for any Soviet leadership—even assuming that it could make the necessary ideological and psychological adjustments—would be all the more onerous for Moscow because it would open the way to a Chinese monopoly in the support of revolution and radicalism.   The Soviets would have yielded a significant position to their Chinese challengers.   The prospects for any such fundamental transformation of alignments are at best dim and can hardly provide a meaningful basis for Western policy in the developing world.

IN addition to the effort to seek balanced and rewarding relations with both communist powers, there have been some attempts to gain the support of one against the other. This is especially, and in some respects uniquely, the case with India, which was perhaps the first country concretely to experience diverging Soviet and Chinese policies. The first clear-cut demonstration of this divergence—as distinct from evidence of differences on ideological and essentially internal communist issues—came in September 1959, when Moscow assumed a virtually neutral position on the Sino-Indian border dispute. In the years since, Moscow has remained neutral on the substance of the border issue but has condemned Chinese attempts to resolve it by force and has stepped up assistance to India, including the supply of military hardware which might be used against China in a new flare-up.

Whether the Indians are correct in regarding themselves as one of the original causes of the Sino-Soviet dispute may be open to question; but diverging policies towards India have certainly become one of the major bones of Sino-Soviet contention. These differences both reflect and contribute to the severity of the antagonism, although it would probably be going too far to say that they could never be composed as part of some broader accommodation.

The Indians clearly view the Sino-Soviet split as beneficial to them in their dispute with the Chinese because it has led the Soviets to withhold backing from the Chinese and to provide assistance to India. India values this assistance both for its own sake and as a counterbalance to help from the West. The Indians seem to believe that close relations with Moscow will help to ensure the maintenance of the split. Moscow, in turn, evidently hopes to contain the spread of Chinese influence in India and to prevent the Sino-Indian dispute from driving India into closer association with the West and thus from undermining Soviet policy objectives. The Soviets may hope, too, that their assistance to India will benefit the Soviet-oriented Communist Party there and will in time increase its influence both on domestic Indian developments and on the orientation of Indian foreign policy. But the Indian leaders seem confident that such risks—if they perceive them as risks at all—are manageable and in any event worth taking for the advantages they believe Moscow's support brings them. This confidence matches and to some extent feeds the confidence of leaders in other developing countries in their ability to maximise the advantages to be derived from Sino-Soviet antagonism and to minimise the risks.

Moscow's willingness to contribute to India's defence capacity against China when Western countries are doing the same raises in more specific form the possibility, noted earlier, that there may be emerging a pattern of collaboration between the countries of the West and the USSR against China, and that, beyond that, the habit of acting in parallel for this particular purpose may in time broaden into a more constructive collaboration on other issues. Even in the case of India, however, it is worth repeating that parallel desires by the West and the USSR to contain the growth of Chinese influence or Chinese aggressiveness in a specific situation would not necessarily imply a convergence of views on other objectives.

Nor, indeed, does Soviet action to contain the Chinese in one place imply a readiness to do so in another. For example, although Soviet willingness and ability to influence the behaviour of the Chinese (and North Vietnamese) in Southeast Asia have undoubtedly declined, and although the Soviets showed little inclination to come to Hanoi's assistance in the Tonkin Gulf incidents, Moscow has taken no visible positive steps to inhibit Hanoi's and Peking's activities in the region. On the contrary, especially since Khrushchev's fall, Soviet demands for US withdrawal from Vietnam have been almost as persistent as Peking's and Hanoi's; and the general Soviet prescriptions for ending the conflicts in the region would, if implemented, open it to Chinese dominance. The Soviets, in short, have shown no inclination to offer to do for pro-Western countries under pressure from the Asian communists what they have been willing to do for India.

While the Indian case is the most clear-cut example of a third power enlisting the support of one party to the Sino-Soviet dispute against the other, there are signs that other countries are probing this possibility too. Thus, some Japanese have sought and received Chinese support for demands that the USSR adjust certain Soviet-Japanese territorial problems left by the Second World War.

Indeed, Mao made it clear in his talk with a Japanese socialist group last summer that he needs little encouragement on this score and that he is willing, in part no doubt because he believes it supports his own territorial claims against the USSR, to encourage other potential claimants against Moscow. But the result has probably been to stiffen Moscow's price for any territorial concession to Japan. For while the East Europeans, at whom Mao's siren song was explicitly directed, are not pressing the USSR for a redrawing of postwar frontiers, and the Rumanians hinted that they remember Bessarabia, Moscow will be extremely reluctant to create precedents in this field. Over the longer run, the Japanese might conceivably by a policy of rapprochement with China produce a more favourable turn in Soviet policy on the territorial issue. But such a rapprochement is likely at some point to come into conflict with Japan's interests vis-à-vis other countries, including the United States. And Moscow, even if it were prepared to reduce its price for territorial concessions, is unlikely to drop completely its demands for a dismantling of Japan's security arrangements with the United States. The Japanese might thus find that to pursue the effort to use Sino-Soviet competition too vigorously carries hazards for their international position (and possibly for their internal stability as well) which may exceed any benefits that they could hope to obtain.

THE foregoing discussion has sought to deal with some of the ways in which various nations have been adjusting their policies in the light of the Sino-Soviet split, now that they have opportunities to manoeuvre between Russia and China, and that the two rivals themselves are inviting other countries to do so. Given the tendency towards greater autonomy in Eastern Europe—which has, of course, been significantly stimulated by the Sino-Soviet split—it seems clear that the day when the countries ruled by communist parties could be properly treated as a uniform camp are gone forever. This fact alone represents a major change in international politics.

Simultaneously, however, other tendencies making for a change in the patterns of international politics have also made their appearance. Thus, the bonds of the Western alliance have tended to become looser. There are many reasons for this; among them is a sense that the break-up of the communist monolith has lessened the danger of aggression, at least in Europe, and a belief that since the Cuban missile crisis the Soviets have a quite realistic awareness of the strategic balance in the world as well as an appreciation of the dangers of nuclear warfare. This loosening of cohesion within alliances also reflects the fact that neither of the two super-powers has been willing or able to utilise its huge preponderence of power to enforce discipline on deviant allies. Along with these trends, the two super-powers appear to have discerned a common interest in finding means of preventing a chain of events from being unleashed that might result in nuclear war—though the means they propose to this end are far from identical and their calculus of what constitutes a risk of war is not necessarily the same.

These and other factors have clearly worked to diversify international relations even if basic alignments persist. The tantalising question is whether one can expect not merely a continued diversification, but more profound changes in relations with communist states. The answer to this question is bound to be extremely speculative and is not, in any event, solely a function of the Sino-Soviet split.

To start with, it should be noted that suggestions have come from the communist countries themselves that there are interests they may share with Western countries. Peking referred to an 'intermediate zone' of imperialist states, whom China could somehow support against the two super-powers. Moscow has suggested a mutuality of interest with the US on the issue of preventing the proliferation of nuclear weapons; it went so far as to sign the test ban treaty over the violent objections of the Chinese, who charged the nuclear powers with a conspiracy to keep them disarmed and helpless. On other aspects of arms control, too, the Soviets have indicated, before and since Khrushchev's fall, readiness to negotiate despite Chinese opposition. Much less direct, though nonetheless perceptible, are Soviet suggestions that there are some shared interests between economically advanced countries, regardless of their economic systems. Among the East

European countries, in turn, one element in their effort to conduct a more autonomous policy has been the desire to improve relations with the West; and the Rumanians have gone some way in the direction of indicating that at least in economic matters they are no less compatible with the West than with their Comecon associates.

Looking first at the possibility of some fundamental change in relations between Western countries and China, it would seem that this is at best a distant prospect. The Chinese are interested in economic benefits and in recognition and, as in the Japanese case, willing enough to give some backing to countries having difficulties with Moscow, but their essential orientation remains deeply hostile to Western interests. It should be recognised that in present circumstances any effort to strengthen the Chinese politically and economically, even if the intended purpose is to enable them to press their challenge against the Soviets, carries with it considerable hazards. For while the Chinese have presumably forfeited what assurance they used to have of Soviet support for military adventures—and it is doubtful they ever had a blank cheque—they are now able to act independently from Moscow. Thus, if they judged the risks acceptable and the penalties manageable, they might well be more prone to consider aggressive action now than when they had to consult with Moscow or perhaps even pay a price for its support. If, in addition, Peking concludes that at least as long as it does not provoke open warfare it can count on increasing economic support and other overtures, especially from Western countries, its propensity for aggression and subversion may rise that much more. It is hard to see how any Western power could have an interest in encouraging such tendencies.

This is not to deny that there may be benefits in taking advantage of the openings provided by Chinese interest in relations with Western countries. Certainly, there is value in maintaining contact in order both to obtain and to impart information. And the West should certainly not foreclose the possibility that perhaps another generation of Chinese leaders will be less committed to international disorder than the present one (the possession of nuclear weapons may, paradoxically, give some impetus in this direction), and that more constructive relations with them may then become feasible.

TURNING to Western relations with the Soviet Union, one finds that despite some improvement there is as yet little evidence that thorough-going changes are in the making. There is undoubtedly scope for additional improvements, but it is far from clear whether and how much the Sino-Soviet split is likely to contribute to a resolution of the critical issues and a narrowing of the gulf of objectives and outlook which remain between the Soviet Union and the Western world.

In Central Europe, the possibility of any durable settlement remains organically tied to a solution of the problem of Germany's division. Moscow shows no sign of being prepared to yield up Pankow to a united

Germany. Moreover, even though some improvements in the lot of the East German population have occurred, the possibility that anything like a viable relationship between regime and citizenry in East Germany can be achieved seems far off. Unlike the East European regimes, which have been able to strike some responsive chords among their populations, by appealing to nationalist impulses and lessening subservience to Moscow, the East German rulers must essentially remain satellites. For them to attempt to arouse national feeling and to seek to shed Soviet tutelage would be to cut down the prop that holds them up.

It might be argued that if the crumbling of Moscow's communist domain proceeds, the Soviets would be increasingly driven to consolidate their own country, to protect their Western flank through a policy of détente, and to transform their relations with Eastern Europe into something approaching a genuine commonwealth of sovereign, national, if still communist states. But even if a healthier kind of relationship between the USSR and Eastern Europe did come into being—including Soviet approval or at least acquiescence in closer associations between East European and Western countries—and relations between the USSR and the West improved, it would still not necessarily follow that Moscow would find it uncongenial or embarrassing or even burdensome to maintain a satellite in East Germany. It may decide that by additional improvements in the lives of the people the East German regime could be maintained without much difficulty and, indeed, that such improvements would give international respectability to that regime. The incentive even to consider a basic remedy of the German problem would be reduced if Moscow found that half-measures or less sufficed, and that it could reap the benefits of détente without doing more. Depending on how much Moscow valued these benefits, Western policy might at this point be able to exert some pressure on the Soviets. But it is unlikely that the Soviets could easily be brought to the conviction that it is more damaging to their interests to hold on to East Germany than to let go of it. Indeed, whatever changes the Russians might be prepared to make in their East European relationships, the Chinese challenge would probably make them even less willing than in the past to see a communist country move into the other camp—which is how the Soviets will continue to view the unification of Germany for a long time to come. And this attitude is, of course, likely to limit their tolerance towards the development of relations between the West and the East European countries as well.

Whether these Soviet views might in time undergo significant change would depend in part on whether progress is made in mitigating the intensity of the East-West military confrontation. It might be argued that fear of China will lead Moscow to search more seriously for agreements with the United States. It is no doubt true that the dispute with China has permitted the Soviet leaders to brush aside Chinese objections when they considered some particular agreement desirable. On the other hand, there may be other agreements in which Moscow might conceivably be interested but which it fears the Chinese might use to reinforce their charge that Moscow colludes with imperialism. The impact of the Sino-Soviet split on Soviet negotiating flexibility is thus ambiguous, although on balance it probably works to increase it.

But apart from the question of tactical flexibility, it is not clear that the split will lead Moscow in the direction of major disarmament agreements. The example of the agreements already reached shows that East-West collaboration in this field does not hamper the growth of Chinese military power. On the contrary, the Chinese spurn the agreements, proceed with their own military programmes, and continue to get economic assistance not only from countries who also spurn the agreements but from those who support them. For Moscow all this probably serves only to reinforce the inhibitions it already has in pursuing far-reaching disarmament. If this is so, it would not necessarily preclude all disarmament or security agreements with the Soviet Union. One can visualise arrangements, including regional ones, which would not affect the Soviet capacity to cope with an eventual Chinese military threat, although there may be other reasons preventing agreement on them. That a series of modest disarmament agreements may in time produce more friendly relations between the USSR and the countries of the West is quite possible; but whether this would amount to a basic reshaping of these relations is doubtful. And it is hard to see how the USSR would be prepared to make arms control agreements by which East Germany would slip out of its grasp, when it is not politically ready to see this occur.

It is not readily apparent how Western policy could bring any compelling pressure to bear upon the Soviets to improve the prospects. What the West can do, however—and this requires perhaps more consistency and harmony in the conduct of Western policies than has been feasible of late—is to keep before the minds of Soviet leaders a realisation that the advantages they seek from their dealings with the West must be reciprocated. Without some move on their part to eliminate the abnormality of the division of Europe, without a more constructive approach towards orderly change in the developing world, and without explicit measures to mitigate the alienation of their own people from those of the West, genuine progress in the détente is unlikely. This may be asking too much; but it remains true that the test for Western policy should be whether a particular step serves to move the Soviet Union and the other communist countries in the direction of more rather than less constructive behaviour, of more rather than less isolation for their peoples. And the challenge for the countries of the West is whether they can pursue such a policy consistently over a long period of time; whether they can avoid working at cross-purposes with each other; and whether they have the capacity neither to be deluded into thinking prematurely that fundamental changes have occurred nor to be so hidebound as not to recognise them when they do come.

APPENDIX

The State of the Parties

Ruling Parties, Europe

ALBANIA: The Albanian Workers Party (pro-Chinese)
Membership: about 53,000

BULGARIA: The Bulgarian Communist Party (pro-Soviet)
Membership: over 500,000

CZECHOSLOVAKIA: The Communist Party of Czechoslovakia (pro-Soviet)
Membership: over 1,500,000

EAST GERMANY: Socialist Unity Party (SED) (pro-Soviet)
Membership: over 1,500,000

HUNGARY: Hungarian Socialist Workers Party (MSZMP) (pro-Soviet)
Membership: over 500,000

POLAND: Polish United Workers Party (PZPR) (pro-Soviet)
Membership: over 1,000,000

RUMANIA: Rumanian Workers Party
Membership: over 1,000,000

USSR: The Communist Party of the Soviet Union (CPSU)
Membership: over 11,000,000

YUGOSLAVIA: League of Communists of Yugoslavia (LCY) (pro-Soviet)
Membership: over 1,000,000

Ruling Parties, Asia

CHINA: The Chinese Communist Party (CCP)
Membership: 18,000,000 (estimate)

NORTH KOREA: The Korean Workers Party (pro-Chinese)
Membership: 1,300,000 (estimate)

NORTH VIETNAM: Vietnam Workers Party (pro-Chinese)
Membership: 600,000–700,000

OUTER MONGOLIA: The Mongolian People's Revolutionary Party (pro-Soviet)
Membership: 46,000 (estimate)

Europe

AUSTRIA: The Communist Party of Austria (KPÖ) (pro-Soviet)
Membership: 35,000 (estimate)
    Anti-Revisionist Communists of Austria (pro-Chinese)
Membership: unknown

BELGIUM: Communist Party of Belgium (BCP) (pro-Soviet)
Membership: 11,000 (estimate)
    The Communist Party of Belgium (BCP) (pro-Chinese)
Membership: unknown

BERLIN (WEST): Socialist Unity Party (SED/West) (pro-Soviet)
Membership: 3,000–5,000
    (N.B.—SED-West is part of the East German SED)

Europe—*continued*

CYPRUS: Reform Party of the Working People (AKEL) (pro-Soviet)
    Membership: 10,000 (estimate)

DENMARK: The Danish Communist Party (DKP) (pro-Soviet)
    Membership: about 5,000
        Communist Study Circle (pro-Chinese)
    Membership: unknown

FINLAND: The Finnish Communist Party (SKP) (pro-Soviet)
    Membership: 40,000 (estimate)

FRANCE: The French Communist Party (PCF) (pro-Soviet)
    Membership: 240,000–280,000

GREAT BRITAIN: The Communist Party of Great Britain (CPGB) (pro-Soviet)
    Membership: 34,300 (estimate)
        British Committee for Communist Unity (pro-Chinese)
    Membership: unknown

GREECE: The Communist Party of Greece (KKE) (pro-Soviet)
    Membership: 20,000 (estimate)
        The United Democratic Left (EDA) (pro-Chinese)
    Membership: unknown

ICELAND: United Socialist Party of Iceland (pro-Soviet)
    Membership: 950–1,000

IRELAND: Irish Workers Party (pro-Soviet)
    Membership: 100–150

ITALY: The Italian Communist Party (PCI) (pro-Soviet)
    Membership: over 1,600,000

LUXEMBOURG: The Luxembourg Communist Party (pro-Soviet)
    Membership: 500 (estimate)

NETHERLANDS: The Communist Party of the Netherlands (CPN) (pro-Soviet)
    Membership: 12,000
        The Socialist Workers Party (pro-Soviet)
    Membership: unknown

NORWAY: The Norwegian Communist Party (NKP) (pro-Soviet)
    Membership: 4,000–5,000

PORTUGAL: The Portuguese Communist Party (PCP) (pro-Soviet)
    Membership: 2,000 (estimate)

SAN MARINO: The Communist Party of San Marino (pro-Soviet)
    Membership: unknown
        (N.B. This party is part of the Italian Communist Party)

SPAIN: The Spanish Communist Party (PCE) (pro-Soviet)
    Membership: 5,000 (estimate)
        Revolutionary Communist Party (pro-Chinese)
    Membership: unknown
        Spanish Marxist-Leninists (pro-Chinese)
    Membership: unknown

SWEDEN: The Swedish Communist Party (SKP) (pro-Soviet)
    Membership: 20,000 (estimate)
        Communist Workers Association (SKA) (pro-Chinese)
    Membership: unknown

Europe—*continued*

SWITZERLAND: Party of Labour (pro-Soviet)
    Membership: below 6,000
        Swiss Communist Party (pro-Chinese)
    Membership: unknown

WEST GERMANY: German Communist Party (KPD) (pro-Soviet)
    Membership: below 50,000 (estimate)

Africa

ALGERIA: The Communist Party of Algeria (pro-Soviet)
    Membership: 5,000–6,000 (estimate)

BASUTOLAND: The Communist Party of Lesotho (CPL) (pro-Soviet)
    Membership: probably less than 100

CAMEROON: Union of the Peoples of Cameroon (UPC) (pro-Chinese)
    Membership: unknown

DAHOMEY: The Party of the Socialist Revolution of Benin
    Membership: negligible

MALAGASY REPUBLIC: The Madagascar Communist Party (PCM) (Titoist)
    Membership: probably less than 100

MOROCCO: The Communist Party of Morocco (pro-Soviet)
    Membership: 1,000–1,500

NIGERIA: The Nigerian Communist Party (NCP)
    Membership: less than 100 (estimate)
        The Nigerian People's Party
        Nigerian Workers and Peasants Party
    Membership: unknown

RÉUNION: The Communist Party of Réunion (PCR) (pro-Soviet)
    Membership: unknown

SENEGAL: African Party of Independence (PAI) (nearing split)
    Membership: unknown

SOMALI REPUBLIC: Somali Democratic Union
    Membership: unknown

REPUBLIC OF SOUTH AFRICA: The South African Communist Party (SACP)
    (pro-Soviet)
    Membership: about 800

SUDAN: The Sudan Communist Party (SCP) (pro-Soviet)
    Membership: 1,500 (estimate)

TUNISIA: The Tunisian Communist Party (PCT)
    Membership: 1,000 (estimate)

North America

CANADA: The Communist Party of Canada (CPC) (pro-Soviet)
    Membership: 3,000–4,000

UNITED STATES: The Communist Party of the United States (CP of US) (pro-
    Soviet)
    Membership: 10,000 (estimated)
        Hammer and Steel Group (pro-Chinese)
    Membership: unknown
        Progressive Labour Movement (pro-Chinese)
    Membership: unknown

Asia

BURMA: The Burma Communist Party (BCP) (pro-Chinese)
  Membership: 1,200 (estimate)
    The Communist Party of Burma (CPB) (pro-Chinese)
  Membership: 300–500
      National United Front (NUF—led by United Workers' Party of Burma)
      (pro-Soviet)
  Membership: unknown

CAMBODIA: Pracheachon Party (pro-Chinese)
  Membership: 1,000 (estimate)

CEYLON: The Communist Party of Ceylon (CCP) (pro-Soviet)
  Membership: 3,000 (estimate)
      Lanka Sama Samaja Party (LSSP) (Trotskyite)
  Membership: 1,400 (estimate)
      People's United Front (MEP) (pro-Soviet)
  Membership: about 600
      Leftist Fighting Front (pro-Chinese)
  Membership: unknown
      Lanka Sama Samaja Party (Revolutionary Section) (Trotskyite, pro-Chinese)
  Membership: unknown
      The Communist Party of Ceylon (CCP) (pro-Chinese)
  Membership: unknown

HONG KONG: The Communist Party of Hong Kong (section of Chinese party)
  Membership: unknown

INDONESIA: The Indonesian Communist Party (PKI) (pro-Chinese)
  Membership: 2,500,000 (estimate)
      The Proletarian Party (MURBA)
  Membership: unknown

INDIA: The Communist Party of India (CPI) (pro-Soviet)
      The Communist Party of India (CPI) (pro-Chinese)
  Membership claimed before split: 120,000

IRAN: The Tudeh Party of Iran (pro-Soviet)
  Membership: 1,000–2,000

IRAQ: People's Union (pro-Soviet)
  Membership: 15,000 (estimate)
      (N.B.—There is a pro-Chinese faction)

ISRAEL: The Communist Party of Israel (MAKI) (pro-Soviet)
  Membership: less than 2,000 (estimate)

JORDAN: The Communist Party of Jordan (CPJ) (pro-Soviet)
  Membership: about 200

JAPAN: The Communist Party of Japan (JCP) (pro-Chinese)
  Membership: 105,000
      Voice of Japan Comrades Group (pro-Soviet)
  Membership: 3,000 (estimate)

LAOS: The Workers Party (PKN) (pro-Chinese)
  Membership: 100
      Neo Lao Hak Xat (NLHX) (pro-Chinese)
  Membership: unknown, but the Pathet Lao, the military arm of the NLHX,
  has 20,000 members (estimate)
      (N.B.—The NLHX is controlled by the PKN)

Asia—*continued*

LEBANON: The Lebanese Communist Party (pro-Soviet)
Membership: 3,000–4,000
> Party of the Socialist Revolution (PSR) (pro-Chinese)
Membership: unknown, very small

MALAYSIA: The Malayan Communist Party (MCP) (pro-Chinese)
> The Clandestine Communist Organization (Sarawak) (CCO) (pro-Chinese)
> The Malayan Communist Party (Singapore) (MCP) (pro-Chinese)
Membership: 2,000 (estimate)

NEPAL: The Communist Party of Nepal (internally split)
Membership: 3,500

PAKISTAN: The Communist Party of Pakistan (no stand taken)
Membership: 2,300–3,500

PHILIPPINES: The Filipino Communist Party (PKP) (no stand taken)
Membership: 1,800–2,500

SYRIA: The Communist Party of Syria (pro-Soviet)
Membership: 4,000–5,000

THAILAND: Thai Communist Party (pro-Chinese)
Membership: unknown
> Chinese Communist Party (Thailand) (pro-Chinese)
Membership: unknown

TURKEY: The Communist Party of Turkey (no stand taken)
Membership: under 1,000

UNITED ARAB REPUBLIC: The Communist Party of the UAR (no stand taken)
Membership: 1,000 (estimate)

SOUTH VIETNAM: The National Front for the Liberation of South Vietnam
(NFLSV) (pro-Chinese)
Membership: up to 20,000
> The People's Revolutionary Party (Marxist-Leninist) (pro-Chinese)
> (N.B.—This is controlled by the NFLSV)

Latin America

ARGENTINA: The Communist Party of Argentina (PCA) (pro-Soviet)
Membership: 40,000–50,000

BOLIVIA: The Communist Party of Bolivia (PCB) (pro-Soviet)
Membership: 4,000–5,000
> Revolutionary Workers' Party (Trotskyite, pro-Chinese)
Membership: 1,500 (estimate)
> Party of the Revolutionary Left (PIR) (pro-Chinese)
Membership: 1,000 (estimate)

BRAZIL: The Brazilian Communist Party (PCB) (pro-Soviet)
Membership: 30,000 (estimate)
> The Communist Party of Brazil (PC do B) (pro-Chinese)
Membership: 1,000 (estimate)
> (N.B. This information refers to the situation before the overthrow of
> the Goulart regime)

CHILE: The Communist Party of Chile (PCCh) (pro-Soviet)
Membership: 25,000–30,000

Latin America—*continued*

COLOMBIA: The Communist Party of Colombia (PCC) (pro-Soviet)
Membership: 10,000–12,000

COSTA RICA: Popular Vanguard Party (PVP) (pro-Soviet)
Membership: about 300

CUBA: United Party of the Socialist Revolution (PURS)
Membership: 28,000

DOMINICAN REPUBLIC: Dominican Popular Socialist Party (PSP) (pro-Soviet)
Dominican Popular Movement (MPP) (Castroist)
14th June Political Grouping (APCJ)
National Revolutionary Party (PNR)
Membership: unknown—APCJ has the largest following

ECUADOR: The Communist Party of Ecuador (PCE) (pro-Soviet)
Membership: 2,000–3,000

EL SALVADOR: The Communist Party of El Salvador (PCES) (pro-Soviet)
Membership: about 500
April and May Revolutionary Party (PRAM)
Membership: unknown

GUATEMALA: Labour Party of Guatemala (PGT) (pro-Soviet)
Membership: 1,300 (estimate)

HAITI: People's Friendship Party (PEP) (pro-Soviet)
People's National Liberation Party (PPLN) (pro-Soviet)
Membership unknown, but negligible

HONDURAS: The Communist Party of Honduras (PCH) (pro-Soviet)
Membership: 2,000 (estimate)
The Revolutionary Party of Honduras (PRH) (pro-Soviet)
Membership: about 400

MARTINIQUE: The Communist Party of Martinique
Membership: about 700

MEXICO: The Communist Party of Mexico (PCM) (pro-Soviet)
Membership: 3,000–3,200
People's Electoral Front (FEP) (pro-Soviet)
Membership: 7,500–10,000
The Bolshevik Communist Party of Mexico (PCBM) (pro-Chinese)
Membership: about 150–200
Spartacus Leninist League (pro-Chinese)
Communist Workers Front (pro-Chinese)
Membership: unknown
The Socialist People's Party (PPS) (pro-Soviet)
Membership: 38,000 (estimate)

NICARAGUA: The Socialist Party of Nicaragua (PSN) (pro-Soviet)
Membership: about 200–300

PANAMA: People's Party (PDP) (pro-Soviet)
Membership: about 300–500

PARAGUAY: The Communist Party of Paraguay (PCP) (pro-Soviet)
Membership: 3,000–4,000
Paraguayan Leninist Communist Party (PCLP) (pro-Chinese)
Membership: unknown

Latin America—*continued*

PERU: The Communist Party of Peru (PCP) (split)
Membership: 8,000–9,000
    Movement of the Revolutionary Left (MIR) (Castroist)
    Revolutionary Left Front (FIR) (Trotskyite, pro-Chinese)
Membership: unknown

URUGUAY: The Communist Party of Uruguay (CPU) (pro-Soviet)
Membership: 10,000 (estimate)
    Movement of Revolutionary Action (MAR) (pro-Chinese)
Membership: unknown

VENEZUELA: The Communist Party of Venezuela (PCV) (Castroist)
Membership: 30,000 (estimate)
    Movement of the Revolutionary Left (MIR) (Castroist)
Membership: unknown

Australasia

AUSTRALIA: The Communist Party of Australia (CPA) (pro-Soviet)
Membership: about 4,000
    The Communist Party of Australia (Marxist-Leninist) (CPA, M-L) (pro-Chinese)
Membership: about 300

NEW ZEALAND: The Communist Party of New Zealand (CPNZ) (pro-Chinese)
Membership: 200–300

Contributors

J. F. BROWN, former Research Fellow at the University of Michigan, now lives in Munich, and has written a number of studies on East European affairs.

KEVIN DEVLIN, formerly on the staff of *The Guardian*, is doing research on the world communist movement.

WILLIAM E. GRIFFITH is lecturer in Political Science and a Research Associate of the Center for International Studies, Massachusetts Institute of Technology. He is the author of *The Sino-Soviet Rift* (Allen & Unwin).

ERNST HALPERIN, a Swiss journalist, author of *The Triumphant Heretic*, is at present in South America preparing a study on Latin American communism.

KYOSUKE HIROTSU is a student of the communist movement in Japan.

RUTH McVEY, of Cornell University, is at present engaged in a study of the Indonesian Communist Party.

T. H. RIGBY, Associate Professor at the Australian National University, Canberra, lectures on Soviet government.

SATHI is the pseudonym of an Indian journalist, once card-holding communist. He has been running a regular weekly column in *Thought*, Delhi, on the developments in the Indian Communist Party.

HELMUT SONNENFELDT teaches at the School of Advanced International Studies, The Johns Hopkins University.

JOSEPH R. STAROBIN, a former prominent member of the U.S. Communist Party, is at present preparing a historical study on it at Columbia University.

PIO ULIASSI, former Senior Fellow at the Research Institute on Communist Affairs at Columbia, is preparing a book on the Italian Communist Party.

ELIZABETH KRIDL VALKENIER is engaged in research, formerly working at Council on Foreign Relations, New York, now at the European Institute, Columbia University.

ERIC WILLENZ teaches political theory and Soviet foreign policy at American University, Washington.

DONALD S. ZAGORIA is Senior Fellow, Research Institute on Communist Affairs, and Assistant Professor of Government at Columbia University. He is the author of *The Sino-Soviet Conflict 1956–1962*.

INDEX

Aarons, L., 135–141, 143
Abrahams, K. G., 180
Accion Democratica (Venezuela), 164
Acosta Salas, Raul, 35, 36
Adhikari, G., 110, 112, 202n.
Adjubei, Alexei, 82
Adoula, Cyrille, 177, 178
Africa, 18, 117, 168–189
  British East Central, former, 174–176
  British West, 173, 174
  Central, 29n., 176, 187
  Chinese policy in, 185–187
  East, 187, 209
  ex-French colonies, 171–173
  ex-Italian colonies, 176
  North, 171
  Portuguese, 176–179
  Sino-Soviet competition, 188, 189
  Soviet policy in, 183–185
  tropical, 171 ff.
  West, 18, 168n., 173, 174, 182, 186, 187
  White Redoubt, 176 ff., esp. 186–189
  see also individual countries
*Africa Latin America Asia —
  Revolution*, 30
Africanus, Terence, 180n.
Afro-Asian communists, 29, 42, 100, 118,
  119, 192, 202, 204, 208
Afro-Asian Journalists Organisation, 188
Afro-Asian People's Solidarity Organisation
  (AAPSO), 188
Afro-Asian Workers Organisation, 188
Afro-Shirazi Party (Zanzibar), 175
Ahmad, Z. A., 106
Aidit, D. N., 17, 23, 49, 99, 114, 117, 118,
  120, 121, 122, 127, 139
Akahata (Japan), 23, 24, 49, 123, 125, 126,
  127, 128, 130
Aksai Chin Road, 107
Albania and Albanian communists, 19, 23,
  37, 49, 52, 62, 66, 78, 82, 83, 86–88,
  94, 131, 134, 136, 148, 162, 163, 164
Alessandri, Jorge, 166
Alexander, Neville, 180
Alexander, Robert J., 36n., 155n., 160
Algeria and Algerian communists, 30, 111,
  171, 194, 195, 199, 204, 206
Algerian war, 56, 172
Ali, Bashir Hajj, 184
Alicata, Mario, 10
All-China Union of Journalists, 30
Allende, Salvador, 166
Alliance for Progress, 159n.
Amazonas, Joao, 33, 34
Amendola, Giorgio, 59n.
American communist party, 7, 29, 144–153
Anderson, Nils, 30

Andhra, India, 90–92, 112
Andrade, Mario de, 177, 178
Andropov, Yuri, 20
Angola, 177, 178, 182, 187, 191n., 204
Anti-colonialism, 110, 168, 172, 194n.
APRA *(Alianza Popular Revolucionaria
  Americana) Rebelde* (Peru), 166
Arab Socialist Union, 194
Arabs, 46, 174–175
Argentina, 165, 166
Asakura, Setsu, 129
Asia and Asian communists, 14, 18, 24, 27,
  89–104, 109, 117, 118, 125, 133n.,
  185, 190, 191n., 192, 194, 202, 207,
  212
Asian-African Film Festival, 119
Asian-African Labour Conference, 119n.
Asian-African Ministers' Conference, 119
Aswan project, 203
Australasia and Australasian communists,
  131–143
  see also Australia and Australian
    communists, New Zealand
    communists
Australia and Australian communists, 32,
  45, 49, 131, 135n., 137
Australian Congress for International
  Cooperation and Disarmament, 138
Australian Seamen's Union, 133
Austrian communist party, 9, 25, 53, 63, 64
Avanti (Italy), 14

Babu, Abdul Rahman Mohamed, 174n.,
  175, 177, 186
Bagdash, Khaled, 185n.
Bakaric, Vladimir, 84n.
Bakongo tribe, 177
Bakunin, Mikhail A., 5, 6, 19
Banda, Dr. Hastings, 175, 178, 183, 187
Bandera Roja (Red Flag) (Peru), 36
Bandung conferences, 118, 119, 186–188,
  208
'Bantustan' plan, 182
Barak, Rudolf, 67
Barnett, A. Doak, 93n.
Basavapunniah, M., 108, 112
Basel Congress, see Second International
Basu, Jyoti, 106, 107, 112
Basutoland, 182, 183
Batista, Fulgencio, 158, 163n., 164
Bechuanaland, 180, 182
Belaunde Terry, Fernando, 158, 166
Belgian communist party, 9, 24, 30, 32, 51,
  52, 63, 64
  split in, 37–39, 47
Belte, F., 5n.
Ben Bella, Ahmed, 171, 172, 184, 196

Bengal communists, 107
Berita Indonesia, 120
Berlin Wall, 54, 81
Berlinguer, Enrico, 25, 61, 64
Bernstein, Eduard, 13–16, 154
Bessarabia, 212
Betancourt, Romulo, 158, 164
Bhilai project, 203
Bhutan, 106
Bianco, Gino, 59n.
Billoux, François, 11
Bodnaras, Emil, 80n.
Bolivia, 157n., 166
Borneo, 101
Bosnia-Herzogovina, 84
Bratislava, 73
Bravo, Douglas, 164
Brazil and Brazilian communists, 8, 32–34,
    49, 154, 155, 163–165, 198n.
Brazilian Labour Party (PTB), 34
Brazzaville, 173
Brezhnev, Leonid, 23, 77, 80, 88, 137
Britain and Indonesia, 115, 116
British communists, 9, 25, 47, 50, 53, 63,
    144, 146
British High Commission Territories, 182
Brizola, Leonel, 34
Browder, Earl, 7, 145, 147, 148
Brussels Federation, 37, 38, 51
Brzezinski, Zbigniew, 168n., 177n., 185n.
Buckle, Desmond, 184n.
Buffalo, 148
Bukharin, N. I., 16
Bulgarian communists, 66–72, 76, 82
Burdwan conference, 109
Burmese communists, 44, 45, 141, 194, 196
Burmese Workers' Party (BWP), 45
Burnelle, Ernest, 38, 64
Burundi, 173, 187

Calcutta, 106
California, American communist leaders in,
    150
Calojanni, Napoleone, 61
Cambodia, 89, 101n.
Cameroons, 186
Canossa, 23
Caracas University, 164
Caribbean-Himalayan crisis (1962), 29
Carillo, Santiago, 11, 41
Carlisle, Fred, 148n.
Castro, Fidel, and Castroism, 32, 154,
    159–165, 167, 169, 173, 186
Catania, Italy, 62
Central America, 200n.
Centre Federation (Spain), 41
Ceylon and Ceylonese communists, 31, 32,
    42–44, 99, 141, 196
Ceylon Federation of Trade Unions
    (CFTU), 43
Ceylon Trade Union Federation (CTUF),
    42, 43
Challenge (U. S. A.), 148
Charleroi, Belgium, 38

Chervenkov, Volko, 70
Chilean communists, 30, 154–156, 158, 163,
    165-167, 196, 198n.
Chinese manifesto (June 14, 1963), 29,
    190, 193, 195, 197
Chinese People's Republic and
    communists, 8, 16, 19, 23, 26, 27,
    31, 33, 37, 82, 125, 127, 141, 162,
    163
La Chispa (The Spark) (Spain), 42
Chit Maung, 45
Chou En-lai, 24, 63, 86, 107, 108, 145n.,
    186, 187, 192, 194, 202, 203
Chou Yang, 6n., 13n., 48
Chusul, India, 107
Codovilla, Vittorio, 166
Cold war, 115, 170, 206
Colombia, 167
Cominform, 8, 65, 96
Comintern, 7, 132, 134, 144–146, 155, 166
Communist International, 7
*Communist Party and India's Path of
    National Regeneration and
    Socialism*, by Adhikari, 112
Communist Political Association, 145
El Communista (Spain), 41
Le Communiste (France), 55, 64
'Communists and Democracy'
    (1963 conference), 196
Congo, ex-Belgian, 18, 170, 173, 177, 178,
    186, 187, 201, 206, 210
Congress of Industrial Organizations
    (CIO), 145, 151
Convention People's Party (CPP)
    (Ghana), 174, 194n.
Cook Islands, 133
Corvalan, Luis, 165, 167
Council for Mutual Economic Assistance
    (Comecon), 9, 68, 69, 85, 214
Cox, Idris, 17
Creydt, Oscar, 46
Croatia, 84
Crozier, Brian, 44n.
Cruz, Viriato da, 177, 178
Cuba and Cuban communists, 10, 14, 25,
    32, 33, 148, 154, 159–163, 166
    crisis of 1962, 26, 29, 161, 163, 167, 185,
    213
    revolution, 151, 164
Czechoslovakian communists, 10, 15, 25,
    41n., 66, 67, 69, 72–74, 76, 78, 82,
    87

Daily Worker (Great Britain), 10, 64
Dalai Lama, 105, 108
Dange, S. A., 17, 24, 92, 93, 105, 106, 108,
    110–112, 118
Danish communists, 25, 63
Das-Gupta, Promode, 109
Davis, Benjamin J., Jr., 147, 148, 152
De Gaulle, Charles, 172
De Luca, Fausto, 59n.
Del Prado, Jorge, 35n., 36, 157, 161n., 200n.
Democratic Socialist Party (Japan), 95

Dennis, Eugene, 145n., 147
Destalinisation, 8, 12, 53, 67, 70, 77, 78,
        133, 167
Dimitrov, Georgi, 65
Dixon, Richard, 136, 137, 139, 141
Djilas, Milovan, 7n.
Dohlus, Horst, 82n.
Dorticos, Osvaldo, 163
Le Drapeau Rouge (Belgium), 14n., 24,
        64, 204
Drysdale, John, 176n.
Duclos, Jacques, 8, 145, 146
Duse, Ugo, 59n.
Dutch communists, 9

East Germany (GDR), 66, 67, 69, 76, 81,
        82, 84, 175, 214–216
Eastern Europe, 8, 25, 97, 132, 172, 212,
        213, 215
    diversity in, 65–88
Eastern studies, communist, 199n.
Ecuador, 166
Egypt, 171, 195, 204
81 Parties' Conference (1960), 3, 8, 111,
        133n., 134, 135, 139, 149, 193,
        195, 197
Engels, Friedrich, 5, 17, 20, 21, 23
Erningpradja, Ahem, 119n.
Espartaco Editores Ltda. (Chile), 30
Ethiopia, 176, 187
L'Etincelle (Paris), 39
Eureka Youth League (Australia), 138
Evans, Arthur, 47

FALN (Fuerzas Armadas de Liberacion
        Nacional) (Venezuela), 164
Federacion Centro de los comunistas
        marxistas-leninistas, 41
Federal Labour Government
        (Australia), 132
Fever, Lewis S., 52n.
Fiji communists, 133
Finnish communists, 51, 53
Finocchiaro, Nello, 59n.
First International, 4, 5, 6, 19–21
Flemish communists, 38
Flynn, Elizabeth Gurley, 144, 145, 149,
        153n.
Foster, William Z., 145–149, 152
    History of the Three Internationals,
        148, 149
Foulahs, the (Guinea), 172
Fourth International, 43n.
France and French communists, 5, 14, 15,
        24, 29, 50, 51, 63, 116, 141, 171,
        172, 206
    dissidents, 54–58
Frei, Eduardo, 158, 166
FRELIMO (Mozambique Liberation
        Front), 179
French-Chinese Friendship Society, 55
French-Chinese Peoples Association, 54–55
French Union of Communist Students
        (UEC), 24, 25, 56

Freymond, Jacques, 5n.
Fundamentals of Marxism-Leninism, 21

Galli, Giorgio, 59n.
Games of the New Emerging Forces, 119
Gates, John, 147
Gaulle, Charles de, 172
Gelman, Harry, 93n.
Gensuikyo (Japan Council Against
        Atomic and Hydrogen Bombs),
        94–96, 98, 130
Georgescu, Teohari, 78
German communists, 26
Germany, 5, 127, 158, 214
    see also East Germany, West Germany
Ghana, 169, 173, 174, 186, 194, 199, 204
Gheorghiu-Dei, Gheorghe, 67, 68, 77–79,
        80n., 84
Ghosh, Ajoy, 93, 106–111
Gibson, Richard, 30n.
Glineur, Henri, 51
Gold Coast, see Ghana
Gomulka, Wladyslaw, 10, 25, 65, 67, 68,
        76, 77, 79–81
Gopalan, A. K., 92, 106
Gottwald, Klement, 72
Goulart, Joao, 34, 163, 165
Grabois, Mauricio, 33, 34
GRAE (Angolan government-in-exile),
        177, 178
Gramsci, Antonio, 140n.
'Great Leap Forward,' 135
Green, Gilbert, 152
Griffith, William E., 66
Grippa, Jacques, 37–39, 47, 51, 52
'Groups of Eleven' (Brazil), 34
The Guardian (Australia), 137
The Guardian (U.S.A.), 151
Guatemala, 154, 167
Guevara, Che, 161n.
Guinea, 169, 170, 172, 174, 184, 186,
        194, 204
Gumane, Paulo J., 179
Gupta, Bhupesh, 107, 108, 110

Hajj Ali, Bashir, 184
Hakamada, Satomi, 124, 125, 129
Hall, Gus, 17, 147–153
Halperin, Ernst, 30n.
Hammer & Steel Newsletter (U.S.A.), 23
Hanga, A. K., 175
Hendrych, Jiri, 74
Hermansson, C. H., 53, 54
Hill, E. F., 133, 135–143 passim
History of the Three Internationals, by
        William Z. Foster, 148, 149
Hoc Tap (North Vietnam), 102
Houphouet-Boigny, Felix, 170
Hoxha, Enver, 81, 86–88
Huberman, Leo, 151–152
Hungary and Hungarian communists, 10,
        66, 67, 69, 74–77, 82, 87
    1956 uprising, 65, 78
Huysmans, Carl, daughter of, 51

228   INDEX

Ide, Takashi, 129
IFCTU (International Confederation of
    Free Trade Unions), 174
Illia, Arturo, 166
India and Indian communists, 8, 31, 45,
    89, 105–112, 117–119, 196, 198n.,
    202n., 211
  spilt in, 90–94
The India-China Border Dispute and the
    Communist Party in India, by
    Ghosh, 108
India-China relations, 92, 93, 105, 107,
    109–111, 208, 211
Indian Congress party, 17
Indonesia and Indonesian communist party,
    14, 17, 20, 26, 48, 49, 88, 98–104,
    113–122, 125, 127, 137, 139, 141,
    144, 191n., 203, 208
Indo-Tibetan border, 105
Ingrao, Pietro, 59n., 63
International Monetary Fund, 99
International Olympic Committee, 119
L'Internationale, 14n.
Ireland, 190
Irish (Republican) Workers Party, 37
Iron Gates project, 84
Islam, 172, 184
Italy and Italian communists, 9–12, 14, 15,
    17, 21, 25, 26, 47n., 50, 51, 53, 56,
    68, 95, 97, 113, 141, 144, 146, 158
  and the Sino-Soviet dispute, 58–62
  see also Togliatti
Ivekovic, Mladen, 10

Jackson, James, 144, 145n.
'Jacobin Left,' 36, 160, 162, 164, 165
Jalée, Pierre, 191n.
James, Victor, 138
Japan and Japanese communists, 22, 48,
    49, 89, 103, 118, 123–130, 141,
    146, 185, 207, 212, 214
  split in, 94–98
Japanese-American Mutual Security Pact,
    94
Japanese People's Liberation League, 127
Japanese Socialist Party, 95–98
  see also Democratic Socialist Party
Japanese 'Workers' Educational
    Association,' 127
Java, 113, 121
Johns, Sheridan, 180n.
Joint Action Committee (Nigeria), 174
Joshi, P. C., 105, 106, 110
Juliao, Francesco, 165

Kadar, Janos, 19, 25, 66, 75, 76, 81, 84
Kalimpong, India, 105, 106
Kamiyama, Shigeo, 94n., 96
Kardelj, Edvard, 83
Karume, Sheik Abeid, 175
Kasuga, Shojiro, 96, 123, 128, 129
Katane, Moses, 181
Kaunda, Dr. Kenneth, 178, 189
Kautsky, Karl, 6n., 14, 16

Keita, Modiba, 172–174
Kennedy, John F., 52, 125
Kennedy, Robert F., 101n.
Kenya, 176, 187, 206
Kenyatta, Jomo, 170, 174, 187
Kerala, India, 90–92, 106
Khrushchev, Nikita S., passim
Kim, G., 201n.
Kivu, ex-Belgian Congo, 173, 187
Koleka, Spiro, 23
Kolesnichenko, T., 200n.
Konar, Harekrishna, 108, 112
Konovalov, Y., 200n.
Korea and Korean communists, 103, 141
  see also North Korean communists,
    South Korea
Korean war, 103, 128
Kostov, Traicho, 70
Kosygin, Alexei, 23, 77, 80, 88
Krishnan, Pravathi, 43n.
Kudriavtsev, V., 191n.
Kumarasiri, P., 42
Kuo Fang, 190n.
Kurahara, Koreto, 128
Kuusinen, O., 16n., 21, 191n.
Kwilu, 173, 187

Lagos, Nigeria (1964 strike), 174
Lahiri, Somnath, 107
Lanka Sama Samaja Party (LSSP)
    (Ceylon), 42, 43
Lao Dong party (North Vietnam), 89
Laos and Laotian communists, 89, 101n.,
    102, 125, 141
Latin America and Latin American
    communists, 29, 30, 117, 118, 151,
    154–167, 185, 190, 191n., 192
  broadcasts from Moscow, 36
  hatred of U.S.A., 158
  split in, 36, 37
Le Duan, 102
Lebanese communists, 46
Lebanese Party of the Socialist
    Revolution, 46
Lechin, Juan, 157n.
Leftist Fighting Front (Ceylon), 43
Legum, C. and M., 180n.
Lenin, V. I., and Leninism, 6, 13, 14–16,
    19, 20, 23, 91, 100n., 101n., 103,
    104, 115, 118, 127, 146, 154, 157,
    190, 199n.
Leroy, Roland, 57
Lesotho Communist Party (Basutoland),
    183
Liberal Party (Sotuh Africa), 180, 182
Libya, 171, 176
Little, Betty, 138
Liu Shao-chi, 108, 132
Loevlien, Emil, 53
Long Live Leninism, 148n.
Longo, Luigi, 10, 63
Lourenco Marques, 176
Lowenthal, Richard, 177n., 185
Luanda, 176, 177

Luca, Fausto de, 59n.
Luca, Vasile, 78
Lukman, M. H., 99, 100
Lumumba, Patrice, 173
Luthuli, Chief A. J., 181

McCreery, Michael, 47, 53
McDonald, G. T., 135n.
Macedonia, 84
MacMahon Line, 107, 111
Madras, India, 92
Malawi, 170, 175, 178, 179, 187
Malaya and Malayan communists, 101, 141
Malaysia, 99, 100–102, 115, 116, 118–121
Mali, 169, 172–174, 186, 187, 194, 199, 204
Malinke, the, 172
Mandela, N. R., 181
Mao Tse-tung, 16, 29, 33, 42, 66, 79,
    100n., 102, 104, 106, 108, 127, 132,
    147, 149, 179, 180, 181, 185, 186,
    202n., 212
Maphilindo concept, 117
Maramatlov Freedom Party (Basutoland),
    183
Mariam, Mesfin Wolde, 176n.
Marin, Gaston, 69
Marks, J. B., 181
Martinet, Giles, 12n.
Marx, Karl, and Marxism, 4–6, 16–28
    passim, 32, 94, 98, 168, 169, 173,
    174, 190
Marxist-Leninist Quarterly (U.S.A.), 148
Matsushima, Harushige, 124, 128
Mau Mau movement, 191n.
Maugeri, Giacomo, 59n.
Maurer, Ion Gheorghe, 69, 79, 80
Mazzini, Giuseppe, 5
Mbeki, Govan, 181
Mendis, M. G., 43
Mensheviks, 154
Mexican communists, 32
Mezhdunarodnaya Zhizn (USSR), 20
Michels, Robert, 15
Mikoyan, Anastas, 119, 203
Millas, Orlando, 164n.
MIR, see Movement of the Revolutionary
    Left (Peru), Movimiento de
    Izquierda Revolucionaria
    (Venezuela)
Miyamoto, Kenji, 22, 24, 49, 97, 125,
    127–130
Mogadishu, 176
Molotov, V., 136
Mondlane, Eduardo, 179
Mongolian communists, 89
Montenegro, 84
Monthly Review, 151, 152
Morison, David L., 168n.
Morocco, 171
Moscow Declaration (India-China
    dispute), 109
Moscow Statement, 126
Moubarek, Youssef, 46
Moumié, Félix, 186

Movement of the Revolutionary Left
    (MIR) (Peru), 36, 166
Movimiento de Izquierda Revolucionaria
    (MIR) (Venezuela), 164, 166
Movimiento Popular de Libertacao de
    Angola (MPLA), 177, 178
Movimiento Revolucionario Peronista, 167
Mozambique, 177–179, 182, 183, 204
Mundo Obrero (Spain), 40, 41
Mundo Obrero Revolucionario (Spain),
    40, 42
Murba party (Indonesia), 120
Muslim League (India), 91, 92

Naito, Tomochika, 128
Nakano, Shigeharu, 94n., 96
Namboodiripad, E. M. S., 92–94, 106, 110
    document, 111, 112
Narita, Tomoni, 97
NASAKOM slogan, 17
Nasser, Gamal Abdel, 160, 171, 184, 187,
    192, 194, 203, 208
Nasution, Abdul H., 121
National Front (Indonesia), 114
National Guardian (U.S.A.), 150, 151, 152
National liberation movement, 60, 104,
    133, 173, 185, 188, 189, 190–204,
    207, 208
    Sino-Soviet rivalry, 190–204
National Marxist Association of India, 106n.
National United Front (Burma), 45
Nationalists (South Africa), 180, 181, 182
NATO, 177, 206
Ne Win, General, 45, 196
Negro movement, U.S., 147, 152
Nehru, Jawaharlal, 93, 106, 108, 118, 187,
    193
Nenni, Pietro, and Nenni Socialists (PSI),
    14, 59, 60, 62
Nepalese communists, 46
Netherlands, 115, 116
Neto, Agostino, 178
New China News Agency (NCNA),
    29, 30, 33, 36
    Brussels office, 37
'New Emerging Forces', Sukarno's,
    99, 118, 119
New Guinea communists, 133
New South Wales, 132
New Times (USSR), 194
New York state, CP USA in, 146, 148
New Zealand communists, 48, 131, 137,
    138, 141
New Zealand Monthly Review, 139
Nigeria, 174
Nkrumah, Kwame, 169, 170, 173, 174
Noma, Hiroshi, 129
Normington-Rawling, J., 132n.
North Korean communists, 89, 102, 120,
    124, 126, 163
North Vietnam communists, 89, 99, 102,
    108, 120, 124, 163, 212
    see also Lao Dong party

Northern Ireland communists, 37
Norwegian communists, 9, 25, 51, 53, 62, 63
Nosaka, Sanzo, 96, 97, 127, 129
Novais, J.-A., 42n.
Novotny, Antonin, 25, 66, 67, 72–74, 78, 84
Nu, U, 45
Nuova Unita (Italy), 39
Ny Dag (Sweden), 63
Nyerere, Julius, 175, 187, 188, 204
Nyoto, 99, 100, 101n.

Obote, Dr. A. M., 187
Oceania, 133
Odinga, Oginga, 176
One day in the life of Ivan Denisovich, 167
Organisation of African Unity (OAU), 177, 178, 181, 204
Osnovy marksizma-leninizma, 193n., 195n.
Otegbeye, Dr. Tunji, 174
Owen, Robert, 5

Padmore, George, 168n., 173
Pajetta, Giancarlo, 59n.
Pakistan, 111, 207
Pan-Africanism, 169, 173, 179, 181, 184
Pan-Africanist Congress (PAC), 181, 187
Pan-Arabism, 185
Papua, 133
Paraguayan communists, 31, 46
Paredes, S., 35, 36
Paris Commune, 5
Parti africain d'indépendance (PAI) (Senegal), 173
Parti Démocratique de Guinée (PDG), 172, 174
Parti du Travail (Switzerland), 52
Patrascanu, Lucretiu, 78
Pauker, Ana, 78
Peace Liaison Committee for the Asian and Pacific Regions, 138
Peasant Leagues (Brazil), 165
Pekin Informa, 29, 30, 35
Pékin Information, 29
Peking Review, 15, 29, 201, 202, 203
People's Comrade Party (Burma), 45
People's Daily, 20, 31, 48, 82, 127, 201
People's Front (U.S.A.), 146
People's United Front (MEP) (Ceylon), 42, 43
Peron, Juan, and Peronista movement, 165, 166
Peru and Peruvian communists, 31, 35–37, 158, 166, 200n.
Peru Juvenil (Young Peru), 36
Philippines, 117
Poland and Polish communists, 7, 10, 67–69, 74–77, 80, 82, 84
  1956 uprising, 65, 78
  treaty with Albania, 87
Political Affairs, (U.S.A.), 150
Pomar, Pedro, 33n.

Ponomarev, Boris, 13n., 19, 24, 137, 142
Popular Front (Chile), 165, 196
Portugal, 51, 178
Portuguese Africa, 176–179
  see also Angola, Mozambique
Potekhin, I. I., 17, 184
Prado, Jorge del, 157, 161n., 200n.
Prestes, Luiz Carlos, 32, 33, 154, 155, 164, 165
Pro-Chinese factions, 23, 24, 29–39, 41, 44, 46–48, 128, 164, 165, 191n., 192n., 196
Progressive Labor Movement (U.S.A.), 148
Progressive Party (South Africa), 182
Progressive Party (U.S.A.), 146, 150
Proletarian Revolution and the Renegade Kautsky, by Lenin, 6, 14
Proletario (Spain), 41, 42
Pro-Soviet factions, 24, 31, 34–36, 40, 43, 46, 48, 192n., 196
Proudhon, P. J., 5
PSIUP (Italy), 59
Punjab, 106, 108

Rabotnichesko Delo (Bulgaria), 71
Radio Free Portugal, 41n.
Radio Moscow, 36
Radio Peking, 140
Rakosi, Matyas, 65, 75
Ramamurti, P., 107, 108, 110
Ranadive, B. T., 109
Rankovic, Aleksandar, 83, 84
RDA (France), 172
'Red Flag' communists, *see* Burmese communists
Revisionism and Dogmatism in the CPI, by Namboodiripad, 112
Révolution, 18, 30, 31, 41, 191n., 196
Révolution Africaine (Algeria), 30
Rhodesia, Southern, 179, 182, 204
Rinascita (Italy), 15
Roberto, Holden, 177–179
Rosen, Milton, 148
Rote Fahne (Austria), 53
Rumanian communists, 10, 25, 66–69, 76–82, 84, 85, 107, 144, 212, 214
  treaty with Albania, 87

Salazar, Antonio de Oliveria, 179
Samoa, Western, 133
Sandri, Renato, 35n.
Sanmugathasan, M., 42, 43
Sao Paulo, Brazil, 33
Sardauna of Sokoto, the, 170
Sata, Ineko, 129
Sawimbi, Jonas, 178
Scalapino, Robert A., 98n.
Schatten, Fritz, 168n.
Schram, Stuart R., 42
Schwartz, Benjamin, 186
Scott, Sid, 132
Second International, 4, 6, 13
Senegal, 173

Senghor, L. S., 170
Serbia, 84
Sharkey, L. L., 132–143 *passim*
Sharpeville shootings, 181, 182
Shehu, Mehmet, 88
Shelepin, A. N., 192, 203
Shepilov, D. T., 183
Shida, Shigeo, 128
Shiga, Yoshio, 24, 49, 94n., 95, 96, 97, 125,
    126, 128–130
Shiga-Suzuki group, 24, 125
Shiino, Etsuro, 128
Shinn, W. T., Jr., 197n.
El Siglo (Chile), 167
Sikkim, 106
Sindermann, Horst, 82
Sino-Albanian dogmatists, 8
Sino-Indian border dispute, *see* India-China
    relations
Sino-Soviet border incidents, 29, 208
Sino-Soviet conflict, 6, 8–10, 15, 19–49
    passim
    December 1964 conference, 21, 22
    international consequences, 205–216
    provoked polycentrism, 3, 4, 12–14
    Western European reaction, 50–64
    see also Pro-Chinese factions, Pro-Soviet
        factions
Sino-Yugoslav dispute, 131
Siroky, Viliam, 73
Slovakia, 72
Slovenia, 84
Smith Act, 146, 152
Sobolev, A., 202n.
SOBSI (Indonesia), 115n., 116n., 121
Sobukwe, Robert, 181
Socialist Programme Party (Burma),
    45, 194, 196
Socialist Workers and Farmers Party
    (SWAFP) (Nigeria), 174
Society of Friends of *The Voice of Japan,*
    49
Soe, Thakin, 44, 45
Sohyo (Japan), 95, 96
Soka Gakkai group (Japan), 98
SOKSI (Indonesia), 121
Somalia, 176, 187, 189, 194, 206
Somoza, A., 158
Sotomayor, Carlos Martinez, 35
South Africa, 9, 10, 179–183, 204
South African Bureau of Relations
    (SABRA), 182
South Korea, 101n., 102, 125
South Vietnam, 89, 101n., 102
Southern Rhodesia, 179, 182, 204
Southwest African Peoples Organisation
    (SWAPO), 180
Soviet-Cyprus arms agreement, 176
Soviet-Nazi Pact, 7
Spanish communists, 11, 29, 39–42, 51
The Spark (Ghana), 174
Spartacus group (Chile), 30
Spartacus League *(Liga Espartaco)*
    (Mexico), 32

Sri Lanka (Freedom) Party (Ceylon), 43
Stalin, J. V., and Stalinism, 19, 23, 28,
    53, 132, 162
    imposed Bolshevik pattern, 7
    revised Lenin, 15
Stanistreet, H. K., 135n.
Stanleyville, 173, 201, 210
Statement of the 81 parties
    see 81 Parties' Conference
Stepanov, V., 44n.
Strobl, Franz, 53
Strong, Anna Louise, 151
Subandrio, Dr., 119
Sudan, 174
Sukarno, Áchmed, 17, 98, 99, 114–122
    passim, 208
Sundarayya, P., 94, 106, 112
Surjeet, Harkishan Singh, 106
Suslov, Mikhail, 49, 71, 81, 109, 110, 125,
    134, 142, 199
Suzuki, Ichiro, 24, 49, 94n., 96, 125, 126,
    128, 130
Swatantra party (India), 91
Swaziland, 182
Sweden and Swedish communists, 50, 51,
    53, 62, 63
Sweezy, Paul, 151
Swiss communists, 25, 30, 31, 39, 46, 47,
    52, 63, 64
Switzerland, 30

Taft, B., 135n.
Tanganyika, 175, 179, 187, 188
Tanzania, 206
Taylor, William, 150, 151
Tenali (India) conference, 93, 112
Thailand communists, 89
Thakin Soe, 44, 45
Than Tun, 44
Third International, 4, 6, 7, 13
Third World, 190–204
Thompson, Robert, 147
Thorez, Maurice, 24, 25, 58, 62, 63
Tibet, 105, 106, 108
Tilanen (Finland), 53
Tito, Josip Broz, 7, 8, 23, 52, 65–68, 83–86,
    117, 123, 151, 165, 171, 187
    see also Yugoslav communists
Todorov, Stanko, 71n.
Togliatti, Palmiro, 17, 19, 144
    and polycentrism, 8, 12, 60, 95
    and Sino-Soviet split, 10–13, 63
    Yalta 'testament,' 11–15, 59, 60
Tokuda, Kyuichi, 125, 128, 129
Tokyo University, 130
Tonkin Bay incident, 116, 212
Touré, Sekou, 169–174
Trotsky, Leon, and Trotskyism, 11, 16, 32,
    42–44, 46, 52, 55, 110, 127, 151,
    162, 180
Trotskyist Socialist Workers' Party
    (U.S.A.), 151
Trujillo, Rafael, 158

Tshombe, Moise, 177, 178, 189, 201
Tun, Than, 44
Tunisia, 171, 187
26-party preparatory commission, 23,
   134, 145

U Nu, 45
Uganda, 187
Ulbricht, Walter, 25, 66, 81, 82, 84
Umkanto We Sizwe (Spear of the Nation)
   (South Africa), 181
Umma Party (Zanzibar), 175
Uniao dos Populacoes de Angola (UPA),
   177, 178
Unidad (Peru), 35, 36
Union of Australian Women, 138
Union of Communist Students (UEC),
   38, 56, 57
Union des Populations du Cameroun
   (UPC), 172, 186
Union Soudanaise, 174
United Arab Republic (UAR), 109, 118,
   171, 184, 188, 192, 203, 204
United Labor Congress (Nigeria), 174
United Left Front (Ceylon), 42, 43, 196
United Nations, 20, 151, 170, 199, 200, 205,
   208, 210
United Party (South Africa), 182
United States, 7, 101n., 102, 172
United States–Japanese Security Treaty,
   128, 212
United Workers Party (Burma), 44, 45, 196
Uruguay, 34

Vanguard (Great Britain), 47
Vanguardia Obrera (Spain), 42
Venezuela and Venezuelan communists,
   154, 158, 163, 164
Vergès, Jacques, 30, 31, 200
La Vérité / De Waarheid (Belgium), 37
Verwoerd, H. F., 179, 182
Vietnam, 103, 125, 144, 148, 200, 201, 212
   see also North Vietnam communists,
   South Vietnam
Voice of Japan Comrades Society, 96, 130
La Voie Communiste (France), 55

Voix du Peuple (Belgium), 14n., 19, 23,
   24, 37–39, 41, 42, 47, 52

Wallace, Henry, 146
Walloon communist party, 38
Wankowicz trial, 76
Warsaw Pact, 68
Waterside Workers' Federation
   (Australia), 138n.
Wells, Fred, 140n.
West Bengal, 91, 92, 106, 108, 109, 112
West Germany and West German
   communists, 51, 82, 111, 116, 172
West Irian (New Guinea) question, 116
Western European communists, 29, 32, 37,
   38, 39
   and the Sino-Soviet dispute, 50–64
'White Flag' (BCP) communists,
   see Burmese communists
White Redoubt, 176–183, 187–189
Wilcox, V. G., 132, 134, 138, 139, 142
Williams, Robert, 152
The Worker (U.S.A.), 144, 150
Workers World (U.S.A.), 23
World Federation of Trade Unions
   (WFTU), 172
Wyszynski, Cardinal Stefan, 76

Yalta memorandum, *see* Togliatti, Yalta
   'testament'
Yamada, Katsujiro, 129, 130
Yasui, Kaoru, 130
Yenan, 127
Yonehara, Itaru, 124
'Yu Chi Chan Club' (South Africa), 180
Yugoslav communists, 7–10, 14, 23, 65, 68,
   70, 78, 79, 81–86, 100, 117, 118, 123
   see also Tito
Yugov, Anton, 70

Zambia, 178, 179
Zanzibar, 173–175, 177, 185–187, 191n.,
   200
Zanzibari Nationalist Party (ZNP), 175
Zeri i Popullit (Albania), 19, 23, 49
Zhivkov, Todor, 25, 66, 70, 71, 72, 76
Zhukov, Marshal Yury, 126